The *Manhattan Tutors* Guide to the

Upper Level ISEE®

Quantitative Reasoning and
Mathematics Achievement

Manhattan Tutors
217 East 70th Street #2291
New York, NY 10021
office@manhattan-tutors.com

Acknowledgements

Special thanks to:

Meghan Flanigan
Max Gilbert
Andrea Gottstein
Alex Polizzotti
Meredith Willis
Richard Wu

Contents

Part I
Introduction

How to Use This Book

This book is designed to help students in grades 8 to 11 master the Quantitative Reasoning and Mathematics Achievement sections on the Upper Level *Independent School Entrance Exam* (ISEE).

Over the years, the team at Manhattan Tutors has found that students are understandably overwhelmed by the enormous amount of information contained in most test prep books. The math sections of the Upper Level ISEE tend to be particularly intimidating for students who are preparing for the test.

The Manhattan Tutors Guide to the Upper Level ISEE: Quantitative Reasoning and Mathematics Achievement was written with you – the student – in mind. Our streamlined guide is designed to provide students with a tailored study plan that they can use to focus their preparation and minimize the amount of time they need to get ready for the ISEE.

Here's your step-by-step guide for using this book:

1. Read through the ISEE Math Strategies in Part II and complete the practice problems.

2. Take the practice tests in Chapters 5 & 6 of Part VI. Review the questions you answered incorrectly, and focus your remaining time on studying those question types and math fundamentals.

3. Six weeks before the real test, take the practice tests in Chapters 7 & 8 of Part VI. Compare your results with those from the first practice tests, and identify areas of improvement and areas you still need to work on.

4. Four weeks before the real test, take the practice test provided by the ERB. This test, *What to Expect on the Upper Level ISEE*, can be found at www.ERBLearn.org/parents/isee-preparation.

5. If necessary, find a trusted adult or tutor to help you understand the topics you are still struggling with.

6. Remember: the ISEE is just one component of a comprehensive application. Schools consider your grades, extracurriculars, teacher recommendations, and personal essays, so try not to stress too much over the test!

Warmest regards,

The Staff of Manhattan Tutors

The Upper Level ISEE: What You Need to Know

The ISEE is a standardized admissions test administered by the Educational Records Bureau (ERB). Many of the independent elementary, middle, and high schools that are members of the ERB require the ISEE, or another standardized test such as the SSAT, as part of their admissions processes.

Test Structure

The ISEE is offered at four levels (primary, lower, middle, and upper), based on the grade to which you are applying. The Upper Level ISEE is for students in grades 8 to 11 who are applying for admission to grades 9 to 12. The test is offered in both online and paper formats and is composed of four multiple-choice sections, as well as an essay prompt. The number of questions and the time allotted for each section can be found in the table below. The free-response essay is not scored, but it is sent to the schools to which you apply.

Section	Number of Questions	Time Allotted (in minutes)
Verbal Reasoning	40	20
Quantitative Reasoning	37	35
Reading Comprehension	36	35
Mathematics Achievement	47	40
Essay	1 prompt	30

Quantitative Reasoning and Mathematics Achievement

Both sections conform to standards set by the National Council of Teachers of Mathematics. *You cannot use a calculator on either math section, and scratch paper is not allowed.* You should plan on performing all your calculations directly on the test booklet.

Quantitative Reasoning (QR), as the name would suggest, is designed to test your reasoning abilities. QR questions ask you to apply your knowledge of math concepts to word problems and real-world situations. You usually aren't expected to memorize equations or math terminology for this section; instead, you may need to estimate numerical values, compare and contrast quantities, use your reasoning abilities to calculate the probability of certain events, and analyze and interpret data. This section is split into two parts: word problems and quantitative comparisons.

Mathematics Achievement (MA) is a more "traditional" math test. You should expect to perform calculations, demonstrate knowledge of math terminology, and convert common metric units, among many other tasks.

Test Logistics

Registering for the ISEE

Students can take the ISEE *once per season*. The Fall, Winter, and Spring / Summer seasons run from August through November, December through March, and April through July, respectively. Most students now take the test once in October or November, and again in December, which gives them two shots at the test before the standard January application deadline. You should double-check the website of every school to which you are applying; some schools prefer that students apply earlier in the fall.

The test is offered in both paper-pencil and online formats and can be taken at local participating schools, ProMetric Test Centers, or ISEE Testing Offices. The most current test dates and locations are found at www.iseetest.org.

Accommodations

The ISEE offers a wide range of testing accommodations to students with documented learning differences or physical challenges. Your parent or guardian must set up an account at https://iseeonline.erblearn.org/ and submit documentation for ERB review. The process can take up to three weeks, so be sure to submit everything far in advance of when you plan to take the test.

The Day Before the Test

Don't plan on cramming the day before the test. You can spend a little time reviewing vocab flashcards and going over key math equations, but you should focus on being as calm and relaxed as possible. You should get as much sleep as you usually do and drink coffee the morning of the test only if that is already part of your routine. Most importantly, you should get all of the necessary items packed up the day before the test so that you don't forget anything as you're headed out the door!

What to Expect on the Day of the Test

When you arrive at your test site, you will need to show a hard copy of your verification letter in order to check in. You must also present an approved form of identification, such as your library card, birth certificate, social security card, school report card, school ID, passport, or green card. Photocopies of these forms of identification are accepted at school testing centers and ISEE testing offices; *hard copies of your ID must be presented at ProMetric Testing Centers.* Your parent or guardian must also have an original copy of his or her own ID if you are testing at a ProMetric Center. The Upper Level ISEE lasts 160 minutes. There is a 5- to 10-minute break after both the Quantitative Reasoning and the Mathematics Achievement sections. *There is no guessing penalty on the Upper Level ISEE,* so you should answer every question on the test!

What to Bring to the Test

Students taking the paper test should bring #2 pencils, as well as pens with blue or black ink. These items are not allowed if you are taking the test on a computer. We recommend you also bring an analog watch in case there is not a clock in the testing room. The following items are prohibited at all testing centers: cell phones and other electronic devices, scratch paper, calculators, calculator watches, rulers, protractors, compasses, dictionaries, and thesauruses.

Understanding Your Scores

The ISEE provides perhaps the most baffling score report of any standardized test. Your results will show four scores for each of the four multiple-choice sections of the test: a scaled score, percentile rank, stanine, and stanine analysis. When friends tell you what they scored on the ISEE, they're almost always talking about the stanines. Schools care most about your stanine and percentile rank.

Scaled Score: ranges from 760 to 940 for each section and is derived from your raw score. Your raw score is how many questions you answered correctly on each section.

Percentile Rank: compares your score in each section to other students in the same grade who have taken the test within the last three years. A percentile rank of 75, for example, means that you did as well as or better than 75 percent of students in your grade who have taken the ISEE within the last three years.

Stanine: ranges from 1 to 9 for each section. A score of 1 to 3 is considered below average, 4 to 6 average, and 7 to 9 above average.

Stanine Analysis: compares your Verbal Reasoning and Reading Comprehension scores and compares your Quantitative Reasoning and Mathematics Achievement scores.

Keep in mind that your score compares you only to students in your grade who have taken the test. Since students from grades 8 to 11 take the Upper Level ISEE, it wouldn't be fair for 8th graders to be scored on the same scale as 11th graders. That also means that the younger you are, the more likely you are to encounter unfamiliar material on the test.

Part II
ISEE Math Strategies

Chapter 1

Strategies for Quantitative Reasoning and Mathematics Achievement

ISEE Math Strategies

As with all standardized tests, you'll often hear that you must possess a thorough understanding of all the topics on the ISEE in order to do well. While this is what the ERB would like you to believe, it simply isn't true. Learning the math fundamentals tested on the ISEE should of course be one of your top priorities. However, mastering the strategies in this section can help boost your score even higher, and you should always be thinking of them as you move through the math sections on the test.

These strategies apply to the entirety of the Quantitative Reasoning and Mathematics Achievement sections of the Upper Level ISEE. There is a mini quiz after each section to help you practice implementing the strategies.

Strategies are listed in order from least difficult to master to most difficult to master.

1. Fill in an answer for every question

There is no penalty for guessing on the ISEE, so you have a 25% chance of getting a question correct by randomly choosing A, B, C, or D. If you're able to eliminate one incorrect answer, your odds increase to 33%, and if you can eliminate two answers, then you have a 50% chance of guessing the correct answer!

You should review your answer key before time is up to make sure you've filled in every single bubble on the answer key. *Make sure you circle your answers in the test booklet, as well.* If you make a mistake when bubbling the answer key, it will be much easier to fix if you can compare the answer key and the circled answers in the test booklet.

Mini Quiz - Strategy #1
Questions: 7
Time Limit: 2.5 minutes

1. Which of the following complex numbers is equal to $(7 + 7i) - (3i^2 - 8i)$, for $i = \sqrt{-1}$?

   (A) $7 + 3i^2 - 15i$
   (B) $21i^2 + 11i - 56i^2$
   (C) $-3i^2 + 15i + 7$
   (D) $15i - 7 - 3i^2$

2. Which of the following expressions is equivalent to $(2x^2 - 5) - (-4x^2 + 2)$?

   (A) $6x^2 - 7$
   (B) $-2x^2 - 7$
   (C) $6x^2 - 3$
   (D) $-2x^2 - 3$

3. Jessie spent 30% of her 9-hour workday in meetings. How many minutes of her workday did she spend in meetings?

   (A)   2.7
   (B)   3
   (C)   162
   (D)   378

4. If $a^{\frac{b}{5}} = 5$ for positive integers a and b, what is one possible value of b?

   (A)   -1
   (B)   5
   (C)   10
   (D)   25

5. A circle in the xy-plane has the equation $(x + 2)^2 + (y - 4)^2 = 16$. Which of the following points does NOT lie in the interior of the circle?

   (A)   (1,4)
   (B)   (-2,7)
   (C)   (-3,5)
   (D)   (-6,5)

6. $5x + x + 2x - 4 - 8 = 9 - x + 4x$

   In the equation above, what is the value of x?

   (A) $\frac{5}{21}$
   (B) $\frac{21}{5}$
   (C)   4
   (D)   8

7. A package requires 4 centimeters of tape to be closed securely. What is the maximum number of packages of this type that can be secured with 5.5 meters of tape? (1 meter = 100 cm)

   (A)   136
   (B)   137
   (C)   138
   (D)   139

Did you find those questions difficult? That's because they were all SAT-level math questions! If you applied Strategy #1, you should have still circled an answer for each question.

2. Pay close attention to what the question asks

Some answers might seem correct but don't address what the question asks. The writers of the ISEE are deliberately trying to trick you - don't fall for it! You should get in the habit of underlining key words in the questions so that you don't miss terms such as *positive*, *negative*, *sum*, etc. Reading comprehension still plays a huge role in the ISEE math sections.

Example #1

Which positive value of x satisfies the equation $(x + 3)(x - 5) = 0$?

(A)   -5
(B)   -3
(C)   3
(D)   5

Choice (B) satisfies the equation, but the question specifically asks for a *positive* value of x. Therefore, you should immediately cross off (A) and (B). **Choice (D) is the only correct answer.**

In the Mini Quiz on the next page, key words are in bold. You should get in the habit of circling similar terms on every math question.

Mini Quiz - Strategy #2
Questions: 5
Time Limit: 2 minutes

1. If $3x + 4 = 16$, then $2x$ = ?

    (A)   4
    (B)   8
    (C)   12
    (D)   16

2. If the probability that it will rain
    tomorrow is 0.4, what is the probability
    it will **not** rain tomorrow?

    (A)   0
    (B)   0.4
    (C)   0.6
    (D)   1

3. If Nicole walks 3 **miles** in 40 **minutes**,
    how many **miles** does she walk in 4
    hours?

    (A)   5
    (B)   8
    (C)   12
    (D)   18

4. Mahmoud won a cash settlement for a
    suit he filed in court. He paid his lawyer
    25% of the original settlement and had
    $30,000 remaining. How much was the
    original settlement?

    (A) $7,500
    (B) $10,000
    (C) $22,500
    (D) $40,000

5. The width of a square is 8 inches. What
    is the square's **area**?

    (A)   8 in^2
    (B)   16 in^2
    (C)   32 in^2
    (D)   64 in^2

These questions weren't overly difficult, but you might have accidentally selected the wrong answer if
you didn't confirm what the question was asking.

3. Be efficient with your time

You have just under one minute to answer each question on both of the math sections. If you've been working on a question for 20 seconds and feel like you haven't made any progress, it's time to move on. You can always go back to it later if you have time.

Each question is worth 1 point, regardless of difficulty. If you spend 15 minutes working on 10 impossible questions at the beginning of a section and you end up not having time to do 10 super easy questions at the end of a section, you just got 20 questions wrong! If you'd had time to work on those last few questions, at least you would have gotten 10 correct overall.

Mini Quiz - Strategy #3
Questions: 10
Time Limit: 4 minutes

1. What are the solutions of the quadratic equation $6x^2 - 12x - 18 = 0$?

   (A) $x = -3$ and $x = 1$
   (B) $x = 6$ and $x = 18$
   (C) $x = 3$ and $x = -1$
   (D) $x = -6$ and $x = 18$

2. If $4x + 3 = 15$, what is the value of $15x - 4$?

   (A)   4
   (B)   15
   (C)   19
   (D)   41

3. When 3 times the number x is added to 10, the result is 34. What number results when 5 times x is added to -30?

   (A)   10
   (B)   25
   (C)   50
   (D)   70

4. Which of the following is equivalent to the sum of the expressions $z^2 + 4$ and $z - 4$?

   (A) $z^2 + z$
   (B) $z^3 - 4$
   (C) $2z^2$
   (D) z^3

5. The atomic weight of an unknown element, in atomic mass units (amu), is approximately 40% more than that of magnesium. The atomic weight of magnesium is 40 amu. Which of the following best approximates the atomic weight, in amu, of the unknown element?

   (A)   16
   (B)   24
   (C)   56
   (D)   64

6. $3(4x + 2)(3x - 6)$

   Which of the following is equivalent to the expression above?

   (A) $36x^2 - 18x - 36$
   (B) $12x^2 + 18x + 12$
   (C) $12x^2 - 18x - 12$
   (D) $36x^2 - 54x - 36$

7. Which of the following is the greatest?

   (A) $6.7 + 4.2$
   (B) $6.7 - 4.2$
   (C) $\dfrac{6.7}{4.2}$
   (D) 6.7×4.2

8. $\sqrt{k+4} - x = 0$

In the equation above, k is a constant. If $x = 5$, what is the value of k ?

(A)   1
(B)   4
(C)   21
(D)   25

9. $2 + 20 =$

(A)   2
(B)   10
(C)   20
(D)   22

10. Which improper fraction is equivalent to $10\frac{1}{2}$?

(A) $\frac{1}{2}$

(B) $\frac{5}{2}$

(C) $\frac{21}{2}$

(D) $\frac{10}{2}$

There were some easy questions sprinkled in toward the end. If you spent all your time on the more difficult questions at the beginning, you may not have had a chance to try the easy ones.

4. Make educated guesses

This strategy is closely related to Strategy #1, but it's a little more advanced. Does an answer seem way too big or too small? Then it probably is - cross it out! This is especially useful on geometry questions. *Unless noted otherwise, ISEE math questions are drawn to scale.* That makes guessing much easier.

Example #1

The square below has a perimeter of 32 inches. The vertices of the two inscribed triangles lie at the midpoints of each side of the square. What is the area of the unshaded region?

(A)   30 in^2
(B)   32 in^2
(C)   48 in^2
(D)   60 in^2

Can you eyeball it? It seems like the unshaded region accounts for about two-thirds of the total area of the square. If the perimeter of the square is 32 inches, then each side is 8 inches, and the area is 64 square inches. Does it make sense that the unshaded area would be almost the same as the total area? Definitely not; go ahead and cross off (D). Because we've already established that the unshaded region is about two-thirds of the total area, (A) and (B) seem too small. At this point, even if you don't know how to solve this question mathematically, you should be able to choose the correct answer, **which is (C).**

Mini Quiz - Strategy #4
Questions: 4
Time Limit: 1 minute

1. If $\overline{AB} = \overline{BC}$, what is the measure of ∠ABC?

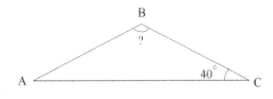

    (A)   40°
    (B)   60°
    (C)   80°
    (D)   100°

2. Three squares are inscribed in the rectangle below. The area of each square is 16 in². What is the area of the shaded region?

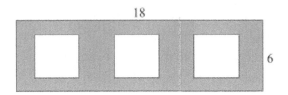

    (A)   60 in²
    (B)   72 in²
    (C)   100 in²
    (D)   108 in²

3. In the figure below, rectangles ABCD and EFGH are similar. If the measure of $\overline{AB}$ is 6 inches, the measure of $\overline{BC}$ is 4 inches, and the measure of $\overline{EF}$ is 9 inches, what is the area of rectangle EFGH?

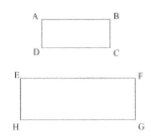

    (A)   24 in²
    (B)   42 in²
    (C)   48 in²
    (D)   54 in²

4. In triangle ABC below, $\overline{AB} = \overline{BC}$ and the measure of ∠B is 80°. What is the measure of ∠C?

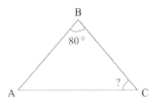

    (A)   30°
    (B)   50°
    (C)   75°
    (D)   90°

The time limit for that one was really short! There's no way you would have been able to actually do the math to figure out the answers. However, you still may have done well by making educated guesses.

5. Don't fall for trick answers

The ERB claims it doesn't include answers that are intended to trick students, but that's misleading. The ERB acknowledges that it includes *common mistakes or misconceptions* in its answer choices. Although there are some genuinely easy questions on the ISEE, be very careful when choosing your answer.

Example #1

If the length of a rectangle is increased by 40 percent and the width is increased by 20 percent, what is the percent increase in the area of the rectangle?

(A)   20%
(B)   52%
(C)   60%
(D)   68%

You might be inclined to choose (C) and move on. 40% + 20% = 60%, right? Unfortunately, things aren't quite so simple when dealing with percent change. Think about a rectangle with a length of 10 and a width of 10. The area of that rectangle would be $10 \times 10 = 100$. Increasing the length by 40 percent and the width by 20 percent results in a rectangle with a length of 14 and a width of 12. The area of that rectangle is 168, an increase of 68% over the original rectangle. Therefore, **the correct choice is (D)**. Notice how choosing your own numbers on that question made solving it much easier! We'll learn more about that strategy soon.

Mini Quiz - Strategy #5
Questions: 6
Time Limit: 5 minutes

1. For what value of x is the equation
    $\frac{3x-9}{x-3} = 0$ true?

    (A)   -3
    (B)   0
    (C)   3
    (D)   There are no values of x that
           make this equation true

2. Which of the following does not
    represent an integer?

    (A) $\sqrt{144} - \sqrt{36}$
    (B) $\sqrt{16 \times 4}$
    (C) $\frac{\sqrt{64}}{4}$
    (D) $\sqrt{\frac{64}{8}}$

3. If the length of a rectangle is decreased
    by 30 percent and the width is increased
    by 30 percent, what is the percent
    decrease in the area of the rectangle?

    (A)   0%
    (B)   9%
    (C)   10%
    (D)   60%

4. For what value of z is the equation
    $\frac{4z-16}{z-4} = 0$ true?

    (A)   -4
    (B)   0
    (C)   4
    (D)   There are no values of z that
           make this equation true

5. For what value of y is the equation
    $\frac{2y-8}{y-2} = 0$ true?

    (A)   0
    (B)   2
    (C)   4
    (D)   There are no values of y that
           make this equation true

6. If the length of a rectangle is increased
    by 50 percent and the width is increased
    by 30 percent, what is the percent
    increase in the area of the rectangle?

    (A)   20%
    (B)   50%
    (C)   80%
    (D)   95%

6. Work backwards

There is one major, helpful difference between the ISEE and the tests you take in school: it's entirely multiple choice. There is exactly one correct answer to each question, and you can use this to your advantage. If you encounter a question you don't know how to solve, try using the answer choices provided by the ISEE to work backwards.

The first example question is very easy. It's included here just to give you an idea of how to use this strategy.

Example #1

If $4x + 2 = 18$, what is the value of x?

(A)   1
(B)   2
(C)   3
(D)   4

$4(1) + 2 = 6$, so (A) is incorrect. $4(2) + 2 = 10$, so (B) is also incorrect. It's probably pretty obvious to you that (C) doesn't work, either. $4(4) + 2 = 18$, so you know **(D) is the correct answer.**

The second example question is more difficult, and it demonstrates how useful working backwards can be on the ISEE.

Example #2

There are 35 students in Mr. Smith's algebra class. $\frac{1}{3}$ of the boys and $\frac{1}{2}$ of the girls own pets, and twice as many girls as boys own pets. How many boys own pets?

(A)   5
(B)   10
(C)   15
(D)   20

Working backwards will make solving this question much easier. Rather than set up a complicated equation to figure out how many boys own pets, start by choosing one of the answer choices. If you choose (B), that means you think there are 10 boys who own pets, and that there are 30 boys total, since $\frac{1}{3}$ of the boys in the class own pets. If 10 boys own pets, and twice as many girls as boys own pets, that means 20 girls own pets. There are 40 girls total, since $\frac{1}{2}$ of the girls own pets. We've just determined that if 10 boys own pets, there are 30 boys and 40 girls in the class, giving us a total of 70 students. However, the question specifically says there are 35 students in the class! Therefore, (B) can't be correct.

Choice (B) gave us a total number of boys and girls that was too large, so let's try picking a smaller number this time. Our only option is choice (A). If 5 boys own pets, there are 15 boys in the class. Since twice as many girls as boys own pets, there must be 10 girls who own pets. That also means there are 20 girls in the class. 15 boys + 20 girls = 35 total students. **The correct answer is (A).**

Example #3

Jeff, Steve, and James live together in a 3-bedroom apartment. Steve and James each pay the same amount every month, but Jeff has the smallest room, so he pays $\frac{1}{3}$ of what Steve pays. If the total rent each month is $1,750, how much does Steve pay?

(A) $250
(B) $400
(C) $750
(D) $800

Let's start with (B). If Steve pays $400 per month, then James also pays $400 per month, and Jeff pays $133.33. The three of them pay $933.33 per month in total. That doesn't add up to $1,750, so we'll need to start with a larger number. Let's try (C). If Steve pays $750 per month, then so does James. Jeff pays $\frac{1}{3}$ of $750, which is $250. $750 + $750 + $250 = $1,750. **The correct answer is (C).**

Mini Quiz - Strategy #6
Questions: 10
Time Limit: none

1. At a liquidation sale, a company discounted its prices by 60%. Joey bought a piece of luggage at the sale for $270. What was the original cost of the luggage?

   (A) $108
   (B) $162
   (C) $450
   (D) $675

2. A rectangular room that is 3 feet longer than it is wide has an area of 130 square feet. How many feet long is the room?

   (A) 5
   (B) 10
   (C) 13
   (D) 26

3. If $3x^2 - 18x = -15$, what are the possible values of x?

   (A) $x = -3$ and $x = 6$
   (B) $x = 6$ and $x = -2$
   (C) $x = -1$ and $x = -5$
   (D) $x = 1$ and $x = 5$

4. What is the smallest possible integer value of x for which $(x + 4)(x - 8) < 0$?

   (A) -4
   (B) -3
   (C) -2
   (D) -1

5. The cost of a gym membership is a one time fee of $100, plus a monthly fee of $30. Jerry wrote a $460 check to pay for his gym membership for a certain number of months, including the one time fee. How many months of membership did he pay for?

   (A) 6
   (B) 12
   (C) 18
   (D) 24

6. Wushin earned 72, 94, 88, and 80 points on the 4 tests (each worth 100 points) given so far this semester. How many points must he earn on his fifth test, which is also worth 100 points, to average 83 points for the 5 tests given this semester?

   (A) 73
   (B) 81
   (C) 87
   (D) 94

7. You ask a friend how old they are, and they say, "If you multiply my age by 23 and subtract the square of my age, the result is 102." How old is your friend?

   (A) 17
   (B) 19
   (C) 20
   (D) 24

8. If $7x = -3(x - 10)$, then $x = ?$

    (A)   3
    (B)   4
    (C)   5
    (D)   6

9. A cannonball is shot from a cannon that
    sits on a turret 15 feet above the ground.
    The height of the cannonball as it falls
    to the ground is modeled by the function
    $h = -3t^2 + 12t + 15$, where t is the
    number of seconds after the cannonball
    is shot. Approximately how many
    seconds will it take for the cannonball to
    hit the ground?

    (A)   3
    (B)   5
    (C)   12
    (D)   15

10. $2x + 3y = 0$
    $6x - 3y = 24$

    What is the solution to the system of
    equations above?

    (A)   (3, -2)
    (B)   (0, 2)
    (C)   (-2, 4)
    (D)   (-1, 3)

Working backwards is an advanced strategy that requires a lot of practice, but it's an extremely powerful
tool once it's mastered. You can only work backwards when each answer choice is a number - if there are
any variables in the answer choices, you can try to use Strategy #7.

7. Input your own number

Sometimes, you'll run into a question that you have no idea how to solve mathematically. Maybe the question tests something that you studied years ago and have now forgotten, like the laws of exponents, or maybe the question is really abstract and uses a lot of variables, making it difficult to solve. If so, it's possible you can input your own numbers to simplify the question.

Example #1

The product of $(2x^2y)(5x^4y^3)$ is equivalent to:

(A) $7x^8y^3$

(B) $8x^8y^3$

(C) $7x^6y^4$

(D) $10x^6y^4$

By choosing your own number, you can solve this question without much knowledge of the laws of exponents! The question does not restrict the values of x and y, so let's say $x = 1$ and $y = 1$. Easy, right? When you put in 1 for x and y in the original expression, you end up with $(2 \times 1^2 \times 1)(5 \times 1^4 \times 1^3) = 10$. Any answer choice that is *equivalent* to $(2x^2y)(5x^4y^3)$ must also equal 10 when you plug in 1 for x and y. (A) and (C) both give you 7, which is wrong. (B) gives you 8, which is also wrong. **The correct answer is (D).**

Example #2

If x and y are positive integers such that $x + y = 8$, then what is the value of $\frac{y-8}{3x}$?

(A) $-\frac{1}{3}$

(B) $-\frac{1}{6}$

(C) $\frac{1}{6}$

(D) $\frac{1}{3}$

Let's pick values for x and y. In this case, they must add up to 8, and they must both be positive. Let's say $x = 6$ and $y = 2$. $\frac{2-8}{3(6)} = \frac{-6}{18} = \frac{-1}{3}$. **The correct answer is (A).** This trick works regardless of what numbers you use for x and y, as long as they are both positive and add up to 8, as the question requires. If we instead said $x = 3$ and $y = 5$, we would get $\frac{5-8}{3(3)} = \frac{-3}{9} = \frac{-1}{3}$. Pretty neat, huh?

Mini Quiz - Strategy #7
Questions: 8
Time Limit: none

1. If $x < 0 < y$, which of the following has the greatest value?

   (A) $x - y$
   (B) $-y - x$
   (C) $y - 2x$
   (D) $2x - y$

2. If $\frac{x}{3} = \frac{y}{5}$, which of the following is equivalent to $\frac{y}{4}$?

   (A) $\frac{x}{5}$
   (B) $\frac{2x}{5}$
   (C) $\frac{5x}{12}$
   (D) $15x$

3. If $x > 4$, which of the following is equivalent to $\dfrac{1}{\frac{1}{x+3} + \frac{1}{x+5}}$?

   (A) $\dfrac{2x + 8}{x^2 + 8x + 15}$

   (B) $\dfrac{x^2 + 8x + 15}{2x + 8}$

   (C) $x^2 + 8x + 15$

   (D) $2x + 8$

4. For all x and y, $(x - 2y)(3x^2 + y) = ?$

   (A) $3x^3 - 2y^2$
   (B) $3x^2 - 2y^2$
   (C) $3x^3 + xy - 6x^2y - 2y^2$
   (D) $3x^3 - xy - 6x^2y + 2y^2$

5. Yesterday, Darius sent x emails each hour for 7 hours, and Austin sent y emails each hour for 5 hours. Which of the following represents the total number of emails sent by Darius and Austin yesterday?

   (A) $7x + 5y$
   (B) $7y + 5x$
   (C) $12xy$
   (D) $35xy$

6. $(x^2)^3$ is equivalent to:

   (A) x^5
   (B) x^6
   (C) x^8
   (D) x^{10}

7. If $\frac{a}{b} = 3$, what is the value of $\frac{3b}{a}$?

   (A)   0
   (B)   1
   (C)   2
   (D)   3

8. $16x^4 + 24x^2y^2 + 9y^4$ is equivalent to which of the following expressions?

   (A) $(4x - 3y)^2$
   (B) $(4x + 3y)^4$
   (C) $(4x^2 - 3y^2)^2$
   (D) $(4x^2 + 3y^2)^2$

Answer Key - ISEE Math Strategies

Strategy #1
1. C
2. A
3. C
4. B
5. D
6. B
7. B

Strategy #2
1. B
2. C
3. D
4. D
5. D

Strategy #3
1. C
2. D
3. A
4. A
5. C
6. D
7. D
8. C
9. D
10. C

Strategy #4
1. D
2. A
3. D
4. B

Strategy #5
1. D
2. D
3. B
4. D
5. C
6. D

Strategy #6
1. D
2. C
3. D
4. B
5. B
6. B
7. A
8. A
9. B
10. A

Strategy #7
1. C
2. C
3. B
4. C
5. A
6. B
7. B
8. D

Chapter 2

Strategies for Quantitative Comparisons

Strategies for Quantitative Comparisons

Quantitative Comparisons are a subsection of Quantitative Reasoning, and the format of the questions is completely different. Each question presents two quantities and asks you to identify which quantity is greater. The questions look like this:

Column A	Column B
200^0	1^0

(A) The quantity in Column A is greater.
(B) The quantity in Column B is greater.
(C) The two quantities are equal.
(D) The relationship cannot be determined from the information given.

Many of the general Math Strategies are applicable to this section, as well. However, there are a few additional strategies that are specific to Quantitative Comparisons.

Strategies are listed in order from least difficult to master to most difficult to master.

1. Memorize the question format and answer choices

Every question on the Quantitative Comparisons subsection displays two quantities that must be compared in order to determine which is greater. Make sure you know what these questions look like so you aren't thrown off when you encounter them on the test.

Example #1

Column A	Column B
$0.7 + 0.2$	$0.7 + 0.02$

Additionally, each question uses the same answer format:

(A) The quantity in Column A is greater.
(B) The quantity in Column B is greater.
(C) The two quantities are equal.
(D) The relationship cannot be determined from the information given.

If you don't memorize this format, you will waste time double-checking every answer on this section to confirm that you've bubbled in correctly.

2. Estimate

Because you're not allowed to use a calculator on the ISEE, estimating is sometimes your only option for solving QC questions.

Example #1

Column A	Column B
$\sqrt{20} + \sqrt{20}$	$\sqrt{50}$

The square root of 20 is between 4 and 5. Let's say it equals 4.5. In that case, $\sqrt{20} + \sqrt{20} = 9$. The square root of 50 would be just over 7. Therefore, **(A) is the correct answer.**

Example #2

Column A	Column B
$5 + 3\sqrt{2}$	$3 + 5\sqrt{2}$

This one is a bit harder, but your only option is to estimate. The square root of 2 is approximately 1.5, and $3 \times 1.5 = 4.5$. Column A = 9.5. $5\sqrt{2} = 5 \times 1.5 = 7.5$, and $7.5 + 3 = 10.5$. **(B) is the correct answer.** If you'd used a calculator, you would have found that column A is equal to 9.24 and column B is equal to 10.07. As you can see, our estimate wasn't too far off!

Mini Quiz - Strategy #2
Questions: 5
Time Limit: 2 minutes

1.

Column A	Column B
$\sqrt{15} + \sqrt{15}$	$\sqrt{36}$

2.

Column A	Column B
$\sqrt{16}$	$\sqrt{8} + \sqrt{8}$

3.

Column A	Column B
$4\sqrt{17}$	16

4.

Column A	Column B
$2 + 3\sqrt{2}$	$3 + 2\sqrt{2}$

5.

Column A	Column B
$10 + 6\sqrt{2}$	$6 + 10\sqrt{2}$

3. Compare pieces from each column

On questions that give you several numbers and seem to require that you perform a lot of calculations, try comparing individual pieces from each column. You should line the numbers up from smallest to largest and compare the smallest pieces in each column, the second smallest pieces in each column, etc.

Example #1

Column A	Column B
$\frac{1}{4} + \frac{2}{3} + \frac{2}{9}$	$\frac{2}{5} + \frac{3}{10} + \frac{3}{4}$

First, put the fractions in column A in order from smallest to largest: $\frac{2}{9} < \frac{1}{4} < \frac{2}{3}$. Do the same thing with the fractions in column B: $\frac{3}{10} < \frac{2}{5} < \frac{3}{4}$. Finally, compare the corresponding fractions from each column: $\frac{2}{9} < \frac{3}{10}$, $\frac{1}{4} < \frac{2}{5}$, and $\frac{2}{3} < \frac{3}{4}$. All of the fractions in column B are larger than the corresponding fractions in column A. **(B) is the correct answer.**

Example #2

Column A	Column B
$\dfrac{2}{5 + \dfrac{1}{4 + \frac{1}{2}}}$	$\dfrac{2}{4 + \dfrac{1}{3 + \frac{1}{3}}}$

This question is much easier than it looks! Let's compare piece by piece. Both fractions have a 2 in the numerator, so you can ignore that. Moving down to the left side of the denominator, column A has a 5 and column B has a 4. If both fractions have the same numerator, then the fraction with the *smaller* denominator is the *larger* fraction. So far, it looks like the fraction in column B is larger, but let's keep comparing to make sure.

On the right side of the denominator, column A has 1 over 4.5, while column B has 1 over $3.\overline{33}$. This piece of column B is also smaller than the corresponding piece of column A, so **the answer is (B).**

Mini Quiz - Strategy #3
Questions: 5
Time Limit: 4 minutes

1.

Column A	Column B
The average of 68, 73, 78, and 92	The average of 70, 76, 78, and 95

2.

Column A	Column B
$\frac{1}{10} + \frac{3}{4} + \frac{19}{20}$	$\frac{3}{4} + \frac{1}{15} + \frac{9}{10}$

3.

Column A	Column B
$\frac{2}{7} + \frac{4}{5} + \frac{3}{6}$	$\frac{3}{5} + \frac{1}{8} + \frac{4}{9}$

4.

$$a < b < c < d$$

Column A	Column B
$b + d$	$a + c$

5.

Column A	Column B
The average of 44, 12, 90, and 57	The average of 9, 57, 88, and 40

4. Make each column look as similar as possible

Sometimes, you'll be given two columns in which the values are presented in different forms.

Example #1

<u>Column A</u>	<u>Column B</u>
.6	$\frac{13}{21}$

You'll need to change both columns into fractions or both columns into decimals. It's easier to change .6 into a fraction than it is to change $\frac{13}{21}$ into a decimal, so start by doing that.

Now you can compare $\frac{6}{10}$ and $\frac{13}{21}$:

$21 \times 6 = 126$ and $10 \times 13 = 130$. $130 > 126$, so $\frac{13}{21}$ is the larger fraction. **The correct answer is (B).**

Mini Quiz - Strategy #4
Questions: 4
Time Limit: 3 minutes

1.

<u>Column A</u>	<u>Column B</u>
.45	$\frac{9}{19}$

2.

<u>Column A</u>	<u>Column B</u>
$\frac{16(2x + 1)}{4}$	$8x + 5$

3.

<u>Column A</u>	<u>Column B</u>
12% of 20	2.5

4.

<u>Column A</u>	<u>Column B</u>
$\frac{27(3x - 4)}{9}$	$9x - 12$

5. Determine if there is enough information to answer the question

This strategy is vitally important, but it also tends to be the most difficult for students. There are a few things to keep in mind:

- If a question contains only numbers, there is *always* enough information to answer the question.
- You can pick your own numbers if there are variables involved.
- If the answer changes depending on which numbers you pick, then the answer is (D).
- Be extra careful when a variable is squared and the answer is positive: the variable could either be positive or negative, since any number times itself will be positive.

Example #1

$$x \text{ is an even integer}$$

Column A	Column B
x^2	x^3

Let's pick a few numbers. If $x = 2$, then column A = 4 and column B = 8. However, if $x = -2$, then column A = 4 and column B = -8. Therefore, we cannot determine which column is larger. **The correct answer is (D).**

Example #2

$$x > 2$$

Column A	Column B
$x - 5$	-1

If $x = 3$, then column A = -2 and column B = -1. But, if $x = 5$, column A = 0 and column B = -1. **The correct answer is (D).**

Mini Quiz - Strategy #5
Questions: 4
Time Limit: 3 minutes

1. $ab = 10$ and $a + b = 7$

   <u>Column A</u>   <u>Column B</u>
       a b

2. x is a positive integer

   <u>Column A</u>   <u>Column B</u>
       x $x + \frac{3}{x}$

3.

   <u>Column A</u>   <u>Column B</u>
       2^5 5^2

4. $z > 1$

   <u>Column A</u>   <u>Column B</u>
      $z + 2$ 8

5.   <u>Column A</u>   <u>Column B</u>
       y $|y|$

Answer Key - Strategies for Quantitative Comparisons

Strategy #2

1. A
2. B
3. A
4. A
5. B

Strategy #3

1. B
2. A
3. A
4. A
5. A

Strategy #4

1. B
2. B
3. B
4. C

Strategy #5

1. D
2. B
3. A
4. D
5. D

Part III
Upper Level ISEE Math Fundamentals

Applied Arithmetic

Math Definitions

You should memorize the following definitions before taking the ISEE. Definitions that students struggle to remember are listed in bold; you should focus your efforts on those.

Vocab Word	Definition	Examples
Integer	A number that does not contain fractions or decimals. Integers can be positive, negative, or zero	-100, -5, 0, 2, 50
Even number	A number that is divisible by two. Zero is even	-34, -10, 0, 8, 92
Odd number	A number that is not divisible by two	-7, 1, 9, 99
Positive number	A number greater than zero	1, 4, 45, 100
Negative number	A number less than zero	-34, -16, -9, -5
Whole number	Positive integers and zero	0, 1, 5, 50, 75
Prime number	A number divisible only by 1 and itself. 1 is not prime. 2 is the only even prime number	2, 3, 5, 7, 11, 13, 17
Consecutive numbers	A series of integers that appear in the same order as they do on the number line	5, 6, 7 -6, -5, -4
Distinct numbers	Numbers that are different from one another	1, 2, 3, 4, 5
Consecutive even numbers	A series of even integers that appear in the same order as they do on the number line	-2, 0, 2, 4 34, 36, 38
Consecutive odd numbers	A series of odd integers that appear in the same order as they do on the number line	-9, -7, -5 3, 5, 7
Sum	The result of addition	The sum of 5 and 7 is 12
Difference	The result of subtraction	The difference between 20 and 5 is 15
Product	The result of multiplication	The product of 3 and 9 is 27
Quotient	The result of division	The quotient of 12 and 4 is 3
Divisible by	A number is divisible by another if there is no remainder	10 is divisible by 2 7 is not divisible by 2
Remainder	The amount that is left over after performing division	When 9 is divided by 2, the remainder is 1
Absolute value	The distance of a number from zero. Absolute value is always positive and is notated as $|x|$	$|10| = 10$ $|-45| = 45$

Vocab Word	Definition	Examples
Digits	The integers from 0 to 9	123 has three digits
Inclusive	Includes all integers in a range	There are 5 integers, inclusive, from 7 to 11 (7, 8, 9, 10, & 11)
Factor	All of the integers that a certain integer is divisible by	The factors of 20 are 1, 2, 4, 5, 10, and 20
Multiple	The result of multiplying an integer by another integer	20 is a multiple of 2 (2×10); 5 is a multiple of 5 (5×1)
Rational number	A number that can be written as a fraction	$4, \frac{2}{3}, .5, -7$
Irrational number	A number that can't be written as a simple fraction	$\sqrt{3}, \pi$
Numerator	The top part of a fraction	The numerator of $\frac{4}{5}$ is 4
Denominator	The bottom part of a fraction	The denominator of $\frac{10}{13}$ is 13
Least common multiple	The smallest number that is a multiple of two other numbers	The least common multiple of 6 and 4 is 12. The least common multiple of 10 and 15 is 30.
Greatest common factor	The greatest number that evenly divides into a set of other numbers	The greatest common factor of 20 and 15 is 5. The greatest common factor of 36 and 48 is 12
Prime factor	The prime numbers that an integer is divisible by	20 has two prime factors: 2 and 5. 6 has two prime factors: 2 and 3

Practice Questions

1. List 5 integers
2. List 5 prime numbers
3. Is 1 prime?
4. Is 2 prime?
5. List 4 consecutive odd integers
6. What is the quotient of 100 and 5?
7. $|-4-8| =$
8. List 4 rational numbers
9. List 3 irrational numbers
10. List 5 multiples of 4
11. What are the prime factors of 30?
12. How many digits does 109,805 have?
13. When 100 is divided by 30, what is the remainder?
14. What is the greatest common factor of 27 and 18?
15. What is the least common multiple of 10 and 12?

Negative Numbers

Adding, subtracting, multiplying, and dividing negative numbers are key skills that you must be able to perform quickly and accurately on the ISEE.

Adding and Subtracting Negative Numbers

You should always think of the number line when you have to add or subtract negative numbers.

Example

$10 + (-5) = ?$

Imagine 10 on the number line. If you add 5 to 10, it would move 5 units to the right, giving you 15. By adding *negative* five, you are adding "negativeness" to the 10, which drags it left on the number line by 5 units. The answer is 5.

Example

$-5 + (-2) = ?$

Imagine -5 on the number line. If you added +2, you would move two units to the right, resulting in -3. However, adding -2 means you move two units to the left. The answer is -7.

Example

$13 - (-7) = ?$

Imagine 13 on the number line. You can think of subtracting negative 7 as taking away "negativeness," which will result in an answer that is more positive than the original number. The answer is 20.

Students generally become confused when they start dealing with subtracting positive numbers from negative numbers. However, the concept is exactly the same!

Example

$-3 - 5 = ?$

First, imagine -3 on the number line. If you subtract 5 from +3, you would move to the left. You should do the same thing when starting with a negative number. Start at -3, and move 5 units to the left. The answer is -8.

Example

$-9 - (-6) = ?$

Any time you have to "minus a negative," you can instead change it to "plus a positive." You can also think of this as subtracting away "negativeness," making the final answer more positive. $-9 - (-6) = -9 + (+6) = -3$.

Multiplying and Dividing Negative Numbers

All you have to remember when you're multiplying and dividing with negative numbers is an even number of negative signs will result in a positive answer, and an odd number of negative signs will result in a negative answer. Other than that, things work exactly the same as they would if you were only dealing with positive numbers.

$10 \times -10 = -100$

$-10 \times -10 = 100$

$2 \times -2 \times -2 = 8$

$\frac{10}{-10} = -1$

$\frac{-10}{-10} = 1$

Practice Questions

1. $5 + 27 =$ ____

2. $4 + 8 =$ ____

3. $101 - 21 =$ ____

4. $45 - 17 =$ ____

5. $10 - 15 =$ ____

6. $0 - 47 =$ ____

7. $10 + (-8) =$ ____

8. $28 + (-11) =$ ____

9. $-18 + (-10) =$ ____

10. $-29 + 15 =$ ____

11. $-36 + 12 =$ ____

12. $-100 + (-200) =$ ____

13. $0 + (-10) =$ ____

14. $10 - (-4) =$ ____

15. $27 - (-8) =$ ____

16. $0 - (-11) =$ ____

17. $-7 - (-20) =$ ____

18. $-82 - (-12) =$ ____

19. $4 \times 7 =$ ____

20. $4 \times -7 =$ ____

21. $-4 \times -7 =$ ____

22. $-4 \times -7 \times 2 =$ ____

23. $-2 \times -2 \times -2 \times -2 \times -2 =$ ____

24. $4 \times -3 \times -3 \times 2 =$ ____

25. $\frac{-20}{-10} =$ ____

26. $\frac{-8}{2} =$ _-4_

27. $\frac{55}{11} =$ _5_

28. $\frac{102}{-2} =$ ____

29. $\frac{-100}{0} =$ ____

30. $\frac{0}{-10} =$ ____

Intro to Exponents

Exponents are used to tell you how many times a certain number should be multiplied by itself. They are composed of a *base*, which is written as a large number, and an *exponent*, which is the small number that indicates how many times the base should be multiplied times itself.

$$2^2 = 2 \times 2 \qquad 2^4 = 2 \times 2 \times 2 \times 2$$

2^2 is referred to as "two squared" or "two to the second," 2^3 is "two to the third," etc.

Multiplying Exponents

To multiply exponents that have the same base, you add the total number of exponents, and the base remains the same.

Example: $2^3 \times 2^4 = 2^7$

This makes a lot of sense if you think about it: $2^3 \times 2^4$ is the same as $(2 \times 2 \times 2) \times (2 \times 2 \times 2 \times 2)$. When written this way, it becomes obvious that there are a total of 7 twos.

Dividing Exponents

When dividing fractions with the same base, you subtract their exponents.

Example: $\dfrac{4^7}{4^3} = 4^4$

Raised Terms

It's easy to confuse raised terms with multiplying exponents. Generally, the difference is the base will only appear once when you are multiplying raised terms. For raised terms, the exponents should be *multiplied*, not added.

Example: $(2^2)^4 = 2^8$

If you wrote this out, it would look like this: $(2 \times 2) \times (2 \times 2) \times (2 \times 2) \times (2 \times 2) = 2^8$

Example: $(3^3)^8 = 3^{24}$

Practice Questions

1. $3^2 = \underline{9}$

2. $6^2 = \underline{36}$

3. $9^2 = \underline{81}$

4. $2^3 = \underline{8}$

5. $4^3 = \underline{64}$

6. $2^4 = \underline{16}$

7. $3^4 \times 3^5 = \underline{3^9}$

8. $4^9 \times 4^8 = \underline{4^{17}}$

9. $6^2 \times 6^{13} = \underline{6^{15}}$

10. $10^5 \times 10^5 = \underline{10^{10}}$

11. $\dfrac{12^5}{12^2} = \underline{12^3}$

12. $\dfrac{9^{15}}{9^3} = \underline{9^{12}}$

13. $\dfrac{5^5}{5^4} = \underline{5^1}$

14. $\dfrac{6^{88}}{6^{50}} = \underline{6^{38}}$

15. $(3^4)^4 = \underline{3^{16}}$

16. $(4^3)^9 = \underline{4^{27}}$

17. $(6^6)^6 = \underline{6^{36}}$

18. $(5^1)^1 = \underline{5^1}$

Advanced Exponents

There are a few other exponent rules that you should memorize.

1. Any number raised to the "zero" power equals one.

   Example: $2^0 = 1$

2. Any number raised to the "first" power equals itself

   Example: $50^1 = 50$

3. If there is a negative sign within parentheses, it should be included in the operation you are performing. If the negative sign is outside the parentheses, it is added on at the end.

   Example: $(-5)^2 = (-5)(-5) = 25$
   $-5^2 = -(5)(5) = -25$

4. A number to a negative exponent is equal to one over that same number to the positive exponent. If a negative exponent is found in the denominator of a fraction, you can flip the fraction and make the exponent positive.

   Example: $2^{-2} = \frac{1}{2^2} = \frac{1}{4}$

   $\frac{1}{x^{-4}} = x^4$

5. A negative number raised to an even exponent will be positive.

   Example: $(-2)^4 = 16$

6. A negative number raised to an odd exponent will be negative.

   Example: $(-4)^3 = -64$

7. A positive integer raised to a fraction between 0 and 1 will be less than the original integer.

   Example: $4^{2/3} \approx 2.52$

8. To simplify a fraction raised to an exponent, apply the exponent to each part of the fraction.

   Example: $\left(\frac{3}{4}\right)^2 = \frac{3^2}{4^2} = \frac{9}{16}$

9. A positive fraction raised to a power higher than one will be less than the original fraction.

   Example: $\left(\frac{1}{4}\right)^2 = \frac{1}{16}$

Practice Questions

1. $(-6)^2 = $ _____
2. $4^1 \times 2^3 = $ _____
3. $3^{-2} = $ _____
4. $4^0 = $ _____
5. $\left(\frac{1}{2}\right)^3 = $ _____

6. $(-3)^3 = $ _____
7. $-7^2 = $ _____
8. $2^{-3} \times 4^2 = $ _____
9. $21^0 \times 3^3 = $ _____
10. $\left(\frac{2}{3}\right)^2 \times 3^2 = $ _____

11. If $x^2 + 1 = y$ and $x = -4$, then $y = $ _____
12. $10^1 = $ _____
13. If $x^3 + 2 = y$ and $x = -2$, then $y = $ _____

Order of Operations / PEMDAS

The order of operations (PEMDAS) tells you what order to solve equations. You're probably already familiar with the mnemonic for remembering PEMDAS:

Please **E**xcuse **M**y **D**ear **A**unt **S**ally

This means that you should always complete **p**arentheses first, then **e**xponents. **M**ultiplication and **d**ivision are then completed from left to right; finally, **a**ddition and **s**ubtraction are completed from left to right.

Correct: $10 - 5 + 3 = 5 + 3 = 8$ ✓
Incorrect: $10 - 5 + 3 = 10 - 8 = 2$ ✗

Correct: $14 \div 7 + 10 \times 4 - 6 + 5 = 2 + 40 - 6 + 5 = 42 - 6 + 5 = 36 + 5 = 41$ ✓
Incorrect: $14 \div 7 + 10 \times 4 - 6 + 5 = 2 + 40 - 6 + 5 = 42 - 6 + 5 = 42 - 11 = 31$ ✗

It is very easy to make careless mistakes when working with PEMDAS. To minimize the risk of errors, you can use the inverted pyramid method of solving PEMDAS problems: only simplify one type of operation per line, and then rewrite the simplified equation on the next line. Repeat as necessary until you have simplified the expression.

Example #1
What is the value of
$(4 - 2)^2 + (5^2 - 23) + 33 - 6$?
(A)   25
(B)   27
(C)   33
(D)   39

$$(4 - 2)^2 + (5^2 - 23) + 33 - 6$$
$$(2)^2 + (5^2 - 23) + 33 - 6$$
$$4 + (5^2 - 23) + 33 - 6$$
$$4 + (25 - 23) + 33 - 6$$
$$4 + (2) + 33 - 6$$
$$6 + 33 - 6$$
$$39 - 6$$
$$33$$

The correct answer is (C).

Practice Questions

1. $15 - 5 + 8 = $ ____
2. $5 + (9 - 4) + 7 = $ ____
3. $(6 + 2) + (3 - 6) + 1 = $ ____
4. $(-4 - 8) - 3 \times 2 = $ ____
5. $4 \times 4 - 6 \times 2 = $ ____

6. $3 \times (5 - 2)^2 \div 9 = $ ____
7. $100 \div (20 \div 4 \times 2) = $ ____
8. $6 \times (2 + 7) \div (3 \times 3) \times (-3 + 6) = $ ____
9. $4 + (2 \times 3)^2 \div (4 \div 2) = $ ____
10. $150 - 120 \div 3 \times 2^3 = $ ____

Fractions

Fractions are numerical quantities that are not whole numbers. They are represented in two parts: the numerator (the top) and the denominator (the bottom). Examples of fractions include $\frac{1}{2}$ and $\frac{16}{5}$. Fractions indicate division. $\frac{1}{2}$, for example, means "one divided by two."

Reducing Fractions

To reduce a fraction, divide the numerator and the denominator by their greatest common factor.

Example

Reduce the fraction $\frac{12}{20}$

The greatest common factor of 12 and 20 is 4. $\frac{12 \div 4}{20 \div 4} = \frac{3}{5}$. This fraction can't be reduced any further. $\frac{3}{5} = \frac{12}{20}$. Both will give you .6 if you plug them into a calculator.

Finding the greatest common factor can be time consuming. If the numerator and denominator are both even, it's usually easiest to divide by 2 first. If they aren't both even, see if you can eyeball a common factor.

Example

Reduce the fraction $\frac{244}{300}$

We can see that both the numerator and denominator are even. Rather than find a greatest common factor, let's divide by two as many times as possible.

$\frac{244 \div 2}{300 \div 2} = \frac{122 \div 2}{150 \div 2} = \frac{61}{75}$. 61 is a prime number and has no factors other than 1 and 61, so we know this fraction cannot be reduced any further.

Example

Reduce the fraction $\frac{27}{81}$

Although 27 and 81 are not even, you might notice that they are both divisible by 9.

$\frac{27 \div 9}{81 \div 9} = \frac{3}{9}$. You're not finished just yet: 3 and 9 are both divisible by 3.

$\frac{3 \div 3}{9 \div 3} = \frac{1}{3}$. This fraction is now fully reduced.

Improper Fractions and Mixed Numbers

So far we have dealt only with fractions in which the numerator is smaller than the denominator. In many instances, however, the numerator will be greater than the denominator. These are known as improper fractions. Because fractions indicate division, this logically means that improper fractions represent numbers larger than 1. $\frac{9}{4}$ means "9 divided by 4." While you might not know the exact value off the top of your head, you do know that 4 goes into 9 more than one time.

You will need to know how to convert between improper fractions and mixed numbers. Mixed numbers are another way of representing improper fractions. To convert an improper fraction into a mixed number, see how many times the denominator goes into the numerator evenly. That number goes on the left. Then, take whatever is left over (the remainder) and put it over the original denominator. This fraction goes on the right.

Example

Convert $\frac{9}{7}$ to a mixed number

7 goes into 9 one time, with a remainder of 2. Place the 1 on the left, then take the remaining 2 and put it on top of your original denominator, which gives you $1 \frac{2}{7}$.

Example

Convert $\frac{30}{11}$ to a mixed number

11 goes into 30 two times, with a remainder of 8. Put the 2 on the left and the 8 on top of the original denominator. The final answer is $2 \frac{8}{11}$.

To convert from a mixed number to a fraction, multiply the denominator of the fraction by the big number on the left. Then, add the numerator to this number. This result becomes the new numerator, while the original denominator remains the same.

Example

Convert $3 \frac{4}{9}$ to an improper fraction

$9 \times 3 = 27$, and $27 + 4 = 31$. 31 is the new numerator, and the denominator is 9. The improper fraction is $\frac{31}{9}$.

Adding and Subtracting Fractions

Adding and subtracting fractions requires a common denominator. When you add or subtract the fractions, only the numbers in the numerator will change.

Example

$\frac{6}{11} + \frac{4}{11} = \frac{10}{11}$

If the numerators are not the same, you have to do more work. What number do both of the denominators go into?

Example

$\frac{3}{7} + \frac{1}{2} = ?$

7 and 2 both go into 14. $7 \times 2 = 14$, so you'll also need to multiply the numerator by 2, giving you $\frac{6}{14}$. $2 \times 7 = 14$, so you'll need to multiply 1 by 7 as well, giving you $\frac{7}{14}$. Now that you've found a common denominator, you can add like you did in the example above. $\frac{3}{7} + \frac{1}{2} = \frac{6}{14} + \frac{7}{14} = \frac{13}{14}$.

Sometimes, it can be tricky to find a common denominator. Using the *bow tie method* will help you easily find a common denominator in any pair of fractions!

Example

$\frac{3}{17} + \frac{4}{19} = ?$

Although you might have a hard time finding the common multiple of 17 and 19, you can easily solve this equation by using the bow tie method. $3 \times 19 = 57$, $17 \times 4 = 68$, and $17 \times 19 = 323$. You can rewrite this equation as $\frac{57}{323} + \frac{68}{323} = \frac{125}{323}$.

Comparing Fractions

You may be asked to compare fractions in the Quantitative Comparisons section. Using a partial bowtie method makes this a piece of cake!

Example

Which is larger: $\frac{2}{11}$ or $\frac{3}{20}$?

$$\frac{2}{11} \oplus \frac{3}{20} = \overset{40}{\underset{11}{2}} \oplus \overset{33}{\underset{20}{3}}$$

Multiply the denominator of one fraction by the numerator of the other fraction, and then write the product above the numerator. Whichever numerator has the larger number above it is the larger fraction. In this case, $\frac{2}{11} > \frac{3}{20}$.

Multiplying and Dividing Fractions

Multiplying and dividing fractions is much easier than adding and subtracting fractions! When multiplying, simply multiply straight across the numerator and straight across the denominator.

Example

$\frac{6}{11} \times \frac{4}{11} = ?$

$$\frac{6}{11} \times \frac{4}{11} = \frac{6 \times 4}{11 \times 11} = \frac{24}{121}$$

Dividing fractions requires one more step than multiplying fractions. First, flip the second fraction. Then, change the division sign to multiplication, and multiply like you did in the previous example.

Example

$\frac{6}{11} \div \frac{4}{11} = ?$

$$\frac{6}{11} \div \frac{4}{11} = \frac{6}{11} \times \frac{11}{4} = \frac{6 \times 11}{11 \times 4} = \frac{66}{44} = \frac{33}{22}$$

Finally, you should know that any fraction that has a 0 in the denominator is *undefined*. The ISEE loves testing this concept and you can be sure it will come up on the test. Fractions like $\frac{0}{0}$ and $\frac{19}{0}$ cannot be solved. Fractions with 0 in the numerator and any number but 0 in the denominator equal 0.

Practice Questions

Reduce

1. $\frac{10}{20} =$ ____

2. $\frac{6}{10} =$ ____

3. $\frac{15}{45} =$ ____

4. $\frac{999}{999} =$ ____

5. $\frac{232}{444} =$ ____

6. $\frac{55}{99} =$ ____

7. $\frac{100}{300} =$ ____

8. $\frac{126}{94} =$ ____

9. $\frac{12}{9} =$ ____

10. $\frac{20}{10} =$ ____

Convert to mixed numbers

1. $\frac{10}{9} =$ ____

2. $\frac{14}{10} =$ ____

3. $\frac{21}{15} =$ ____

4. $\frac{100}{85} =$ ____

5. $\frac{13}{6} =$ ____

6. $\frac{92}{14} =$ ____

7. $\frac{66}{11} =$ ____

8. $\frac{121}{100} =$ ____

9. $\frac{3}{2} =$ ____

10. $\frac{12}{5} =$ ____

Convert to improper fractions

1. $2\frac{3}{7} =$ ____

2. $5\frac{9}{10} =$ ____

3. $4\frac{3}{4} =$ ____

4. $5\frac{1}{6} =$ ____

5. $11\frac{1}{3} =$ ____

6. $2\frac{19}{20} =$ ____

7. $3\frac{7}{8} =$ ____

8. $10\frac{3}{10} =$ ____

9. $11\frac{4}{5} =$ ____

10. $100\frac{99}{100} =$ ____

Which fraction is larger?

1. $\frac{2}{7}$ or $\frac{3}{8} =$ ____

2. $\frac{3}{4}$ or $\frac{7}{10} =$ ____

3. $\frac{9}{13}$ or $\frac{15}{20} =$ ____

4. $\frac{3}{8}$ or $\frac{26}{71} =$ ____

5. $\frac{6}{17}$ or $\frac{20}{60} =$ ____

Add, subtract, multiply, or divide

1. $\frac{5}{9} + \frac{2}{9} =$ ____

2. $\frac{5}{11} \div \frac{4}{9} =$ ____

3. $\frac{3}{7} \times \frac{6}{7} =$ ____

4. $\frac{11}{12} - \frac{3}{4} =$ ____

5. $\frac{19}{20} \div \frac{2}{3} =$ ____

6. $\frac{23}{25} + \frac{1}{5} =$ ____

7. $\frac{8}{13} - \frac{4}{16} =$ ____

8. $\frac{5}{17} - \frac{4}{20} =$ ____

9. $\frac{9}{11} \div \frac{3}{4} =$ ____

10. $\frac{12}{13} \times \frac{1}{2} =$ ____

11. $\frac{3}{14} + \frac{4}{21} =$ ____

12. $\frac{6}{5} \times \frac{5}{6} =$ ____

13. $\frac{8}{9} \div \frac{2}{5} =$ ____

14. $\frac{8}{9} - \frac{2}{5} =$ ____

15. $\frac{7}{11} + \frac{3}{12} =$ ____

16. $\frac{4}{9} \times \frac{4}{9} =$ ____

Decimals

You will need to be able to add, subtract, multiply, and divide decimals on the ISEE.

Adding and Subtracting
To add and subtract decimals, line up the decimal points and then add or subtract as you normally would.

Examples

$$\begin{array}{r} 17.670 \\ +\ \ 4.321 \\ \hline 21.991 \end{array} \qquad\qquad \begin{array}{r} 9.0100 \\ -\ \ \ .0221 \\ \hline 8.9879 \end{array}$$

Multiplying
To multiply decimals, remove all of the decimals from the equation and then multiply as you normally would. When you're finished, add back in the total number of decimal places that were in the original numbers.

Example

$$2.34 \times 3.5 = 234 \times 35 = 8{,}190 = 8.190 = 8.190$$

There were 3 decimal places in the original equation (.34 and .5), so 3 decimal places must be added in at the end.

Dividing
To divide decimals, move the decimals in both numbers over the same number of spaces until there are no longer any decimals in the equation. Then, divide as you normally would.

Examples

$$\frac{14.52}{.04} = \frac{1452}{4} = 363 \qquad\qquad \frac{2.656}{41.5} = \frac{2656}{41500} = .064$$

Practice Questions

1. $4.954 - 2.91 =$ _____
2. $3.2 \times 1.1 =$ _____
3. $3.21 + 0.1202 =$ _____
4. $0.0052 \div 0.0002 =$ _____
5. $11.43 - 5.921 =$ _____
6. $12.5 + 6.34 =$ _____
7. $1.02 \times 3.1 =$ _____

8. $0.491 - 0.199 =$ _____
9. $2.43 \div 0.03 =$ _____
10. $0.999 \div 0.009 =$ _____
11. $10.9 + 0.04 =$ _____
12. $5.8 \times 2.32 =$ _____
13. $0.5 \div 0.25 =$ _____
14. $4.4 \times 2 =$ ___

Factors and Multiples

Factors are integers that can be multiplied together to get another integer. For example, $2 \times 3 = 6$, so 2 and 3 are factors of 6. Making a chart is a fail proof way of identifying all the factors of a certain integer. The chart below shows all the factors of 24:

24	
1	24
2	12
3	8
4	6

When making your chart, always start with 1 and work your way down. 1 times 24 equals 24, so put 1 and 24 in the first row. 2 times 12 equals 24, so put 2 and 12 in the second row, and so on. 24 is not divisible by 5, so 5 is the first integer that you don't put in the chart. 24 is divisible by 6, but you already entered 6 into the chart when you found that 4 was a factor of 24. Now that the integers have "met in the middle," you've found all the factors of 24.

Multiples are what you get when you multiply an integer by another integer. $6 \times 5 = 30$, so 30 is a multiple of 6 and 5. Each integer has an infinite number of multiples, because you can keep on multiplying that number by larger and larger integers all the way to infinity! Multiples of 15 include 15, 30, 45, 90, 105, 240, and so on. Note that 15 is a multiple of 15 because $15 \times 1 = 15$.

The classic way of remembering the difference between factors and multiples is "fewer factors, many multiples." An integer will have a limited number of factors, but an unlimited number of multiples.

The *greatest common factor* (GCF) of two integers is the largest integer that divides evenly into both of the two integers. For example, the greatest common factor of 60 and 90 is 30. To find the greatest common factor of two integers, make a factor tree for both integers, circle all the prime factors that those integers share in common, and multiply those shared prime factors together.

The *least common multiple* (LCM) of two integers is the smallest integer that is a multiple of both numbers. On the ISEE, it's easiest to write out the multiples of two integers until you get a match.

Example #1

What is the greatest common factor of 52 and 36?

(A)   2

(B)   4

(C)   8

(D)   36

Make a factor tree:

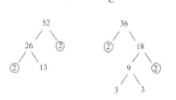

These two integers share 2 twos in common. $2 \times 2 = 4$. The greatest common factor of 52 and 36 is 4, so **the correct answer is (B).**

Example #2

What is the least common multiple of 6 and 8?

(A)   2

(B)   8

(C)   16

(D)   24

Write out the multiples of each number until you find a match:

6: 6, 12, 18, **24**, 30...

8: 8, 16, **24**, 32, 40...

The correct answer is (D).

There's also an "official" way of finding the least common multiple. First, find the prime factorization of each integer. If the integers share a prime factor, include that factor only once when you multiply. For prime factors that only one number has, include that prime factor one time when you multiply.

Example #3

Find the least common multiple of 36 and 42

(A)   2

(B)   6

(C)   84

(D)   252

Find the prime factorization of each number:

36: $2 \times 2 \times 3 \times 3$

42: $2 \times 3 \times 7$

36 and 42 share one 2 and one 3, so include each of those one time. This leaves 2, 3, and 7 remaining. $2 \times 3 \times 2 \times 3 \times 7 = 252$. **The correct answer is (D).**

Practice Questions

1. List all the factors of 25: 1, 25, 5

2. List all the factors of 36: 4, 2, 1, 36, 9, 18 12, 3

3. List all the factors of 100: 1, 100, 2, 50, 4, 25, 5, 20 10

4. 24 has how many distinct prime factors?: 2

5. 40 has how many distinct prime factors?: 2

6. List the first five multiples of 6: 6, 12, 18, 24, 30, 36

7. List the first 5 multiples of 4: 4, 8, 12, 16, 20

8. Find the GCF of 12 and 18: 6

9. Find the GCF of 36 and 96: 12

10. Find the GCF of 45 and 50: 5

11. Find the LCM of 10 and 12: 60

12. Find the LCM of 4 and 9: 36

13. Find the LCM of 18 and 5: 90

14. Find the LCM of 30 and 36: 180

Scientific Notation

Scientific notation is used to make it easier to write very large and very small numbers. For example, writing 5,923,000,000,000 is time consuming and wastes a lot of space. Using scientific notation, you can rewrite that number as 5.923×10^{12}. Here are the basics:

1) If the exponent next to 10 is positive, the number is greater than 1.
2) If the exponent next to 10 is negative, the number is smaller than 1.
3) The number to the left of the times sign must always be between 1 and 10.
4) The number to the right of the times sign will always be 10 raised to some power.

Converting to Scientific Notation

To convert a number to scientific notation, determine where you must place a decimal in order to make a number that is between 1 and 10. In the example above, we placed a decimal between 5 and 9, giving us 5.923. Then, determine how many decimal places you had to move in order to create that number. To transform 5,923,000,000,000.00 into 5.923000000000, the decimal was moved 12 places to the left. Your final answer is 5.923×10^{12}.

Examples: $142,000 = 1.42 \times 10^5$ $.0000576 = 5.76 \times 10^{-5}$

Addition and Subtraction with Scientific Notation

While there are several methods for adding and subtracting numbers expressed in scientific notation, our favorite is converting each number into standard notation, stacking them, adding them, and then converting back to scientific notation!

Examples: $(4.215 \times 10^{-2}) + (3.2 \times 10^{-4}) =$ $\begin{array}{r} .04215 \\ + .00032 \\ \hline .04247 \end{array}$ $= 4.247 \times 10^{-2}$

                 $(8.97 \times 10^4) - (2.62 \times 10^3) =$ $\begin{array}{r} 89,700 \\ - \ 2,620 \\ \hline 87,080 \end{array}$ $= 8.708 \times 10^4$

Be careful when using this method - you must make sure the decimals or commas of the two numbers line up when adding or subtracting.

Multiplication and Division with Scientific Notation

When multiplying or dividing numbers expressed in scientific notation, deal with the numbers to the left of the times sign individually and with the numbers to the right of the times sign individually. The same rules about exponents apply: when multiplying exponents that have the same base, you should add them.

Examples: $\dfrac{4.5 \times 10^8}{1.5 \times 10^5} = \dfrac{4.5}{1.5} \times \dfrac{10^8}{10^5} = 3 \times 10^3$ $(4 \times 10^4) \times (2 \times 10^3) = (4 \times 2) \times (10^4 \times 10^3) = 8 \times 10^7$

Practice Questions

Convert to scientific notation

1. $4,000,800,000 = 4.008 \times 10^9$
2. $200 = 10^2 \times 2$
3. $62,900,000 = 62.9 \times 10^7$
4. $.000945 = 9.45 \times 10^{-4}$
5. $.0123 = 1.23 \times 10^{-2}$
6. $.00007698 = 7.698 \times 10^{-5}$

Convert to standard notation

7. $9.34 \times 10^8 = 934,000,000$
8. $1.11 \times 10^4 = 11,100$
9. $4.7843 \times 10^{12} = 4,784,300,000,000$
10. $3.45 \times 10^{-5} = .0000345$
11. $2.42 \times 10^{-2} = .0242$
12. $7.7054 \times 10^{-8} = .000000077054$

Simplify

13. $\dfrac{9 \times 10^4}{4.5 \times 10^8} = 2 \times 10^{-4}$
14. $\dfrac{4.8 \times 10^8}{1.2 \times 10^3} = 4 \times 10^5$
15. $\dfrac{6.6 \times 10^4}{1.1 \times 10^9} = 6 \times 10^{-6}$
16. $\dfrac{3 \times 10^{12}}{2 \times 10^7} = 1.5 \times 10^5$
17. $(1.5 \times 10^4) \times (3 \times 10^8) = 4.5 \times 10^{12}$
18. $(2 \times 10^3) \times (2 \times 10^5) = 4 \times 10^8$
19. $(4.5 \times 10^5) \times (3 \times 10^6) = 1.5 \times 10^{12}$
20. $(2.4 \times 10^5) \times (3.2 \times 10^6) = 7.68 \times 10^{11}$
21. $(1.23 \times 10^4) + (3.1 \times 10^7) = 3.10123 \times 10^7$
22. $(2.23 \times 10^2) + (1.22 \times 10^5) = 1.22223 \times 10^5$
23. $(1.4 \times 10^8) + (9.27 \times 10^7) = 2.327 \times 10^8$
24. $(4.5 \times 10^5) - (4.1 \times 10^5) = 4.4 \times 10^4$
25. $(7.77 \times 10^6) - (7.77 \times 10^2) = 7.769223 \times 10^6$

4.50000   4.10000

0.4

$\div \dfrac{9}{4.5} \times \dfrac{10^4}{10^8} = 2 \times 10^{-4}$

$\div \dfrac{4.8}{1.2}$ $\dfrac{10^8}{10^3}$

$12\overline{)48}$ 1010.0000

$9 \div 4.5 = 2$ $\dfrac{3}{2} = 1.5$

$1.5 \times 10^4 \times 3 \times 10^8$

$4.5 \times 10^6 \times 3 \times 10^6$

$\dfrac{+7}{\times 5}$

4.5×10^{12}

$4.5 \div 3$ $10^6 \times 10^6$

7.770000   7.77
-7.770000
-7.77 =   7.769223

1.5 $1.4 \cdot 10^8 + 9.27 \cdot 10^7$

(7,769) 992.23   2   .9127   .140   .927
   + 1.4
   2.327

59

Operations with Roots

You can think of roots as the opposite of exponents. $2^2 = 4$, and $\sqrt{4} = 2$. When you see a number under the $\sqrt{}$ sign, you must ask yourself what number times itself equals that number.

Example: $\sqrt{25} = 5$ $\sqrt{169} = 13$ $\sqrt{x^2} = x$

For cube roots ($\sqrt[3]{}$), you must determine what number times itself two times equals the number under the cube root.

Example: $\sqrt[3]{125} = 5$ $\sqrt[3]{8} = 2$ $\sqrt[3]{x^3} = x$

Converting Roots to Fractional Exponents
On certain questions, it may be necessary to convert from roots to fractional exponents or vice versa.

Examples: $x^{\frac{4}{3}} = \sqrt[3]{x^4}$ $27^{\frac{1}{3}} = \sqrt[3]{27^1}$ $\sqrt[3]{64^2} = 64^{\frac{2}{3}}$ $\sqrt[4]{x^5} = x^{\frac{5}{4}}$

Do you notice a pattern? When converting a fractional exponent into a root, the bottom part of the fraction "goes down," while the top part "stays up." In other words, the denominator becomes the root, while the numerator stays attached to the big number as an exponent. When converting from a root to a fractional exponent, the root becomes the denominator of the fraction, while the exponent becomes the numerator.

The order in which you solve these *does not matter*. In $\sqrt[3]{64^2}$, for example, you can first take the cube root of 64 and then square that answer, or you can square 64 and then find the cube root of that answer. Since you can't use a calculator on the ISEE, it makes much more sense to find the cube root of 64, which is 4, and then do 4 squared.

Simplifying Roots
To simplify roots, you must find all the prime factors of the number under the root sign. Then, pull out any number pairs and rewrite them as one number outside the root sign.

Example: $\sqrt{40} = \sqrt{2 \times 2 \times 2 \times 5} = 2\sqrt{2 \times 5} = 2\sqrt{10}$ $\sqrt{50} = \sqrt{5 \times 5 \times 2} = 5\sqrt{2}$
                $\sqrt{75} = \sqrt{5 \times 5 \times 3} = 5\sqrt{3}$

Adding and Subtracting Roots
If the numbers under two roots are the same, you can add and subtract the numbers in front of the roots and leave the numbers under the roots alone. If they are not the same, you must simplify them until they are.

Example: $6\sqrt{2} + 3\sqrt{2} = 9\sqrt{2}$ $4\sqrt{4} - 10\sqrt{4} = -6\sqrt{4}$
                $\sqrt{20} + \sqrt{80} = \sqrt{2 \times 2 \times 5} + \sqrt{2 \times 2 \times 2 \times 2 \times 5} = 2\sqrt{5} + 4\sqrt{5} = 6\sqrt{5}$

Multiplying and Dividing Roots

Multiplying and dividing roots is easier than adding and subtracting them. You can multiply or divide the terms under the roots as though the roots are not there and then simplify your answer.

Example: $\sqrt{20} \times \sqrt{3} = \sqrt{60} = \sqrt{2 \times 2 \times 3 \times 5} = 2\sqrt{15}$ $\sqrt{7} \times \sqrt{12} = \sqrt{84} = \sqrt{2 \times 2 \times 3 \times 7} = 2\sqrt{21}$

$\dfrac{\sqrt{24}}{\sqrt{6}} = \sqrt{\dfrac{24}{6}} = \sqrt{4} = 2$ $\dfrac{\sqrt{100}}{\sqrt{10}} = \sqrt{\dfrac{100}{10}} = \sqrt{10}$

Multiplying and Dividing Roots with Coefficients

If the roots have coefficients next to them, you deal with the coefficients and the roots separately

Example: $2\sqrt{20} \times 3\sqrt{3} = 6\sqrt{60} = 6(2\sqrt{15}) = 12\sqrt{15}$ $\dfrac{50\sqrt{24}}{25\sqrt{6}} = 2\sqrt{4} = 2(2) = 4$

Practice Questions

1. $\sqrt{16} = $ _4_

2. $\sqrt{81} = $ _9_

3. $\sqrt[3]{27} = $ _3_

4. $\sqrt[4]{16} = $ _4_

5. $\sqrt{28}$ $2\sqrt{7}$

6. $\sqrt{68}$ $2\sqrt{17}$

7. $\sqrt{44} = $ $2\sqrt{11}$

8. $4\sqrt{3} + 2\sqrt{3} = $ $6\sqrt{3}$

9. $9\sqrt{7} - 4\sqrt{7} = $ $5\sqrt{7}$

10. $\sqrt{18} + \sqrt{72}$ $9\sqrt{2}$

11. $\sqrt{48} + \sqrt{300} = $ $14\sqrt{3}$

12. $\sqrt{40} - \sqrt{20} = $ $2\sqrt{10} - 2\sqrt{5}$

13. $\sqrt{8} \times \sqrt{6} = $ 48

14. $\sqrt{2} \times \sqrt{8} = $ $\sqrt{16} = 4$

15. $\dfrac{\sqrt{30}}{\sqrt{6}}$ $\sqrt{\dfrac{30}{6}} = \sqrt{5}$

16. $\dfrac{\sqrt{40}}{\sqrt{4}} = \sqrt{\dfrac{40}{4}} = \sqrt{10}$

17. $\dfrac{\sqrt{99}}{\sqrt{11}} = \sqrt{\dfrac{99}{11}} = \sqrt[2]{9} = 3$

18. $\dfrac{10\sqrt{28}}{2\sqrt{7}} = 5\sqrt{4} = 2$ $5\times2 = 10$

19. $\dfrac{75\sqrt{90}}{25\sqrt{2}} = $ $3^{45}\sqrt{\frac{90}{2}} = 9\sqrt{5}$

20. $9\dfrac{45\sqrt{18}}{5\sqrt{2}} 3 = $ _27_

21. $\sqrt{27x^3} = $ $3x\sqrt{3x}$

22. $\sqrt{64x^2} = $ $8x$

23. $2x\dfrac{4x\sqrt{9x^4}}{2\sqrt{3x^2}} = 2x^3\sqrt{3}$

24. $\dfrac{x^5\sqrt{x^8}}{x^3\sqrt{x^5}} = x\sqrt[3]{x}$ $\dfrac{x^6}{x^3}$ $\dfrac{\sqrt{x^8}}{\sqrt{x^5}} = x^2\sqrt[3]{x}$
     $x^2\cdot\sqrt{x^2}\cdot\sqrt{x}$
     $(\sqrt{x^3})^{\frac{1}{2}} x^2\cdot x\cdot\sqrt{x} = x^3\sqrt{x}$

25. $\dfrac{5\sqrt{20x^5}}{25\sqrt{4x^2}} = x\sqrt{5x}$ $\dfrac{1}{5}$ $\dfrac{5}{5}$

48 16×3 300
$\sqrt{2\times2\times2\times6}$ $+100\times3$
$8\times8\times3$ $8\sqrt{3}$ $6\sqrt{3}$ 16800

20×2
$2\sqrt{10} \rightarrow 2\sqrt{5}$ $\frac{20}{}$

Ratios

Ratios show a relationship between two amounts and show the number of times one value is contained within the other. You're familiar with ratios, even if you haven't formally studied them before. For example, if there are 8 girls and 9 boys in your class, you would say the ratio of girls to boys is 8 to 9. This information can be represented in several ways:

$$8 \text{ to } 9 \qquad\qquad 8 : 9 \qquad\qquad \frac{8}{9}$$

Ratios should be written in their most reduced form. Also note that a ratio of 8 to 9 is different than a ratio of 9 to 8! Misleading answer choices will definitely be included on the ISEE.

Example #1

There are 5 pencils and 4 pens in your bookbag. What is the ratio of pens to writing utensils?

There are 4 pens and 9 writing utensils total. Therefore, the ratio is 4 : 9.

Example #2

There are 6 drummers and 12 trombonists in the school band. What is the ratio of trombonists to drummers?

There are 12 trombonists for every 6 drummers, so the ratio is 12 : 6. You should reduce this so your final answer is 2 : 1.

Harder questions involving ratios will give you a ratio and one actual number and then ask you to solve for the rest of the missing information. In order to do this, you will need to find something that is known as a *multiplier*. For example, if the ratio of girls to boys in a classroom is 2 : 1 and there are 16 girls in the classroom, that means the multiplier is 8, because $2 \times 8 = 16$. Therefore, there are 8 boys in the classroom, because $8 \times 1 = 8$.

In the most difficult questions, you will be given a multi-part ratio and asked to find real numbers. In these questions, add up all the numbers in the ratio, then divide the total number of objects by that number. This gives you the multiplier. Multiply each part of the ratio by that multiplier in order to find the real number of objects in each category.

Example #3

There are 120 animals in the zoo, and the ratio of lions to tigers to polar bears is 1 : 2 : 3. How many tigers are there in the zoo?

$1 + 2 + 3 = 6$. $\frac{120}{6} = 20$. The multiplier is 20. Therefore, there are 20 lions, 40 tigers, and 60 polar bears. In these questions, you can always double check your work at the end. $20 + 40 + 60 = 120$, so you know you have done the work correctly. Make sure to pay close attention to the order of the ratio!

Practice Questions

1. There are 13 boys and 15 girls in a classroom. What is the ratio of boys to the total number of students?

2. If the ratio of fourth graders to fifth graders is 3 : 4, could there be 14 total students?

3. If a box of chocolates has 4 dark chocolates, 9 milk chocolates, and 3 white chocolates, what is the ratio of dark chocolate to white chocolate after one third of the white chocolates have been removed?

4. The ratio of strawberries to blueberries is 3 : 7. If there are 15 strawberries, how many blueberries are there?

5. There are 40 students in a classroom. If the ratio of girls to boys is 3 : 1, how many girls are in the classroom?

6. There are 63 shirts, pants, and shorts in your closet. If the ratio of shirts to pants to shorts is 1 : 5 : 3, how many pants are there?

Rates

A rate is a measure, quantity, or frequency, and it is usually expressed in terms of one measurement compared to some other measurement. A classic example of a rate is "miles per hour." This phrase indicates how many miles something travels in one hour. You can also measure "miles per minute," "kilometers per second," or "cost per unit."

Rates can be expressed as fractions:

$$\frac{miles}{hour} \qquad \frac{dollars}{minute}$$

Questions involving rates on the ISEE will usually give you a rate and then ask you to solve for one part of the fraction in another, related rate. You can use your knowledge of cross multiplying to create two fractions, set them equal to one another, and then solve for the missing piece of information.

Example #1

A car drives 60 miles in two hours. How many miles does the car travel in 3.5 hours?

Set up your fractions, making sure that corresponding pieces of information go in the same place in each fraction:

$$\frac{60\ miles}{2\ hours} = \frac{x\ miles}{3.5\ hours}$$
$$(60)(3.5) = (2)(x)$$
$$210 = 2x$$
$$105 = x$$

The car travels 105 miles in 3.5 hours. On multiple choice questions, think about whether your answer choice makes sense. In this example, if your answer was 45 miles, would that make sense? Of course not - the car won't travel a shorter distance over a longer period of time! Likewise, if you found an answer of 500 miles, that would be way too big.

Practice Questions

1. If you can buy 7 pens for 30 cents, how many pens can you buy with $1.20?

2. A chef is able to bake 5 cakes every 2 hours. How many cakes will the chef bake in 12 hours?

3. Your friend drives 40 miles in 30 minutes. How many minutes will it take your friend to drive 220 miles?

4. You can write 2 pages of an essay in 3 hours. How many hours does it take to write 8.75 pages?

5. A cheetah runs 80 miles per hour. How many miles does it travel in 1 minute?

6. On a map, 2.5 cm equals 125 miles. If two cities are 11 cm apart on the map, what is the actual distance between them?

Percents and Percent Change

Percent means "out of 100." When you are asked to find a percent, it's the same thing as finding how many times out of 100 times something happens. Once you've mastered fractions and decimals, dealing with percents is easy. You just have to make a fraction, convert that fraction to a decimal, and then multiply the decimal by 100. If possible, you should try to make the denominator of the fraction 100 since this will make converting to a decimal much easier.

Example #1

If a test has 25 questions on it, and you answer 18 questions correctly, what was your score on the test?

$$\frac{18}{25} \times \frac{4}{4} = \frac{72}{100} = .72 \times 100 = 72\%$$

Example #2

On a math test, you answer all 20 questions correctly, and you also answer the extra credit question correctly, which adds 3 points to your score. What was your score on the test?

$$\frac{23}{20} \times \frac{5}{5} = \frac{115}{100} = 1.15 \times 100 = 115\%$$

You will also be asked to work with percents in real world situations.

Example #3

A $150 dress is marked down 30%. What is the sale price?

First, find 30% of $150 by multiplying: $150 \times .30 = 45$. Then subtract 45 from 150. The sale price is $105. To save yourself some work, you can also multiply 150 by 70%, since 30% *off* the original price is the same as 70% *of* the original price.

Example #4

The price of a $2.50 cup of coffee increases by 26%. What is the new price?

First, find 26% of $2.50 by multiplying: $2.50 \times .26 = 0.65$. Then, add 0.65 to 2.50. The new price is $3.15. You can also multiply 2.50 by 1.26 and save yourself a step.

Practice Questions

1. What is 60% of 150?   *90*
2. If you answer 44 questions correctly out of 55 on a test, what percent did you get right? *80%*
3. What is 125% of 22? *27.50*
4. What is 12% of 44? *5.28*
5. If you answer 27 questions correctly out of 30 on a test, what percent did you get right? *$\frac{27}{30} = .9 = 90\%$*

6. The price of a $12.00 entree increases 15%. What is the new price? *13.80*
7. The price of a $9,000 car decreases 10%. What is the new price? *8,100*
8. A $65 shirt goes on sale for 20% off. What is the sale price? *$65 \times .20 = 13$ 52*
9. What is 100% of 99? *99*

1.50 × .60
$\frac{44}{55} \times 0.8 \times 100$
80%

$1.25 \times 22 = 27.50$
.12 × 44 = 5.28

$9,000 \times .10 = 900$
$9,000 - 900$
$8,100$

Percent Change

The *percent change formula* will help you find percent change when you aren't dealing with easy numbers like 10 and 100:

$$\frac{change}{original} \times 100$$

As you can see, the percent change formula doesn't look like most formulas since it only contains one number. What do the words in this equation mean? It's pretty simple: when you have a number that is increased or decreased to a different number, the *difference* between those two numbers goes on the top of the fraction, while the first, original number goes on the bottom.

Example #1
Robbie drank 80 mL of water from a bottle filled with 120 mL of water. What was the percent decrease in the amount of water in the bottle?

The *change* is 80. The *original* number is 120. $\frac{80}{120} = 0.\overline{66} \times 100 = 66.66\%$. The amount of water in the bottle decreased by 66.66%.

Example #2
The population of a town increased from 25 to 75. What is the percent change in the population?

The *change* is 75 – 25 = 50. The *original* number is 25. $\frac{50}{25} = 2 \times 100 = 200\%$. The population of the town increased by 200%. Notice how using the percent change formula makes dealing with percent change of 100%, 200%, 300% etc much easier than trying to do it in your head.

Practice Questions

10. This year, 9 new students join Jack's class of 45 students. What is the percent increase in the size of Jack's class?

11. The price of an entree increases from $14 to $21. What is the percent increase in the entree's price?

12. The population of a rural town decreases from 84 people to 63 people. What is the percent decrease in the town's Population?

13. Charlie's rent increases from $1,200 per month to $1,350 per month. What is the percent increase in his rent?

14. 12 pencils are added to a pencil box that already contains 20 pencils. What is the percent increase in the number of pencils?

15. A student eats 7 french fries from a basket of 25 french fries. What is the percent decrease in the number of french fries?

Mean, Median, Mode, and Range

Mean, median, mode, and range are statistical measures.

Mean is the same as an average. To find the mean of a data set, add up all the numbers and divide by the total number of numbers.

Example: the mean of 3, 7, 4, 5, 9, and 2 is

$$\frac{3+7+4+5+9+2}{6} = 5$$

Median is the middle number in a data set when you line all the numbers up in order from smallest to largest. If there are an even number of numbers, then the median is the average of the two numbers in the middle.

Example: the median of 2, 1, 7, 5, and 10 is 5. When you line the numbers up, you get 1, 2, 5, 7, 10. 5 is in the middle.

Mode is the number that shows up most often in a data set. You can commit this to memory by noting that **mo**de and **mo**st both start with **mo-**.

Example: the mode of 4, 7, 100, 3, 7, 5, and 8 is 7, because this number appears twice.

Range is the largest number minus the smallest number in a data set.

Example: the range of 60, 78, 3, 9, 44, and 57 is 75, because $78 - 3 = 75$.

The questions about mean, median, mode, and range on the ISEE will not be as simple as the examples above. It is very important to consider these questions carefully and logically. You should always line up the numbers in order from smallest to largest to avoid making careless mistakes.

Example #1

What is the average of the set of integers $\{x, x + 4, x + 8, x + 12\}$?

Although there are variables in this data set, you can still find the average just like you would normally.

$$\frac{x + x + 4 + x + 8 + x + 12}{4} = \frac{4x + 24}{4} = x + 6.$$

Example #2

Because the scores on his students' most recent math test were so poor, Mr. Jeffries decided to add 20 points to each student's test. Which measure of central tendency would change the least?

Think logically: the mean would go up quite a bit. The median and the mode would also increase. However, the range would not change at all. It may be easiest to create your own data set so you can see how this works. Pretend that the students scored 10, 15, 15, 25, and 35 on the test. The mean is 20, the median is 15, the mode is 15, and the range is 25. Now, add 20 points to each score. Your new data set is 30, 35, 35, 45, and 55. The mean is 40, the median is 35, the mode is 35, and the range is still 25.

Example #3

If the mean of 3 different positive integers is 15 and the median is 10, which of the following could not be the value of the largest integer?

(A)   25

(B)   26

(C)   30

(D)   32

Think through this carefully; the question actually provides more information than you might think at first glance. You know that there are three different integers, and the middle integer is 10. We also know that the sum of the three integers is 45, because $\frac{45}{3} = 15$, and we are told that 15 is the average. So, start with 26. If 10 is the middle integer and 26 is the largest integer, then the third integer must be 9. This gives 3 different integers: 9, 10, and 26. That isn't our answer. What about (A)? If 10 is the middle integer and 25 is the largest integer, the third integer must be 10. This is not acceptable, because the question tells us that the integers are all different. Therefore, **(A) is the correct answer.**

Example #4

The following set of numbers is missing one entry: 4, 5, 5, 7, 7, 9. If the median of the set is 7, which of the following could be the missing number?

(A)   1

(B)   4

(C)   5

(D)   9

You can work backwards on this question. If 1 is the missing number, then the median would be 5. If 4 is the missing number, the median would be 5. If 5 is the missing number, the median would be 5. If 9 is the missing number, the median would be 7. **The correct answer is (D).**

Practice Questions

1.   At a family reunion, each person took an average of 13 pictures. If 156 total pictures were taken, how many people were at the reunion?

2.   The average of 6 numbers is 6. When a seventh number is added, the average of the seven numbers is also 6. What is the seventh number?

3.   Four friends have the following number of chocolate bars: 15, 13, 20, and 24. What is the mean number of chocolate bars?

4.   In the following data set, which is the greatest: mean, median, mode, or range? {2, 2, 7, 11, 19, 55}

5.   The average of 3 numbers is 72. If two of the numbers are 40 and 66, what is the third number?

6.   What is the average of the set of integers {a, $a + 8$, $a - 6$, and $a + 14$}?

7.   If the mean of three different positive integers is 44, what is the greatest possible value of one of the integers?

Probability

Probability tells you the likelihood of something happening. It is expressed as a number between zero (event never occurs) and one (event always occurs). Probability can be expressed as a fraction, decimal, or percent. The formula for probability is:

$$\text{Probability} = \frac{number\ of\ favorable\ outcomes}{total\ number\ of\ possible\ outcomes}$$

Example #1

What is the probability of flipping heads on a coin?

This one is easy. There are two possible outcomes: heads or tails. Heads is a "favorable outcome," so it goes in the numerator. The probability of flipping heads is $\frac{1}{2}$.

Example #2

What is the probability of rolling a 3 or a 4 on a die?

Another easy one! There are six possible outcomes, and two of them are "favorable." The probability of rolling a 3 or a 4 on a die is $\frac{2}{6} = \frac{1}{3}$.

The examples above show the most basic fundamentals of probability, but the questions on the ISEE won't be so easy. It's more likely that you'll be asked about the probability of two events happening simultaneously. In these questions, find the probability of each event occurring by itself, and then multiply the two probabilities to find the chances of both events happening.

Example #3

What is the probability of rolling a 6 on a die and flipping heads on a coin?

The probability of rolling a 6 is $\frac{1}{6}$ and the probability of flipping heads is $\frac{1}{2}$. $\frac{1}{6} \times \frac{1}{2} = \frac{1}{12}$.

Example #4

You roll a 6 on a die. What is the probability that you will then flip heads on a coin?

This is a trick question! If you've already rolled 6 on a die, that has no relationship at all to whether you'll flip heads on a coin. In this example, the answer is simply $\frac{1}{2}$.

Practice Questions

1. There is a .4 probability that it will rain tomorrow. What is the probability that it will not rain tomorrow?
2. What is the probability of rolling an even number on a die and flipping heads on a coin?

3. What is the probability of rolling a 6 twice in a row?
4. What is the probability of flipping heads 4 times in a row?

Permutations and Combinations

Permutations and combinations refer to lists and groups. Both of these terms are easiest to understand after looking at a few examples. *Permutations* indicate all possible ways of doing something.

Example #1

There are five contestants in a school competition. How many possible ways can these five students be awarded a gold, silver, and bronze medal?

There are five students who could be awarded a gold medal. Once you've awarded a student a gold medal, there are four remaining students who could receive a silver medal. Once you've awarded the silver medal, there are three students who could win the bronze medal. Multiply these numbers together to get your final answer: $5 \times 4 \times 3 = 60$.

Example #2

Shantae wants to arrange four of her six books on a bookshelf. How many possible ways can these six books be arranged?

Here, you could draw a slot for each position to help yourself visualize the question:

Each slot represents a book on the bookshelf. How many choices does Shantae have for the leftmost position? She has six books, so she has six choices for that first position. Once she has placed a book in the first position, she has five remaining to choose from for the second position, and so on. Therefore, she has $6 \times 5 \times 4 \times 3 = 360$ possible ways in which to arrange her books.

Combinations are for groups of objects where order doesn't matter. Think of it this way: if you're picking friends to be on a basketball team, choosing Sammy, Sage, and Sally is exactly the same as choosing Sage, Sally, and Sammy. These two groups make 2 permutations but only 1 combination!

Example #3

A pizza shop owner plans to give out 3 identical pizzas to 3 different people in a group of 8 people. How many ways could the owner give out the pizzas?

Find the permutations first. The first pizza could go to 8 people, the second pizza could go to 7 people, and the third pizza could go to 6 people: $8 \times 7 \times 6 = 336$. However, within those permutations there will be redundancies. Giving pizzas to people #1, #2, and #3 is the same as giving pizzas to people #2, #1, and #3. Therefore, we need to divide out the redundancies. To do this, ask yourself how many ways there are to arrange 3 pizzas. The answer is $3 \times 2 \times 1 = 6$. When you divide 336 by 6, you find that there are 56 possible ways the owner could give out the pizzas.

Example #4

The local pizza shop has five kinds of toppings. You and your friend will each choose a topping to go on the pizza, and neither of you will choose the same topping. How many combinations of pizza toppings could you make?

In this example, there are $5 \times 4 = 20$ permutations. However, because choosing pepperoni and sausage is the same as choosing sausage and pepperoni, you must divide out the redundancies. How many ways can 2 toppings be arranged? The answer is $2 \times 1 = 2$ ways. 20 divided by 2 = 10. There are 10 combinations of toppings that you and your friend could choose.

Example #5

A teacher will place 10 books on a shelf. She has 4 science books, 3 math books, and 3 English books. If the teacher wants to put the math books on the left, the science books in the middle, and the English books on the right, in how many ways can she place the books on the shelf?

Imagine 10 slots. The math books must go on the left, so there are $3 \times 2 \times 1 = 6$ possible ways for them to be arranged. The science books must go in the middle, so there are $4 \times 3 \times 2 \times 1 = 24$ ways for them to be arranged. The English books must go on the right, so there are $3 \times 2 \times 1 = 6$ ways for them to be arranged. Multiplying $6 \times 24 \times 6$ gives us 864 possible ways to arrange the books.

Example #6

At a party, each of the 7 guests will shake hands with every other guest exactly one time. How many handshakes are exchanged during the party?

Each person shakes 6 people's hands, so at first guess that's $7 \times 6 = 42$ handshakes. However, this double counts the number of handshakes since we count the handshake between person A and B once when we count A's 6 handshakes and a second time when we count B's 6 handshakes. Therefore, we divide our answer by 2 and get 21.

There are a few takeaways from these examples:
1. In identical situations, there will always be more permutations than combinations.
2. Questions on the ISEE will not necessarily reference *permutations* or *combinations*. More often, they will ask about arrangements of groups of objects.
3. You can identify permutations vs. combinations by asking yourself whether the order matters. In this situation, is A, B, C, the same as C, A, B? If the answer is yes, it is a combination. If the answer is no, it is a permutation.

Practice Questions

1. How many ways can first place and second place prizes be awarded to ten people?

2. Joey's grandma will let him choose 3 different ice cream toppings from 7 available ice cream toppings. How many different combinations of toppings can Joey make?

3. When getting dressed for school, you choose from four shirts, three pairs of pants, and four pairs of socks. How many different outfits are possible?

4. The 7-member debate team plans to send 3 of its members to a conference. How many combinations of 3 members are possible from the 7-member team?

5. Jamie wants to put four of her books on a shelf. The history book must be placed in the leftmost position, while the math book must be placed in the rightmost position. How many ways can her books be arranged

6. You are asked to create a 4-character password using the 26 letters of the alphabet. The first three letters must be consonants, while the last letter must be a vowel. If no letter can be used more than once, how many different passwords can you make? Express your answer using the "slot" method.

7. Your father has five types of vegetable seeds and wants to plant a garden that contains three different types of vegetables. How many combinations of vegetables could he plant in the garden?

8. Clara wants to put seven of her books on a shelf. She wants to put *13 Reasons Why* in the middle. How many ways can her books be arranged? Express your answer using the "slot" method.

9. You are asked to create a 7-character password using the 26 letters of the alphabet. The first four letters must be vowels, while the last three letters must be consonants. If each letter can be used multiple times, how many possible passwords can you make? Express your answer using the "slot" method.

10. An ice cream shop sells 11 kinds of ice cream and 7 kinds of toppings. If you must also choose between a cone or a cup, how many different options does the store offer?

11. The 8-member soccer team plans to send 4 of its members to the championship. How many combinations of 4 members are possible from the 8-member team?

Translating English into Math

Many algebra word problems will require that you create your own equation. You should memorize the terms on the chart below.

English	Math	Example	Translation
What, a number	Any variable (x, y, etc)	A number is equal to three divided by four	$n = \frac{3}{4}$
Equals, is, was, has, costs, are	=	x equals 10 An apple costs 4 dollars	$x = 10$ $a = \$4$
Sum, greater than, more, added to, increased by, total	+	Ben is four years older than Steve Ben and Steve have a total of $16	$b = s + 4$ $b + s = \$16$
Decreased by, difference, less than, fewer	–	Mary has four fewer toys than Cain x is 9 less than y	$m = c - 4$ $x = y - 9$
Product, times, of, twice, triple, half of	×	An apple costs twice as much as a pear x is the product of y and 7	$a = 2p$ $x = 7y$
Per, for, out of, divided by, ratio	÷	The ratio of apples to oranges is 4 to 7 Harry drives 40 miles per hour	$\frac{a}{o} = \frac{4}{7}$ $h = \frac{40 \ miles}{hour}$

Example #1

The sum of Laurie and Joanna's income is $400 less than three times Joanna's income. Rewrite as an equation.

Underline the key words: *sum, is, less than, times*. "Is," which can be rewritten as an equals sign, goes in the middle. On the left, there will be a plus sign: $l + j$. On the right, three times Joanna's income = $3j$. Finally, subtract 400 from $3j$. The final equation is $l + j = 3j - 400$.

You'll notice that the question above isn't exactly easy to solve now that you've converted it into an equation. On the ISEE, it is often beneficial to work backwards or choose your own numbers on algebra word problems.

Example #2

Joyce has two more candy bars than Remy, and Remy has half as many candy bars as Amy. If j is the number of candy bars that Joyce has, then in terms of j, how many candy bars does Amy have?

(A) $j - 2$
(B) $2j$
(C) $2j - 2$
(D) $2j - 4$

$r = j - 2$, and $a = 2r$. In the second equation, replace r with $j - 2$ to get $2(j - 2) = 2j - 4$. Alternatively, use your own numbers. If $j = 5$, then $r = 3$ and $a = 6$. The target number is 6. Plugging $j = 5$ into (D) gives you $2(5) - 4 = 6$.

Practice Questions

1. A 39-foot piece of wood is cut into three pieces. The second piece is 3 times as long as the first piece. The third piece is 6 feet shorter than the first piece. How many feet long is the second piece?
   (A) 3
   (B) 9
   (C) 18
   (D) 27

2. Bruce has 4 dollars more than Osho, but 7 dollars less than Errol. If Bruce has b dollars, how many dollars do Osho and Errol have together?
   (A) $b + 7$
   (B) $2b - 4$
   (C) $2b + 3$
   (D) $4b - 7$

3. The sum of two numbers is two more than four times the smaller number, and the sum of the two numbers is 22. What is the value of the smaller number?
   (A) 2
   (B) 3
   (C) 4
   (D) 5

4. The sum of two numbers is equal to 79 less than their product. If one of the numbers is 11, what is the other number?
   (A) 8
   (B) 9
   (C) 11
   (D) 15

5. Kurt has 12 more books than Vaughn. Liz has one third as many books as Kurt. If v is the number of books Vaughn has, then how many books does Liz have, in terms of v?
   (A) $\frac{v}{3} + 4$
   (B) $v + 12$
   (C) $\frac{v}{3} + 12$
   (D) $v - 6$

6. A 250-foot wire is cut into three pieces. The third piece is 9 times as long as the first piece. The second piece is 140 feet longer than the first piece. How many feet long is the first piece?
   (A) 10
   (B) 15
   (C) 20
   (D) 90

Units of Measurement

You should memorize the following units of measurement before taking the ISEE. Related questions on the test most often ask for the appropriate units of measurement for a specific item.

Length

Standard unit of measure:

meter

1 meter is approximately 3 feet.

Related units:

Millimeter - the thickness of a credit card
Centimeter - a bit less than half an inch
Kilometer - a bit more than half a mile

Mass

Standard unit of measure:

gram

1 gram is approximately the weight of a sugar packet

Related units:

Milligram - about the weight of a snowflake
Kilogram - a little more than two pounds

Volume

Standard unit of measure:

liter

The large bottles of soda that people buy for birthday parties are 2 liters

Related units:

Milliliter: there are about 5 milliliters in a teaspoon

Prefixes

You may have noticed that the related units above all use the same prefixes.

Milli: one thousandth
Centi: one hundredth
Kilo: one thousand

Memorizing these prefixes will help you recognize any units of measurement that appear on the ISEE.

Practice Questions

1.   What units are most appropriate for measuring the length of a leaf?
2.   What units are most appropriate for measuring the weight of a basketball?
3.   What units are most appropriate for measuring the volume of a small bottle of medicine?
4.   What units are most appropriate for measuring the volume of a bathtub?
5.   What units are most appropriate for measuring the weight of a car?
6.   What units are most appropriate for measuring the length of a basketball court?

Answer Key - Applied Arithmetic

Math Definitions

1. Possible answers include -50, -8, 0, 1, 2, 34, etc
2. Possible answers include 2, 3, 5, 7, 11, 13, 17, 19, etc
3. No
4. Yes
5. Possible answers include 1, 3, 5, 7, or -11, -9, -7, -5
6. 20
7. 12
8. Possible answers include -9, 0, 5, and $\frac{1}{2}$

9. Possible answers include $\sqrt{2}$, $\sqrt{3}$, $\frac{\sqrt{2}}{2}$, and π
10. Possible answers include 4, 8, 12, 16, 20, 40, and 100
11. 2, 3, and 5
12. 6
13. 10
14. 9
15. 60

Negative Numbers

1. 32
2. 12
3. 80
4. 28
5. -5
6. -47
7. 2
8. 17
9. -28
10. -14
11. -24
12. -300
13. -10
14. 14
15. 35

16. 11
17. 13
18. -70
19. 28
20. -28
21. 28
22. 56
23. -32
24. 72
25. 2
26. -4
27. 5
28. -51
29. Undefined
30. 0

Exponents - Fundamentals

1.   9
2.   36
3.   81
4.   8
5.   64
6.   16
7. 3^9
8. 4^{17}
9. 6^{15}
10. 10^{10}
11. 12^3
12. 9^{12}
13. 5
14. 6^{38}
15. 3^{16}
16. 4^{27}
17. 6^{36}
18. 5

Advanced Exponents

1.   36
2.   32
3. $\frac{1}{9}$
4.   1
5. $\frac{1}{8}$
6.   -27
7.   -49
8.   2
9.   27
10. 4
11. 17
12. 10
13. -6

PEMDAS

1.   18
2.   17
3.   6
4.   -18
5.   4
6.   3
7.   10
8.   18
9.   22
10. -170

Fractions

Reduce

1. $\frac{1}{2}$
2. $\frac{3}{5}$
3. $\frac{1}{3}$
4. 1
5. $\frac{58}{111}$
6. $\frac{5}{9}$
7. $\frac{1}{3}$
8. $\frac{63}{47}$
9. $\frac{4}{3}$
10. 2

Convert

1. $1\frac{1}{9}$
2. $1\frac{2}{5}$
3. $1\frac{2}{5}$
4. $1\frac{3}{17}$
5. $2\frac{1}{6}$
6. $6\frac{4}{7}$
7. 6
8. $1\frac{21}{100}$
9. $1\frac{1}{2}$
10. $2\frac{2}{5}$

Convert

1. $\frac{17}{7}$
2. $\frac{59}{10}$
3. $\frac{19}{4}$
4. $\frac{31}{6}$
5. $\frac{34}{3}$
6. $\frac{59}{20}$
7. $\frac{31}{8}$
8. $\frac{103}{10}$
9. $\frac{59}{5}$
10. $\frac{10,099}{100}$

Compare

1. $\frac{3}{8}$
2. $\frac{3}{4}$
3. $\frac{15}{20}$
4. $\frac{3}{8}$
5. $\frac{6}{17}$

Add, subtract, multiply, or divide

1. $\frac{7}{9}$
2. $\frac{45}{44}$
3. $\frac{18}{49}$
4. $\frac{1}{6}$
5. $\frac{57}{40}$
6. $\frac{28}{25}$
7. $\frac{19}{52}$
8. $\frac{8}{85}$
9. $\frac{12}{11}$
10. $\frac{6}{13}$
11. $\frac{17}{42}$
12. 1
13. $\frac{20}{9}$
14. $\frac{22}{45}$
15. $\frac{39}{44}$
16. $\frac{16}{81}$

Decimals

1. 2.044
2. 3.52
3. 3.3302
4. 26
5. 5.509
6. 18.84
7. 3.162
8. .292
9. 81
10. 111
11. 10.94
12. 13.456
13. 2
14. 8.8

Factors and Multiples

1. 1, 5, 25
2. 1, 2, 3, 4, 6, 9, 12, 18, 36
3. 1, 2, 4, 5, 10, 20, 25, 50, 100
4. 2 (3 & 2)
5. 2 (5 & 2)
6. 6, 12, 18, 24, 30
7. 4, 8, 12, 16, 20
8. 6
9. 12
10. 5
11. 60
12. 36
13. 90
14. 180

Scientific Notation

1. 4.0008×10^9
2. 2×10^2
3. 6.29×10^7
4. 9.45×10^{-4}
5. 1.23×10^{-2}
6. 7.698×10^{-5}
7. 934,000,000
8. 11,100
9. 4,784,300,000,000
10. .0000345
11. .0242
12. .000000077054
13. 2×10^{-4}
14. 4×10^5
15. 6×10^{-5}
16. 1.5×10^5
17. 4.5×10^{12}
18. 4×10^8
19. 1.35×10^{12}
20. 7.68×10^{11}
21. 3.10123×10^7
22. 1.2223×10^5
23. 2.327×10^8
24. 4×10^4
25. 7.769223×10^6

Operations with Roots

1. 4
2. 9
3. 3
4. 2
5. $2\sqrt{7}$
6. $2\sqrt{17}$
7. $2\sqrt{11}$
8. $6\sqrt{3}$
9. $5\sqrt{7}$
10. $9\sqrt{2}$
11. $14\sqrt{3}$
12. $2\sqrt{10} - 2\sqrt{5}$
13. $4\sqrt{3}$
14. 4
15. $\sqrt{5}$
16. $\sqrt{10}$
17. 3
18. 10
19. $9\sqrt{5}$
20. 27
21. $3x\sqrt{3x}$
22. $8x$
23. $2x^3\sqrt{3}$
24. $x^3\sqrt{x}$
25. $\frac{x\sqrt{5x}}{5}$

80

Ratios

1.   13 : 28
2.   Yes. There could be 6 fourth graders and 8 fifth graders.
3.   2 : 1
4.   35
5.   30
6.   35

Rates

1.   28 pens
2.   30 cakes
3.   165 minutes
4.   13.125 hours
5.   1.33 miles
6.   550 miles

Percents and Percent Change

1.   90
2.   80%
3.   27.50
4.   5.28
5.   90%
6. $13.80
7. $8,100
8. $52

9.   99
10. 20%
11. 50%
12. 25%
13. 12.5%
14. 60%
15. 28%

Mean, Median, Mode, and Range

1.   12
2.   6
3.   18
4.   Range
5.   110
6. $a + 4$
7.   129

Probability

1.   .6
2. $\frac{1}{4}$
3. $\frac{1}{36}$
4. $\frac{1}{16}$

Permutations and Combinations

1.   90
2.   35
3.   48
4.   35
5.   2
6. $21 \times 20 \times 19 \times 5$

7.   10
8. $6 \times 5 \times 4 \times 1 \times 3 \times 2 \times 1$
9. $5 \times 5 \times 5 \times 5 \times 21 \times 21 \times 21$
10. 154
11. 70

Translating English into Math

1.   D
2.   C
3.   D
4.   B
5.   A
6.   A

Units of Measurement

1.   Inches, centimeters
2.   Grams, kilograms, pounds
3.   Ounces, milliliters
4.   Liters, gallons
5.   Pounds, kilograms
6.   Feet, meters

Algebra

Basic Algebra

In algebra, letters or symbols are used to represent numbers in an equation.

There are a few definitions you should be familiar with before beginning this section:
- *variable*: a letter used to represent a number (x, y, etc)
- *coefficient*: a number that appears before a variable ($5x$, $10y$, etc)
- *expression*: a mathematical phrase that can contain numbers, variables, and operators such as addition, subtraction, multiplication, or division ($x + 5$, $3y - 6$, etc)
- *equation*: an expression that has been set equal to something ($x + 5 = 6$, $3y - 6 = 10$, etc)

Combining Like Terms

Some questions on the ISEE will ask you to simplify an expression or ask you which of the answer choices is equivalent to a given expression. The most important thing to remember is that only "like terms" can be simplified. That means that a variable like x can only be combined with another variable x, y^2 can only be combined with y^2, and so on. These questions are only tricky because it can be difficult to keep track of all the like terms. *You should cross off terms as you go so that you don't get confused!*

Examples: $a + a = 2a$ $7z + 10z = 17z$ $2x^2 + 3x^2 = 5x^2$ $6y^3 + 4x - 2y^3 = 4y^3 + 4x$
$2x^2y^2 + 5ab^4 + 4x^2y^2 - 3ab^4 = 6x^2y^2 + 2ab^4$

Bear in mind that you only have to worry about like terms when adding or subtracting. If you are asked to multiply or divide, you just need to think about the rules of exponents.

Examples: $4x^2(x^3) = 4x^5$ $2k^4(3y^2) = 6k^4y^2$ $\dfrac{3m^2n^4}{6mn} = \dfrac{mn^3}{2}$

Evaluating Algebraic Expressions

Even if you've never taken algebra before, you most likely have an innate understanding of how it works. If you know that x is equal to some number, and $x + 4 = 6$, it should be obvious that $x = 2$. Some questions will simply test your ability to plug in a number for a variable and simplify the expression. Here, it is most important that you remember your order of operations and that you show your work.

Examples:
If $y = 4$, what is the value of $4y^2$?   If $x = -2$, what is the value of $x^4 - 2 + 3x$?
$4(4)^2 = 4(16) = 64$ $(-2)^4 - 2 + 3(-2) = 16 - 2 + (-6) = 8$

Solving Equations with One Variable

In the simplest equations, you can eyeball what the answer should be.

Example: $x + 2 = 7$

In this example, just ask yourself *"two plus what equals seven?"*

In an algebraic equation, you need to isolate the variable. You can do this if you know that addition and subtraction are opposites, multiplication and division are opposites, and squaring and taking the square root are opposites.

Example: $4x + 8 = 16$

This example is slightly more difficult because it requires two steps. First, subtract 8 from both sides of the equation to get $4x = 8$. Then, divide by 4 on both sides of the equation to get $x = 2$.

Example: $\frac{x^2}{4} - 7 = 18$

First, add 7 to both sides to get $\frac{x^2}{4} = 25$. Then, multiply both sides by 4 to get $x^2 = 100$. Finally, take the square root of both sides to get $x = 10$.

One thing students have trouble with is determining which step to take first. If you remember PEMDAS, you might think you should have taken the square root first in the example above. The best way to figure this out is to ask yourself which part of the equation affects the *whole* equation. In the final example, the exponent only applies to x, but not to anything else. Likewise, the 4 only affects the x^2. However, the -7 affects the entire equation, so that's what you need to deal with first.

Finally, remember that in many instances you can work backwards using the answer choices if you're having a difficult time solving mathematically.

Practice Questions

Simplify

1. $2z^3 + 9z^3$ $11z^3$
2. $8k^4 - 10k^4$
3. $2p^3 + 9xy - 6xy - p^3$
4. $-x^2y^3 + 4x^3y^2 + 8x^3y^2 + 2x^2y^3 + 4$
5. $-lm^2n^3 + 4m^3n^2 - (-2lm^2n^3 + 6m^3n^2)$
6. $2j^4k - 3jk^4 + (jk^4 + 2j^4k)$
7. $-5x^3y^4(2x^4y^3)$
8. $\frac{24y^5z^3}{8y^3z^4}$

Solve

9. If $z = 2$, what is the value of $3z + 4z^2$?
10. If $a = 3$, what is the value of $2a(a - 2)$?
11. If $x = 2.5$, what is the value of $3x + (x - 2)$?
12. If $y = -3$, what is the value of $2y - 2(3 - y)$?
13. $\frac{3x}{2} + 7 = 13$
14. $x^2 - 7 = -6$
15. $\frac{\sqrt{x}}{6} + \frac{3}{2} = 2$
16. $\frac{8}{x} - 6 = -8$
17. $-2x + 8 = -6$

First, Outer, Inner, Last (FOIL)

FOIL is an acronym to help you remember how to multiply two binomials together.

Here are a few definitions that will help you on this section:

Binomial: an algebraic expression of the sum or difference of two terms
Examples: $a + b$ or $2 - x$

Quadratic equation: any equation having the form $ax^2 + bx + c = 0$
Examples: $x^2 + 3x + 2 = 0$ or $2x^2 + 4x - 5 = 0$

We'll explore the formula $ax^2 + bx + c$ in much more detail in Chapter IV. For now, let's focus on multiplying two binomials together.

Example #1
Rewrite the following expression as a quadratic equation:

$(x + 2)(x + 3) = 0$

To rewrite this expression, use FOIL. Multiply the **F**irst terms of each binomial, then the **O**uter terms, then the **I**nner terms, and finally the **L**ast terms. It will look like this:

$(x)(x) + (x)(3) + (2)(x) + (2)(3) = 0$
$x^2 + 3x + 2x + 6 = 0$
$x^2 + 5x + 6 = 0$

Example #2
Rewrite the following expression as a quadratic equation:

$(x - 4)(x + 1) = 0$

It's very important to be careful about any negative signs in the binomials!
$(x)(x) + (x)(1) + (-4)(x) + (-4)(1) = 0$
$x^2 + 1x + (-4x) + (-4) = 0$
$x^2 + 1x - 4x - 4 = 0$
$x^2 - 3x - 4 = 0$

It's important to understand what the binomial version of the quadratic equation means. If we had to actually solve $(x + 2)(x + 3) = 0$, what values of x would work? Plugging in -2 would give you $(-2 + 2)(-2 + 3) = (0)(1) = 0$, while plugging in -3 would give you $(-3 + 2)(-3 + 3) = (-1)(0) = 0$. Therefore, there are two answers: -2 and -3.

There are a few common quadratics that you should memorize:
$(a + b)(a - b) = a^2 - b^2$
$(a + b)^2 = a^2 + 2ab + b^2$
$(a - b)^2 = a^2 - 2ab + b^2$

Examples: $(x + 2)(x - 2) = x^2 - 4$ $(x + 3)^2 = x^2 + 2(x)(3) + 3^2 = x^2 + 6x + 9$
$(x - 5)^2 = x^2 - 2(x)(5) + 5^2 = x^2 - 10x + 25$

Reverse FOIL is a method for changing a quadratic equation into two binomials. Remember that the general format of a quadratic equation is $ax^2 + bx + c$. To change this into binomials, you should find the numbers that "add to b and multiply to c."

Example #3
Rewrite the following quadratic equation using binomials: $x^2 + 5x + 6 = 0$

In this equation, 5 has taken the place of b and 6 has taken the place of c. You must find two numbers that equal 5 when added together and equal 6 when multiplied together. In this case, the numbers are 2 and 3. $2 + 3 = 5$ and $2 \times 3 = 6$, so we can rewrite this expression as $(x + 2)(x + 3) = 0$

Example #4
Rewrite the following quadratic equation using binomials: $x^2 + 4x - 32 = 0$

This example is a bit harder. It's not as easy to find the two numbers we need, and there are negatives involved. Your best strategy is to think of the factors of c, write them out, and choose numbers until you find the ones that work. The factors of 32 are 1, 2, 4, 8, 16, and 32. You need two numbers that multiply to c, so your options are 1×32, 2×16, or 4×8, and one of the numbers must be negative. They must also add to positive 4. The only option that works is -4×8, so your final answer is $(x + 8)(x - 4) = 0$. As you can see, this may take some trial and error.

Practice Questions

FOIL the following expressions:

1. $(x + 1)(x + 1)$
2. $(x + 2)(x + 2)$
3. $(x + 1)(x - 4)$
4. $(x - 5)(x - 3)$
5. $(x + 3)(x - 3)$
6. $(x + 4)(x - 4)$
7. $(x + 5)^2$
8. $(x + 6)^2$
9. $(x - 1)^2$
10. $(x - 10)^2$

Find the solutions to the following quadratic equations:

11. $(x + 4)(x + 1) = 0$
12. $(x - 3)(x + 2) = 0$
13. $(x - 10)(x - 12) = 0$
14. $(x + 6)(x - 2) = 0$

Reverse FOIL the following quadratics:

15. $x^2 + 5x + 6$
16. $x^2 + 4x - 45$
17. $x^2 - 25$
18. $x^2 + 10x + 25$
19. $x^2 - 8x + 16$
20. $x^2 - 49$
21. $x^2 - 14x + 49$
22. $x^2 + 20x + 100$
23. $x^2 - 9x + 14$
24. $x^2 - 10x + 24$
25. $x^2 + 6x + 8$
26. $x^2 - 3x - 10$
27. $x^2 - 3x - 18$

Inequalities

Solving inequalities is very similar to solving algebraic equations, but instead of finding one value of x, you will find a range of values of x that satisfy the inequality.

First, let's look at an algebraic equation:

$$2x + 1 = 5$$

To solve this expression, subtract 1 from both sides and then divide both sides by 2. You'll find that $x = 2$.

Now, let's change things up a little:

$$2x + 1 < 5$$

The only difference is that "=" has been changed to "$<$." This sign means that $2x + 1$ is *less than* 5. Once again, we can solve algebraically:

$$2x + 1 < 5$$
$$2x < 4$$
$$x < 2$$

This answer means that x must be less than 2. Any number less than 2 will satisfy this inequality: if you plug in 0 for x, you get $1 < 5$; if you plug in -2 for x, you get $-3 < 5$, etc. In this equation, 2 **does not** satisfy the equation, because that would give you $5 < 5$, which is not true.

There are 3 other signs you need to be familiar with: $>$, $\leq$, and $\geq$. The signs with the lines under them are "*less than or equal to*" and "*greater than or equal to*." These two signs are *inclusive*.

Let's look at another example:

$$4x - 4 \geq 20$$
$$4x \geq 24$$
$$x \geq 6$$

In the example above, any number 6 or greater satisfies the inequality.

If you get confused about the direction of the inequality, remember that the mouth always opens in the direction of the larger quantity.

The other thing that you need to remember when dealing with inequalities is that if you multiply or divide by a negative number at any point in the process of solving the equation, *the sign will change direction.*

Example

$$-5x + 2 \geq 7$$
$$-5x \geq 5$$
$$x \leq -1$$

Pay close attention to how the sign changed in the last step! Forgetting to change the sign when multiplying or dividing by a negative number is the most common mistake that students make when working with inequalities.

Three-part inequalities

More advanced inequalities questions may test your knowledge of three-part inequalities. On these questions, you just need to remember to perform each operation to all parts of the inequality.

Example

$$-4 \leq 2x < 10$$
$$-2 \leq x < 5$$

In the inequality above, you should divide each of the three parts of the inequality by 2 in order to get your final answer. Pay close attention to both of the inequality signs in these question types. If you were to graph your answer on a number line, it would look like this:

Note that the hole is filled in when it represents *greater than or equal to* and *less than or equal to*, and the hole is open when it represents *greater than* or *less than.*

Example

$$4 < \frac{-3x - 1}{5} \leq 7$$
$$20 < -3x - 1 \leq 35$$
$$21 < -3x \leq 36$$
$$-7 > x \geq -12$$

The most important thing to notice in this example is that the rule about switching the direction of the inequalities when you multiply or divide by a negative number still applies!

Practice Questions

Solve

1. $3x + 4 > 10$

2. $2x + 7 < 17$

3. $-4 + 3x \leq 23$

4. $-9x - 5 \geq -95$

5. $5x - 6 < 54$

6. $15 \leq 7x + 1$

7. $-4x \geq 48$

8. $-3x + 4 > -5$

9. $-5 \leq 3x + 1 < 13$

10. $-14 \leq -4x - 2 < 10$

11. $-2 < \frac{-x - 2}{3} \leq 1$

12. $4 < \frac{4x}{5} < 8$

Absolute Value

Absolute value tells you the distance of a number from 0. Absolute value is denoted by $|x|$, and it is *always positive*. For example, $|-5|$ ("the absolute value of negative 5") is 5, because -5 is 5 units from 0 on the number line.

$$|10| = 10 \qquad\qquad\qquad |-11| = 11 \qquad\qquad\qquad |-x| = x$$

Most absolute value questions on the ISEE will require several steps to solve. The most important thing to remember is that every equation that contains an absolute value has two answers. Your first step should always be isolating the absolute value. Then, create two equations. In one equation, remove the absolute value signs and solve. In the second equation, remove the absolute value signs AND multiply the right side by negative one. See the examples below:

$4|x + 3| = 20$ $3|x - 2| + 4 = 7$

$|x + 3| = 5$ $3|x - 2| = 3$

$x + 3 = 5$ and $x + 3 = -5$ $|x - 2| = 1$

$x = 2$ and $x = -8$ $x - 2 = 1$ and $x - 2 = -1$

                                                   $x = 3$ and $x = 1$

You also need to be comfortable working with absolute value inequalities. These work mostly the same as the examples above. Once again, you will get two answers. On the first equation, remove the absolute value sign and solve as you usually would. On the second equation, remove the absolute value sign, flip the inequality, AND multiply the right side by negative one.

$4|x + 3| \leq 20$ $3|x - 2| + 4 \geq 7$ $2|x + 3| - 6 \leq 4$

$|x + 3| \leq 5$ $3|x - 2| \geq 3$ $2|x + 3| \leq 10$

$x + 3 \leq 5$ and $x + 3 \geq -5$ $|x - 2| \geq 1$ $|x + 3| \leq 5$

$x \leq 2$ and $x \geq -8$ $x - 2 \geq 1$ and $x - 2 \leq -1$ $x + 3 \leq 5$ and $x + 3 \geq -5$

                                   $x \geq 3$ and $x \leq 1$ $x \leq 2$ and $x \geq -8$

You can usually double-check your answers on absolute value questions. Once you've found a range of numbers that x could be equal to, plug a few of them in to the original equation and see if they work!

Practice Questions

1. $|10v| \leq 100$ 5. $|-x| > -1$

2. $|10 + 4x| \leq 14$ 6. $2|3x - 1| - 1 \leq 7$

3. $|t - 8| + 10 \geq 22$ 7. $|2x + 4| \leq -4$

4. $\dfrac{|2 + 3x|}{2} > 5$ 8. $-3|x - 5| + 15 < -15$

Answer Key - Algebra

Basic Algebra

1. $11z^3$
2. $-2k^4$
3. $p^3 + 3xy$
4. $x^2y^3 + 12x^3y^2 + 4$
5. $lm^2n^3 - 2m^3n^2$
6. $4j^4k - 2jk^4$
7. $-10x^7y^7$
8. $\dfrac{3y^2}{z}$

9. 22
10. 6
11. 8
12. -18
13. $x = 4$
14. $x = \pm 1$
15. $x = 9$
16. $x = -4$
17. $x = 7$

FOIL and Reverse FOIL

1. $x^2 + 2x + 1$
2. $x^2 + 4x + 4$
3. $x^2 - 3x - 4$
4. $x^2 - 8x + 15$
5. $x^2 - 9$
6. $x^2 - 16$
7. $x^2 + 10x + 25$
8. $x^2 + 12x + 36$
9. $x^2 - 2x + 1$

10. $x^2 - 20x + 100$
11. -4 and -1
12. 3 and -2
13. 10 and 12
14. -6 and 2
15. $(x + 2)(x + 3)$
16. $(x - 5)(x + 9)$
17. $(x + 5)(x - 5)$
18. $(x + 5)^2$

19. $(x - 4)^2$
20. $(x + 7)(x - 7)$
21. $(x - 7)^2$
22. $(x + 10)^2$
23. $(x - 2)(x - 7)$
24. $(x - 4)(x - 6)$
25. $(x + 2)(x + 4)$
26. $(x - 5)(x + 2)$
27. $(x + 3)(x - 6)$

Inequalities

1. $x > 2$
2. $x < 5$
3. $x \leq 9$
4. $x \leq 10$
5. $x < 12$
6. $2 \leq x$

7. $x \leq -12$
8. $x < 3$
9. $-2 \leq x < 4$
10. $-3 < x \leq 3$
11. $-5 \leq x < 4$
12. $5 < x < 10$

Absolute Value

1. $-10 \leq v \leq 10$
2. $-6 \leq x \leq 1$
3. $20 \leq t$ and $t \leq -4$
4. $x < -4$ and $x > \frac{8}{3}$

5. All real numbers
6. $-1 \leq x \leq \frac{5}{3}$
7. No solution
8. $x < -5$ and $x > 15$

Geometry

Lines and Angles

Finding Missing Degrees

The ISEE requires that you memorize the degrees in lines, triangles, circles, and quadrilaterals.

$$lines = 180°$$
$$triangles = 180°$$

$$circles = 360°$$
$$quadrilaterals = 360°$$

Example #1

In the figure below, x = ?

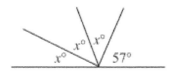

(A)   30°
(B)   41°
(C)   90°
(D)   123°

There are 180° in a line, and the angle on the right takes up 57°. That means $3x = 123°$. $\frac{123}{3} = 41°$. **The correct answer is (B).**

Remember, you can use guesstimating strategies on many geometry questions. Does angle x look bigger or smaller than the 57° angle? It seems smaller, so you should eliminate (C) and (D). Then, you can guess between (A) and (B) if you're not sure how to complete the question!

Vertical Angles

Vertical angles are the angles that are opposite one another when two lines intersect. Vertical angles are always equal to one another.

Example #2

In the figure below, what is the value of $a + b + c + d$?

(A)   75°
(B)   180°
(C)   270°
(D)   360°

You should first note that in questions that ask for the value of multiple angles added together, it is often impossible to find the value of the individual angles, so don't bother trying to solve for them. However, you can use your knowledge of vertical angles to solve this question. The blank angle across from b is a vertical angle and is equal to b. The angle across from c is a vertical angle and is equal to c. Now, you can see that angles a, b, c, and d compose one straight line. Since there are 180° in a straight line, **the correct answer is (B).**

Parallel Lines and Transversals

Parallel lines have the same distance continuously between them and will never intersect. A question will either tell you if lines are parallel, say *A // B*, or indicate lines are parallel with the following symbol:

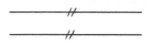

On tougher questions, the parallel lines will intersect a transversal.

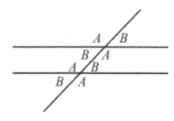

There is a lot of information that can be gleaned from this figure. Each angle *A* is equal to the others, and each angle *B* is equal to the others. Furthermore, *A* + *B* = 180°, because those angles added together create one straight line.

Example #3

A triangle is shown below. $\overline{BE}$ is parallel to $\overline{CD}$. $\angle BAE = 30°$, and $\angle ABE = 75°$. What is the measure of $\angle EDC$?

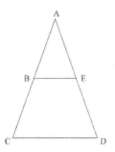

First, look at triangle ABE. If $\angle BAE = 30°$ and $\angle ABE = 75°$, then $\angle AEB = 75°$, because there are 180° in a triangle. Then, because $\overline{BE}$ is parallel to $\overline{CD}$, $\angle AEB$ and $\angle EDC$ must be equal, because they are two parallel lines cut by a transversal. $\angle EDC = 75°$

Example #4

Lines A and B are parallel. What is the value of *x*?

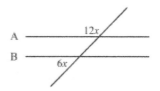

Once again, it looks as though there is not enough information to answer this question. However, we know that the sum of the two angles in question equals 180°, because they correlate with angles A and B in the transversals figure at the top of the page. Therefore, $18x = 180°$, and $x = 10°$.

94

Practice Questions

1.   In the figure below, what is the value of $t + s$?

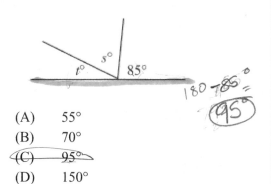

$180 - 85 = $

(95)

   (A)   55°
   (B)   70°
   (C)   95°
   (D)   150°

2.   In the figure below, what is the value of $y - x$?

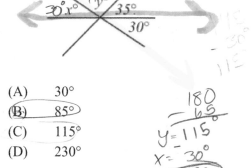

   (A)   30°
   (B)   85°
   (C)   115°
   (D)   230°

180
$- 65$
$y = 115$
$x = 30°$
$85°$

3.   In the figure below, $X \parallel Y$. What is the value of $3n$?

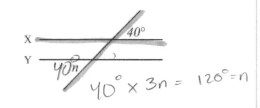

$40° \times 3n = 120° = n$

   (A)   20°
   (B)   40°
   (C)   80°
   (D)   120°

4.   In the figure below, lines A, B, and C are parallel. What is the value of $r + s$?

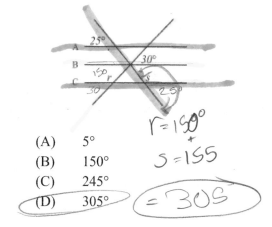

$r = 150°$
$+$
$s = 155$

   (A)   5°
   (B)   150°
   (C)   245°
   (D)   305° $= 305$

5.   In the figure below, lines M and N are parallel. If $a = 45°$ and $b = 40°$, what is the value of c?

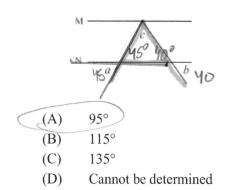

   (A)   95°
   (B)   115°
   (C)   135°
   (D)   Cannot be determined

6.   In the figure below, $M \parallel N$. What is the value of x?

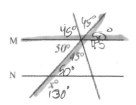

   (A)   95°
   (B)   130°
   (C)   145°
   (D)   160°

Triangles

Triangles are plane figures with three straight sides and three angles. Triangles always contain a total of 180°.

Perimeter

Like all other shapes, to find the perimeter of a triangle you must add together the lengths of its sides. Slightly more difficult perimeter questions may ask you to find missing side lengths based on your knowledge of special side and special angle triangles, and then ask that you solve for perimeter.

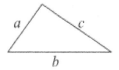

$$a + b + c = \text{perimeter}$$

Inequality Theorem

The triangle inequality theorem states that the length of the third side of a triangle must be less than the sum of and greater than the difference of the other two sides.

Example #1

What is the range of possible values for side x of the triangle below?

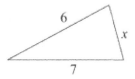

The length of side x must be between 1 $(7 - 1)$ and 13 $(7 + 6)$. This range is not inclusive; x could not be equal to exactly 1 or 13.

$$1 < x < 13$$

Area

The equation for finding the area of a triangle is $\frac{bh}{2}$, where b = base and h = height. Height must be perpendicular to the base.

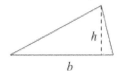   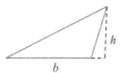

Special Side Triangles

Isosceles Triangles

An isosceles triangle has two sides that are the same length; the angles opposite these sides are also congruent. A question might tell you that a given triangle is isosceles. Otherwise, you might see markings like those in the figure above which indicate two equal sides and two equal angles. Finally, if the question tells you that a triangle has two congruent angles (50° and 50°, for example) or two congruent sides, you can deduce that it is an isosceles triangle.

Equilateral Triangles

The sides of an equilateral triangle are all the same length, and the angles are all equal to 60°. A figure may indicate a triangle is equilateral using the dashes shown in the figure above. The question might also tell you a given triangle is equilateral.

The Pythagorean Theorem

The Pythagorean theorem allows you to find the length of a missing side of a right triangle.

The theorem states: $a^2 + b^2 = c^2$

C always represents the hypotenuse of the triangle, while a and b represent the legs.

Example #2

What is the length of side a in the triangle below?

Use the Pythagorean theorem:

$a^2 + b^2 = c^2$
$a^2 + 4^2 = 5^2$
$a^2 + 16 = 25$
$a^2 = 9$
$a = 3$

Special Angle Triangles

45-45-90 Triangles

A 45-45-90 triangle is formed when a square is cut in half diagonally.

45-45-90 triangles are a type of isosceles triangle because their two legs are always the same length. The relationship between the length of the legs and the length of the hypotenuse is expressed as $x : x : x\sqrt{2}$. If one leg of a 45-45-90 triangle is 4, then the length of the second leg is also 4, and the length of the hypotenuse is $4\sqrt{2}$.

30-60-90 Triangles

A 30-60-90 triangle is formed when an equilateral triangle is split in half.

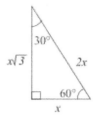

The relationship between the length of the legs and the length of the hypotenuse is expressed as $x : x\sqrt{3} : 2x$. If the shortest leg of a 30-60-90 triangle is 4, then the length of the second leg is $4\sqrt{3}$, and the length of the hypotenuse is 8.

More Special Side Triangles

The two triangles below are common special side triangles that often appear on the ISEE. You can use the Pythagorean theorem to solve for a missing side in one of these triangles, but we recommend memorizing them in order to save time.

3-4-5 Triangles

5-12-13 Triangles

Example #3
What is the length of the diagonal of the square below?

If you've memorized your special triangles, you'll recognize that this square has been split into two 45-45-90 triangles. The legs are equal to x, and the hypotenuse is equal to $x\sqrt{2}$. In this example, the legs = 10, so the hypotenuse equals $10\sqrt{2}$.

Similar Triangles

Two triangles are similar if the measures of their corresponding angles are congruent. These triangles will have the same shape, but their sizes may be different. Their corresponding sides are proportional.

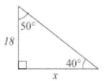

The triangles above are similar because the measures of their corresponding angles are congruent. Therefore, their corresponding sides must be proportional. $12 \times 1.5 = 18$, so the multiplier is 1.5. 14×1.5 is 21, so $x = 21$.

Sometimes, a question will tell you two triangles are similar, or it will be obvious because all of the angles are labeled. Otherwise, you may have to recognize a situation in which two triangles are similar.

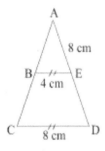

In this triangle, because $\overline{BE}$ is parallel to $\overline{CD}$, $\triangle ABE$ is similar to $\triangle ACD$. The multiplier is 2, since the base of the smaller triangle is 4 cm and the base of the larger triangle is 8 cm. Using this information, we can find $\overline{ED}$. If $\overline{AD}$ is twice as long as $\overline{AE}$, then $\overline{ED}$ must equal 8 cm.

This figure is more complicated because it contains three triangles. First, you should "unpack" this figure and redraw all the triangles.

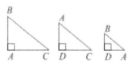

These three triangles are all similar to one another!

Example #4

In the figure below, $\overline{AB} = 8$ and $\overline{BC} = 16$. What is the length of $\overline{BD}$?

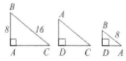

Unpacking the triangles makes it obvious that the relationship between the biggest and smallest triangles is 2 : 1. Therefore, if $\overline{AB} = 8$, then $\overline{BD} = 4$.

Practice Questions

1. A triangle's base is 10 inches and its height is 12 inches. What is its area?

$10 \times 12 = 120$ 60 inches^2

2. What is the length of side c in the triangle shown below?

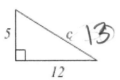

13

3. What is the range of possible lengths of the third side of the triangle shown below?

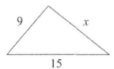

4. A triangle's area is 180 cm^2 and its height is 24 cm. What is the length of its base?

15 cm

$A = \frac{bh}{2}$

5. What is the length of x in the triangle below?

6. The triangles shown below are similar. What is the length of $\overline{YZ}$?

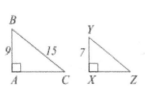

7. A triangle has two sides that measure 6 inches and 12 inches, respectively. What is the possible range of lengths of the third side?

8. If one side of an equilateral triangle is 10 inches long, what is the perimeter of the triangle?   30 inches

9. In the triangle below, what is the length of x?

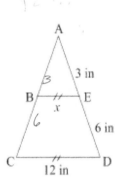

10. What is the perimeter of the triangle shown below?

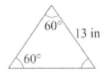

11. If $\overline{AB}$ = 10, and $\overline{BC}$ = 26, then what is the length of $\overline{AD}$?

100

12. What is the length of side *b* in the triangle shown below?

13. The triangle shown below is equilateral. What is the triangle's height?

14. What is the perimeter of the square below?

24

15. An equilateral triangle has a perimeter of 25. What is the length of each side?

16. What is the length of side *x* in the triangle below?

17. Is it possible for a triangle to have sides measuring 6 inches, 2 inches, and 3 inches?

18. What is the measure of ∠ABC?

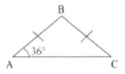

(Height) *a* ⌐◺ *c*
b
(base)

Coordinate Geometry

Coordinate geometry is the study of algebraic equations on graphs. It involves plotting points, curves, and lines on an *x*- and *y*-axis. The figure below shows an example of a coordinate plane.

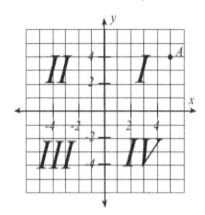

Coordinate planes are divided into four quadrants. They are composed of an *x*-axis, which runs horizontally, and a *y*-axis, which runs vertically. The axes intersect at the origin.

To find the location of a point on the coordinate plane, start at the origin and count how far you must move on the *x*-axis. If you move to the right, the coordinate is positive. If you move to the left, the coordinate is negative. Then, count how far up and down you must move on the *y*-axis. If you move up, the coordinate is positive. If you move down, the coordinate is negative.

Point A is labeled in the plane above. Beginning at the origin, move right 5 spaces, then move up 4 spaces. The coordinates of Point A are (5, 4).

Example #1

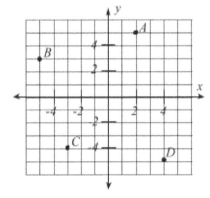

Point A is located at (2, 5)
Point B is located at (-5, 3)
Point C is located at (-3, -4)
Point D is located at (4, -5)

Label the following points: E (-2, 4); F (6, 6); G (3, -5); and H (-4, -6)

Slope

Slope tells us how steep a line is. Before we learn how to find the equation of a line, we must first learn how to find slope. There are three common ways of writing the equation for slope:

$$\frac{rise}{run} \qquad\qquad \frac{\Delta y}{\Delta x} \qquad\qquad \frac{y_2 - y_1}{x_2 - x_1}$$

These three equations all boil down to the same thing: what is the ratio between the change in y and the change in x?

Example #2

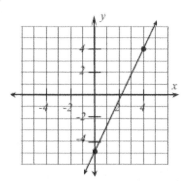

In this coordinate plane, there is a line that intersects two points: (0, -5) and (4, 4). You can use any of the equations to find the slope of this line. The line rises 9 spaces (from -5 to 4) and runs 4 spaces (from 0 to 4). Therefore, the slope is $\frac{9}{4}$. If you use the third equation, then

$$\frac{y_2 - y_1}{x_2 - x_1} = \frac{4 - (-5)}{4 - 0} = \frac{9}{4} .$$

Slope is represented using the variable m. This will be important once you learn how to find the full equation of a line!

Example #3

What is the slope of the line below?

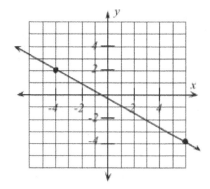

(A) $\frac{-5}{3}$

(B) $\frac{-3}{5}$

(C) $\frac{3}{5}$

(D) $\frac{5}{3}$

The points are at (-4, 2) and (6, -4). Use $\frac{y_2 - y_1}{x_2 - x_1}$ and plug in the missing variables:

$\frac{-4 - 2}{6 - (-4)} = \frac{-6}{10} = \frac{-3}{5}$. **The correct answer is (B).**

Notice the slope in Example #3 is negative. If a line goes from bottom left to top right, it is positive; if it goes from top left to bottom right, it is negative. *Vertical lines have no slope, and horizontal lines have zero slope.*

Practice Questions

1.   In what quadrant is Point A located?

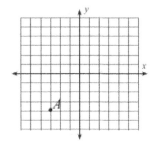

(A)   I
(B)   II
(C)   III
(D)   IV

2.   What are the coordinates of Point F?

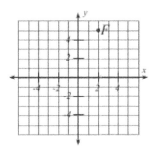

(A)   (-2, -5)
(B)   (-2, 5)
(C)   (2, -5)
(D)   (2, 5)

3.   A line has points at (-5, -10) and (6, 12). What is the slope of the line?
(A)   -1
(B)   0
(C)   1
(D)   2

4.   A line has points at (1, 7) and (-2, -8). What is the slope of the line?
(A)   -7
(B)   -1
(C)   5
(D)   7

5.   What is the slope of the line below?

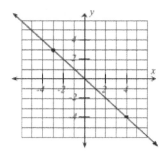

(A)   -2
(B)   -1
(C)   1
(D)   2

6.   In what quadrant is Point Z located?

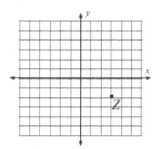

(A)   I
(B)   II
(C)   III
(D)   IV

7.   What are the coordinates of Point U?

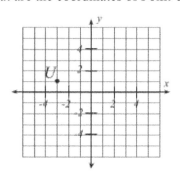

(A)   (-3, 1)
(B)   (-2, 1)
(C)   (1, -2)
(D)   (3, -1)

Y-intercept

The *y*-intercept is where a line crosses the *y* axis. It can be positive, negative, or zero.

Example #4

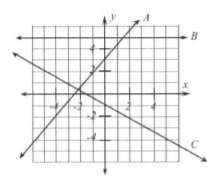

In the coordinate plane above, the *y*-intercept of line A is 3. The *y*-intercept of line B is 5. The *y*-intercept of line C is -1.

The Equation of a Line

Now that you're familiar with slope, *y*-intercept, and plotting points on a graph, you know enough to graph lines! On the ISEE, the equations of lines will most commonly be written in slope-intercept form:

$$y = mx + b$$

m represents the line's slope, *b* represents its *y*-intercept, and *x* and *y* represent the coordinates of any two points on the line.

Example #5

What is the equation of the line shown below?

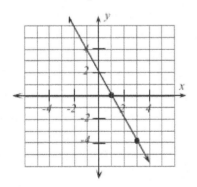

(A) $y = -2x + 2$

(B) $y = \frac{-x}{2} - 2$

(C) $y = \frac{x}{2} + 2$

(D) $y = 2x - 2$

Start with the easiest part: this line crosses the *y* axis at (0, 2), so $b = 2$. Then, find the slope. This line contains points at (1, 0) and (3, -4). Using one of our equations for slope, we find that $m = \frac{-4 - 0}{3 - 1} = \frac{-4}{2} = $ -2. If $b = 2$ and $m = $ -2, then the formula of this line is $y = -2x + 2$. **The correct answer is (A).**

Note how you can eliminate (C) and (D) simply by recognizing that the given line has a negative slope. You can also eliminate (B) because the *y*-intercept is negative.

The Equation of a Line, continued

Trickier questions might only give you one or two pieces of information and require that you find the equation of a line using those.

Example #6
A line has points at (6, -1) and (-3, 5). What is the equation of the line?

Find the slope of the line. $m = \frac{5-(-1)}{-3-6} = \frac{6}{-9} = \frac{-2}{3}$. In the equation $y = mx + b$, replace m with $\frac{-2}{3}$ and replace x and y with either of the given coordinate pairs. For example, $-1 = \frac{-2}{3}(6) + b$. Then, solve for b.

$$-1 = \frac{-12}{3} + b$$
$$-1 = -4 + b$$
$$3 = b$$

The equation of the line is $y = \frac{-2x}{3} + 3$

Parallel and Perpendicular Slope

Parallel lines run side by side and never intersect one another. Perpendicular lines intersect at 90° angles. Lines are parallel if their slopes are identical; they are perpendicular if their slopes are negative reciprocals. That means if the slope of one line is m, the slope of a perpendicular line will be $\frac{-1}{m}$.

Parallel Lines

$y = 2x + 4$
$y = 2x - 7$

Perpendicular Lines

$y = 2x + 4$
$y = \frac{-1}{2}x + 2$

When dealing with lines, it's important to remember that y must be isolated on one side of the equation before you can find the line's slope and y-intercept.

Example #7
Find the slope and y-intercept of a line with the equation $3x + 4y = 12$. Then, identify the slope of a line that is parallel and a line that is perpendicular to $3x + 4y = 12$.

Rearrange the equation to isolate y:

$$y = \frac{-3x}{4} + 3$$

This line's slope is $\frac{-3}{4}$ and its y-intercept is 3. A line parallel to this one could be $y = \frac{-3x}{4} + 1$, and a line perpendicular to this one could be $y = \frac{4x}{3} + 6$.

Practice Questions

8. What is the *y*-intercept of the line?

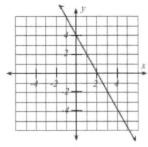

  (A) 0
  (B) 2
  (C) 4
  (D) 6

9. What is the slope of a line whose equation is $2x - 3y = 4$?

  (A) -2
  (B) $\frac{-2}{3}$
  (C) $\frac{2}{3}$
  (D) 2

10. What is the *y*-intercept of a line whose equation is $-4y + 2x = 16$?

  (A) -4
  (B) 2
  (C) 4
  (D) 16

11. What is the slope of the line below?

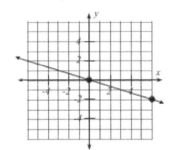

  (A) -3
  (B) $\frac{-1}{3}$
  (C) 0
  (D) 3

12. What is the *y*-intercept of a line whose equation is $y = 2x + 8$?

  (A) 2
  (B) 4
  (C) 6
  (D) 8

13. Which of the following lines is perpendicular to the one graphed below?

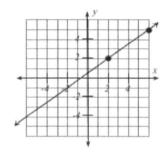

  (A) $y = \frac{-4x}{3} + 2$
  (B) $y = \frac{-3x}{4} + 5$
  (C) $y = \frac{3x}{4} + 3$
  (D) $y = \frac{4x}{3} + 4$

14. A line has points at (-3, -13) and (5, 11). What is the equation of the line?

  (A) $y = 2x - 7$
  (B) $y = 3x - 4$
  (C) $y = 4x - 1$
  (D) $y = 5x + 2$

15. A line has a point at (3, -5) and its *y*-intercept is 1. What is the equation of the line?

  (A) $y = -x + 3$
  (B) $y = 4x - 5$
  (C) $y = -2x + 1$
  (D) $y = 3x + 4$

16. The slope of a line that passes through points $(b, 4)$ and $(3, 8)$ in the coordinate plane is 2. What is the value of b?
    (A)   0
    (B)   1
    (C)   2
    (D)   3

17. If the points $A(2, 3)$, $B(10, 3)$, and $C(6, 8)$ are vertices of a triangle in the coordinate plane, what is the area of the triangle?
    (A)   5
    (B)   10
    (C)   15
    (D)   20

18. Rectangle $ABCD$ is graphed in the coordinate plane as shown.

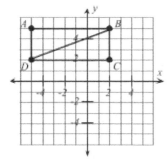

What is the area of triangle ABD in square units?
    (A)   3
    (B)   7.5
    (C)   10.5
    (D)   21

19. In the graph below, the line segment joins two vertices of a square.

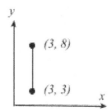

Which of the following could be the coordinates of another vertex of the square?
    (A)   (-2, 8)
    (B)   (-3, -3)
    (C)   (8, 7)
    (D)   (3, -2)

20. The slope of line A graphed in the coordinate plane shown is $\frac{2}{3}$.

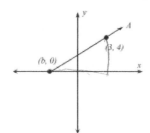

What is the value of b?
    (A)   -3
    (B)   -2
    (C)   -1
    (D)   2

Circles

You must memorize all the parts of a circle and all of the equations related to circles for the ISEE. The diagram below shows the main components of a circle with which you must be familiar.

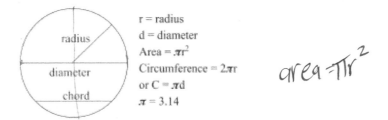

r = radius
d = diameter
Area = πr^2
Circumference = $2\pi r$
or $C = \pi d$
$\pi = 3.14$

$area = \pi r^2$

Radius: the distance from the center of a circle to its edge.

Chord: a straight line segment whose endpoints both lie on the edge of a circle.

Diameter: any straight line segment that passes through the center of the circle and whose endpoints lie on the circle. The diameter is the longest chord of a circle.

Pi (π): the ratio of a circle's circumference to its diameter. Pi is approximately equal to 3.14.

Circumference: the distance around the circle. Circumference is usually expressed in terms of pi.

Area: In circles, area is equal to πr^2.

Examples

1. What is the area of a circle with a radius of 5 inches?

The equation for the area of a circle is πr^2. If the radius is 5 in, then the area is 25π in^2.

$5\pi r^2 = 25\pi \text{ in}^2$

2. What is the length of the radius of a circle whose circumference is 10π?

The equation for the circumference of a circle is $2\pi r$. If $C = 10\pi$, then the radius equals 5.

On circle questions, one of the most important things to do is underline key vocab words. If you are asked to find the radius, don't give the diameter! The answer choices will inevitably include options designed to trick you. You should also draw out the circle if it is not drawn for you already.

Practice Questions

1. What is the area of a circle with a radius of 10 cm? $10 \times 10 = 100\pi \text{ cm}^2$

2. What is the length of the radius of a circle whose circumference is 26π? 13π

3. What is the area of a circle with a diameter of 18 cm?

4. What is the length of the diameter of a circle whose circumference is 50π in? 50 in

5. A circle is inscribed in a square. Each side of the square is 10 m. What is the area of the circle?

6. A circle is inscribed in a square. Each side of the square is 8 cm. What is the diameter of the circle?

7. A circle is inscribed in a square. Each side of the square is 20 in. What is the length of the radius of the largest circle that could be inscribed in the square?

Quadrilaterals

A quadrilateral is a four-sided figure. There are four quadrilaterals that you should be familiar with on the ISEE.

Squares

A square is a quadrilateral with four equal sides and four right angles.

- Perimeter $= 4s$
- Area $= s^2$
- Diagonal $= s\sqrt{2}$. You learned this in the section on triangles

Rectangles

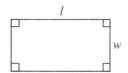

A rectangle is a quadrilateral with two pairs of equal sides and four right angles.

- Opposite sides are equal
- Perimeter $= 2l + 2w =$ the sum of all four sides
- Area $= l \times w$

Parallelograms

A parallelogram is a quadrilateral with two pairs of parallel sides.

- Opposite sides are equal
- Opposite angles are equal
- The sum of consecutive angles $= 180°$
- Perimeter $= 2a + 2b$
- Area $= b \times h$. Note that h is the vertical distance from the top to the bottom of the parallelogram, not the length of side a

Trapezoids

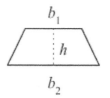

A trapezoid is a quadrilateral with one pair of parallel sides.

- Perimeter = the sum of all four sides
- Area $= \dfrac{b_1 + b_2}{2} \times h$. You can think of this as the average of the two bases times the height

Example #1

What is the area of a square whose diagonal measures 12 inches?

(A) $24\sqrt{2}$ inches

(B)   48 inches

(C)   72 inches

(D)   144 inches

A square cut by a diagonal forms two 45-45-90 triangles. The diagonal corresponds to the hypotenuse of each triangle, and its length is $x\sqrt{2}$. If $x\sqrt{2} = 12$, then $x = 6\sqrt{2}$. Each side of the square measures $6\sqrt{2}$. To find the area of the square, multiply $6\sqrt{2}$ by $6\sqrt{2}$ to get 72. **The correct answer is (C).**

Example #2

In the figure below, *ABCE* is a parallelogram and *CDE* is a triangle. If *CD* = 12 and each side of *ABCE* is 13, what is the area of *ABCD*?

(A)   126

(B)   156

(C)   169

(D)   186

The area of the parallelogram is 156. To find *ED*, use the Pythagorean theorem. *ED* = 5, so the area of CDE = 30. 156 + 30 = 186. **The correct answer is (D).**

Example #3

If there is no waste, how many square yards of carpeting are needed to cover a rectangular floor that is 24 feet by 72 feet? (1 yard = 3 feet)

(A)   192

(B)   360

(C)   576

(D)   1,728

First, convert the measurements to yards by dividing the length and width by 3. The floor is 8 yards by 24 yards. Multiply them together to find the area. **The correct answer is (A).**

Example #4

If the area of the trapezoid shown below is 66, what is the length of b_1?

(A)   2

(B)   9

(C)   11

(D)   13

Use the trapezoid area formula and plug in the pieces of information you know: $\dfrac{b_1 + 13}{2} \times 6 = 66$. Solving for b_1 results in 9. **The correct answer is (B).**

Practice Questions

1. *ABCD* is a square. What is the area of the unshaded region?

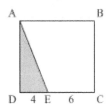

   (A) 20
   (B) 50
   (C) 80
   (D) 100

2. In a parallelogram, which of the following is not necessarily true?
   (A) Opposite angles are congruent
   (B) The sum of consecutive angles = 180°
   (C) Opposite sides are congruent
   (D) Consecutive sides are congruent

3. If the length of each leg of a square is increased by 20%, what is the percent increase in the square's area?
   (A) 20%
   (B) 44%
   (C) 50%
   (D) 96%

4. In rectangle *WXYZ*, point *A* is the midpoint of side *XY*. If the area of trapezoid *WXAZ* is 54 and the length of *WX* is 12, what is the area of rectangle *WXYZ*?
   (A) 48
   (B) 72
   (C) 96
   (D) 108

5. In the figure below, square *LMNO* has a side length of 12, and each of the smaller shaded squares has a side length of 3.

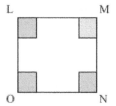

   What is the area of the unshaded region, in square units?
   (A) 36
   (B) 72
   (C) 108
   (D) 144

6. If there is no waste, how many square feet of carpeting are required to cover a rectangular floor that is 18 yards by 48 yards? (1 yard = 3 feet)
   (A) 96
   (B) 864
   (C) 4,486
   (D) 7,776

7. In the rectangle below, *QR* = *RS* + 6.

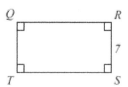

   What is the area of rectangle *QRST*?
   (A) 91
   (B) 108
   (C) 116
   (D) 124

Answer Key - Geometry

Lines and Angles

1. C
2. B
3. D
4. D
5. A
6. B

Triangles

1. 60 in^2
2. 13
3. $6<x<24$
4. 15 cm
5. $7\sqrt{2}$
6. 11.66
7. 6 in$<x<$18 in
8. 30 in
9. 4 in
10. 39 in
11. 9.23 or $\dfrac{120}{13}$
12. $\sqrt{63}$
13. $9\sqrt{3}$
14. $24\sqrt{2}$
15. 8.333
16. $8\sqrt{3}$
17. No
18. 108°

Coordinate Geometry

1. C
2. D
3. D
4. C
5. B
6. D
7. A
8. C
9. C
10. A
11. B
12. D
13. A
14. B
15. C
16. B
17. D
18. C
19. A
20. A

Circles

1. 100π cm^2
2. 13
3. 81π cm^2
4. 50 in
5. 25π m^2
6. 8 cm
7. 10 in

Quadrilaterals

1. C
2. D
3. B
4. B
5. C
6. D
7. A

Part IV
Upper Level ISEE QR and MA Question Types

Chapter 3

Quantitative Reasoning Question Types

Applied Mean Questions

In general, the ISEE will not simply ask you to find the mean, or average, of a set of numbers. Instead, you may need to apply your knowledge of averages to a scenario.

Example #1
Yuyang's friends took a total of 1,440 pictures at her birthday party. The friends took an average of 45 pictures each. How many friends attended Yuyang's party?
(A)   32
(B)   45
(C)   50
(D)   57

Here, you can pretend that the actual number of pictures taken by each friend and the average number of pictures taken by each friend were the same. Think of it this way: if the average of five integers is 5, then the five integers could be 1, 1, 1, 1, and 21; they could be 0, 0, 0, 0, and 25; they could be 5, 5, 5, 5, and 5, etc. No matter what, the sum of the five integers must be 25.

You can apply this logic to Example #1 and assume that each friend took exactly 45 pictures. If each friend took 45 pictures and the total number of pictures taken was 1,440, how many friends were at the party?

45 pictures × 32 guests = 1,440. **The correct answer is (A).**

Example #2
Jamal had a mean score of 94 on his first 5 math tests. What score does he need to get on his sixth test to bring the mean for all 6 scores up to a 95?
(A)   94
(B)   96
(C)   98
(D)   100

Step 1: Set up your equation.
$$\frac{sum\ of\ all\ scores}{total\ number\ of\ scores} = \text{average score}$$

Step 2: Input the information you have.
$$\frac{94 + 94 + 94 + 94 + 94 + score\ of\ Test\ \#6}{6} = 95$$

Step 3: Simplify. $\frac{470 + score\ of\ Test\ \#6}{6} = 95$

Step 4: Continue to simplify.
470 + score of Test #6 = 570.
Step 5: Solve. *Score of test #6 = 100.*

The correct answer is (D).

You could also work backwards. Start with (C).
$\frac{94 + 94 + 94 + 94 + 94 + 98}{6} = 94.66$. This answer is too small, so the score of the sixth test must be higher than 98.

Summary
How to recognize *applied mean* questions:
1) You are presented with a scenario in which a series of scores are added up
2) You are asked how many points must be scored in a final game / test in order to achieve a minimum / maximum average score

What you should keep in mind:
1) Set up the equation for averages as you normally would, then solve for the missing information
2) You can try working backwards on these questions

Practice Problems

1. On a field trip to the museum, Ms. Wood's 7th grade class took a total of 505 pictures. The students took an average of 101 pictures each. How many students are in the class?
   (A)   4
   (B)   5
   (C)   6
   (D)   7

2. James was trying to calculate the mean of his test scores. He did not know what he had scored on each of the first 4 tests but knew that the sum of his scores was 340. If James scored a 95 on his fifth test, then what was the mean of all five scores?
   (A)   85
   (B)   87
   (C)   89
   (D)   91

3. Susan got an average score of 78 on her four math tests this year. Her teacher is going to drop her lowest score, which is 54, before calculating her final average grade. What will be Susan's final math grade?
   (A)   80
   (B)   84
   (C)   86
   (D)   88

4. Ben is playing a game in which the goal is to have the lowest score. After his first six games, his average score is 18 points per game. What is the amount he must score on the next game in order to lower his total average to 16 points?
   (A)   4
   (B)   8
   (C)   12
   (D)   16

5. Mohammad worked an average of 20 hours per week for two weeks and then an average of 28 hours per week for six weeks. What was his average number of hours worked per week over all eight weeks?
   (A)   20
   (B)   24
   (C)   26
   (D)   30

6. Jessie had a mean score of 88 on her first three math tests. What is the lowest score she can possibly get on her fourth and final test while still finishing with a mean score of at least 83 on all her tests?
   (A)   60
   (B)   68
   (C)   70
   (D)   74

7. Jorge is playing a game in which the goal is to have the lowest score. After his first five games, his average score is 28 points per game. What is the amount he must score on the next game in order to lower his average to 25 points per game?
   (A)   10
   (B)   15
   (C)   20
   (D)   25

8. DeShawn got an average score of 86 on his five chemistry tests this year. His teacher is going to drop his lowest score, which is 78, before calculating his final average grade. What will be DeShawn's final chemistry grade?
   (A)   86
   (B)   87
   (C)   88
   (D)   92

9. Jordan worked an average of 10 hours per week for six weeks and then an average of 30 hours per week for six weeks. What was his average number of hours worked per week over all 12 weeks?
   (A) 12
   (B) 16
   (C) 20
   (D) 24

10. Jermaine is playing a game in which the goal is to have the lowest score. After his first four games, his average score is 19 points per game. What is the amount he must score on the next game in order to lower his average to 17 points per game?
    (A) 7
    (B) 9
    (C) 11
    (D) 13

11. Amy had a mean score of 77 on her first four math tests. What score does she need to get on her fifth test to bring the mean for all five scores up to an 80?
    (A) 90
    (B) 92
    (C) 94
    (D) 96

12. Xiaoying had a mean score of 84 on her first two math tests. What score does she need to get on her third test to bring the mean for all three scores up to an 86?
    (A) 90
    (B) 92
    (C) 94
    (D) 96

13. Arturo worked an average of 15 hours per week for four weeks and then an average of 22 hours per week for six weeks. What was his average number of hours worked per week over all ten weeks?
    (A) 19.20
    (B) 20.50
    (C) 21.25
    (D) 21.80

14. Stephen was trying to calculate the mean of his test scores. He did not know what he had scored on each of the first five tests but knew that the sum of his scores was 300. If Stephen scored a 75 on his sixth test, then what was the mean of all six scores?
    (A) 60.25
    (B) 62.00
    (C) 62.50
    (D) 63.25

15. Riku had a mean score of 75 on his first six math tests. What is the lowest score he can possibly get on his seventh and final test while still finishing with a mean score of at least 72 on all his tests?
    (A) 48
    (B) 50
    (C) 52
    (D) 54

16. Wang Su was trying to calculate the mean of his test scores. He did not know what he had scored on each of the first three tests but knew that the sum of his scores was 270. If Wang Su scored a 60 on his fourth test, then what was the mean of all four scores?
    (A) 82.00
    (B) 82.50
    (C) 83.25
    (D) 84.00

$ax^2 + bx + c$

Have you ever worked with FOIL, quadratic equations, or parabolas? If so, $ax^2 + bx + c$ questions aren't as unfamiliar as you might think. Let's say you're given the expression $(2x - 2)(2x - 3)$. Once you expand this using FOIL, it simplifies to $4x^2 - 10x + 6$. Compare $4x^2 - 10x + 6$ with $ax^2 + bx + c$. You'll notice that 4 takes the place of a, -10 takes the place of b, and 6 takes the place of c. Therefore, the coefficient in front of x^2 corresponds to a, the coefficient in front of x corresponds to b, and the constant corresponds to c!

Example #1

If n is a nonnegative integer and
$(x + 7)(x - 7) = x^2 - n$, what is the value of n?

(A)   0

(B)   7

(C)   14

(D)   49

FOILing $(x + 7)(x - 7)$ gives us
$x^2 - 7x + 7x - 49$, which simplifies to $x^2 - 49$.
Comparing that result to $x^2 - n$ shows that 49 has replaced n. **The answer is (D).**

Example #2

If $(x + n)^2 = x^2 - 8x + b$, what is the value of b?

(A)   -16

(B)   -8

(C)   8

(D)   16

This question is more difficult. First, FOIL $(x + n)^2$, which results in $x^2 + xn + xn + n^2$. Comparing that result to $x^2 - 8x + b$ shows that "$xn + xn$" corresponds to $8x$, and n^2 corresponds to b. If $2xn = 8x$, then $n = 4$. That means that $n^2 = 16$, and because n^2 corresponds to b, b equals 16. **The answer is (D).**

Summary

How to recognize $ax^2 + bx + c$ questions:

1) You see the expression $ax^2 + bx + c$, $y^2 + mx + b$, $(x + n)(x - n) = x^2 - n$, or something similar

What you should keep in mind:

1) The number next to x^2 corresponds to a, the number next to x corresponds to b, and the number by itself corresponds to c.

2) You may need to FOIL: **First, Outer, Inner, Last**

3) $-2x^2$ means $a =$ **-2**; likewise, $4x$ means $b =$ **4**, and -8 means $c =$ **-8**. Don't get your signs mixed up!

4) You can often plug your answer back into the original equation to check your work

Practice Questions

1. If m is a positive integer and $(x + 5)^2 = x^2 + mx + 25$, what is the value of m?
   - (A) 5
   - (B) 10
   - (C) 25
   - (D) 50

2. If m is a positive integer and $(x - 3)^2 = x^2 - mx + 9$, what is the value of m?
   - (A) 3
   - (B) 6
   - (C) 9
   - (D) 12

3. If m is a positive integer and $(x + 8)^2 = x^2 + mx + 64$, what is the value of m?
   - (A) 0
   - (B) 8
   - (C) 16
   - (D) 64

4. If $(x + n)^2 = x^2 + 4x + b$, what is the value of b?
   - (A) 2
   - (B) 4
   - (C) 6
   - (D) 8

5. If $(x + n)^2 = x^2 - 20x + b$, what is the value of b?
   - (A) -20
   - (B) 10
   - (C) 20
   - (D) 100

6. If $(x + 10)(x - 4) = ax^2 + bx + c$, what is the value of c?
   - (A) -40
   - (B) -4
   - (C) 4
   - (D) 40

7. If $(x - 6)(x - 3) = ax^2 + bx + c$, what is the value of c?
   - (A) 3
   - (B) 6
   - (C) 9
   - (D) 18

8. If $(x - 7)(x - 9) = ax^2 + bx + c$, what is the value of c?
   - (A) 7
   - (B) 9
   - (C) 16
   - (D) 63

9. If b is a nonnegative integer and $(y - 6)^2 = y^2 + ay + b$, then what is the value of b?
   - (A) 6
   - (B) 12
   - (C) 18
   - (D) 36

10. If b is a nonnegative integer and $(y - 3)^2 = y^2 + ay + b$, then what is the value of b?
    - (A) 2
    - (B) 9
    - (C) 12
    - (D) 16

11. If b is a nonnegative integer and $(y + 9)^2 = y^2 + ay + b$, then what is the value of b?
    - (A) 9
    - (B) 18
    - (C) 81
    - (D) 90

12. If n is a nonnegative integer and $(x + 6)(x - 6) = x^2 - n$, what is the value of n?
    - (A) 0
    - (B) 6
    - (C) 36
    - (D) 72

Isolating Variables

Isolating variables questions contain two or more variables and ask you to solve for one variable in terms of another.

Example #1

If $x - y = 5$, then which expression is equal to y?

(A) $x + 5$

(B) $x - 5$

(C) $-x + 5$

(D) $-x - 5$

Solve algebraically: Because y does not appear in the answer choices, that's the variable you need to isolate. To do that, subtract 5 from both sides of the equation, which gives you $x - y - 5 = 0$. Then, add y to both sides of the equation, which gives you $x - 5 = y$. **(B) is the correct answer.**

Input your own number: Pick a number for x. It can be anything you want, but since you can't use a calculator on the ISEE, choose numbers that are easy to work with. Let's say $x = 10$. If $x = 10$, and $x - y = 5$, that means $y = 5$. Now, take a look at your answer choices. In (A), plugging in 10 for x gives us $10 + 5 = 15$. However, we already determined that $y = 5$, and since $15 \neq 5$, this answer can't be correct. In (B), plugging in 10 for x gives us $10 - 5 = 5$. We determined that $y = 5$, so we've found the correct answer!

Example #2

If $\frac{ab}{4} = 30$, then which expression is equal to b?

(A) $30 - a$

(B) $30 + a$

(C) $120a$

(D) $\frac{120}{a}$

In Example #2, the goal is to isolate b. You should first multiply by 4 on both sides of the equation, which simplifies to $ab = 120$. To isolate b, divide by a on both sides. Your final answer is $b = \frac{120}{a}$. **The correct answer is (D).**

Summary

How to recognize *isolating variables* questions:
1) There will be at least two variables arranged in some kind of algebraic expression
2) You are asked *which expression is equal to _?* or *what is ___ in terms of___?*

What you should keep in mind:
1) Look at the answer choices to determine which variable you're supposed to isolate. The variable you *don't* see in the answer choices is the one you're isolating
2) Solve algebraically or input your own number

121

Practice Questions

1. If $xy^2 - 2 = y$, what is x in terms of y?

    (A) $\frac{y}{y^2} + 2$

    (B) $\frac{y + 2}{y}$

    (C) $\frac{1}{y} + \frac{2}{y^2}$

    (D) $\frac{y}{y^2} - 2$

2. If $\sqrt{z} + 4y = 12$, what is z in terms of y?

    (A) $\sqrt{12} - 4y$

    (B) $12 - 4y$

    (C) $12 - 4y^2$

    (D) $144 - 96y + 16y^2$

3. If $\frac{c^2 + d}{4} = 4$, then which expression is equal to d?

    (A) $\sqrt{2 + c}$

    (B) $\sqrt{2 - c}$

    (C) $16 + c^2$

    (D) $16 - c^2$

4. If $\frac{x - y}{7} = y$, then which of the following is equal to x?

    (A) 7

    (B) y

    (C) $8y$

    (D) $6y$

5. If $\frac{ab}{2} = 10$, then which expression is equal to b?

    (A) $20 - a$

    (B) $20 + a$

    (C) $\frac{20}{a}$

    (D) $20a$

6. If $\frac{m - 6n}{6} = 7$, then which expression is equal to m?

    (A) $42n - 6$

    (B) $42n + 6$

    (C) $42 - 6n$

    (D) $42 + 6n$

7. If $\left(\frac{a}{b}\right)^2 = 100$, then what is b in terms of a?

    (A) $\frac{a}{10}$

    (B) $\frac{10}{a}$

    (C) $10a$

    (D) $100a$

8. If $\sqrt{x + y} + 2 = 6$, then which expression is equal to x?

    (A) $16 - y$

    (B) $16 + y$

    (C) $34 + y$

    (D) $34 - y$

9. If $\frac{4a - b}{5} = 20$, what is a in terms of b?

    (A) $25 - b$

    (B) $25 + \frac{b}{4}$

    (C) $100 - 4b$

    (D) $100 + 3b$

10. If $\frac{10}{x} + y = 20$, what is x in terms of y?

    (A) $\frac{10}{20 + y}$

    (B) $\frac{1}{2} - y$

    (C) $\frac{10}{20 - y}$

    (D) $\frac{1}{2} + y$

Maximizing and Minimizing the Area and Perimeter of Quadrilaterals

To maximize the area of a quadrilateral, the lengths of its sides should be equal. To maximize the perimeter of a quadrilateral, set the width equal to 1. The length should be whatever is left over from the total perimeter.

To minimize a quadrilateral's area, set width equal to 1 and use the remaining perimeter to set the length. To minimize a quadrilateral's perimeter, the lengths of the sides of the rectangle should be equal.

Example #1

A rectangle has an area of 30 in^2. If the length and the width of the rectangle are measured in whole inches, what is the least possible perimeter of the rectangle?

(A)   5 in
(B)   6 in
(C)   22 in
(D)   30 in

To minimize perimeter, the lengths of the sides need to be as close together as possible. 30 is not divisible by 4, so the length and width won't be exactly the same. You could say that length = 5 and width = 6. That gives us an area of 30 in^2 and a perimeter of 22 inches. **(C) is correct.**

Example #2

A room has a perimeter of 20 feet. If the length and width are measured in whole feet, what is the greatest possible area of the room?

(A)   9 ft^2
(B)   20 ft^2
(C)   25 ft^2
(D)   30 ft^2

To maximize area, the sides of the quadrilateral should be equal. 20 is divisible by 4, which means the length and width are equal to 5. The area is 25 ft^2. **The correct answer is (C).**

Summary

How to recognize *maximizing and minimizing area and perimeter of quadrilaterals* questions:

1) The question asks *what is the least possible area, what is the greatest possible area, what is the least possible perimeter*, or *what is the greatest possible perimeter?*
2) The answer choices are all in square units (in^2, cm^2, etc) or lengths (in, cm, etc)

What you should keep in mind:

1) To maximize area, length and width should be equal
2) To minimize area, set width equal to 1 and length equal to whatever is left over from the original perimeter
3) To maximize perimeter, set width equal to 1 and length equal to whatever is left over from the original perimeter
4) To minimize perimeter, length and width should be equal

Practice Questions

1. A rectangle has a perimeter of 18 centimeters. If the length and the width of the rectangle are measured in whole centimeters, what is the least possible area of the rectangle?
   - (A) 6 cm^2
   - (B) 8 cm^2
   - (C) 16 cm^2
   - (D) 18 cm^2

2. A rectangle has an area of 90 in^2. If the length and the width of the rectangle are measured in whole inches, what is the least possible perimeter of the rectangle?
   - (A) 18 in
   - (B) 25 in
   - (C) 38 in
   - (D) 48 in

3. If a rectangle has an area of 30 cm^2 and a length and width that are whole numbers, what is the greatest possible perimeter of that rectangle?
   - (A) 15 cm
   - (B) 29 cm
   - (C) 30 cm
   - (D) 62 cm

4. A rectangle has an area of 56 in^2. If the length and width are both measured in whole inches, what is the greatest possible perimeter of the rectangle?
   - (A) 56 in
   - (B) 112 in
   - (C) 114 in
   - (D) 228 in

5. A room has a perimeter of 46 feet. If the length and width are measured in whole feet, what is the greatest possible area of the room?
   - (A) 22 ft^2
   - (B) 46 ft^2
   - (C) 121 ft^2
   - (D) 132 ft^2

6. A rectangle has a perimeter of 40 centimeters. If the length and the width of the rectangle are measured in whole centimeters, what is the least possible area of the rectangle?
   - (A) 8 cm^2
   - (B) 15 cm^2
   - (C) 19 cm^2
   - (D) 40 cm^2

7. A rectangle has an area of 12 in^2. If the length and width are both measured in whole inches, what is the greatest possible perimeter of the rectangle?
   - (A) 26 in
   - (B) 48 in
   - (C) 96 in
   - (D) 108 in

8. If a rectangle has an area of 99 cm^2 and a length and width that are whole numbers, what is the greatest possible perimeter of that rectangle?
   - (A) 99 cm
   - (B) 100 cm
   - (C) 198 cm
   - (D) 200 cm

9. A rectangle has an area of 182 in². If the length and the width of the rectangle are measured in whole inches, what is the least possible perimeter of the rectangle?
    (A)   26 in
    (B)   38 in
    (C)   45 in
    (D)   54 in

10. A rectangle has a perimeter of 100 centimeters. If the length and the width of the rectangle are measured in whole centimeters, what is the least possible area of the rectangle?
    (A)   49 cm²
    (B)   100 cm²
    (C)   200 cm²
    (D)   625 cm²

11. A rectangle has an area of 144 in². If the length and width are both measured in whole inches, what is the greatest possible perimeter of the rectangle?
    (A)   48 in
    (B)   144 in
    (C)   288 in
    (D)   290 in

12. A room has a perimeter of 72 feet. If the length and width are measured in whole feet, what is the greatest possible area of the room?
    (A)   18 ft²
    (B)   35 ft²
    (C)   108 ft²
    (D)   324 ft²

13. A rectangle has an area of 56 inches². If the length and the width of the rectangle are measured in whole inches, what is the least possible perimeter of the rectangle?
    (A)   30 in
    (B)   32 in
    (C)   36 in
    (D)   38 in

14. If a rectangle has an area of 47 square centimeters and a length and width that are whole numbers, what is the greatest possible perimeter of that rectangle?
    (A)   47 cm
    (B)   50 cm
    (C)   96 cm
    (D)   98 cm

15. Mr. Smith needs to fence off a square football field, which has an area of 400 ft². How many feet of fencing must he buy to construct his fence?
    (A)   20 ft
    (B)   80 ft
    (C)   160 ft
    (D)   200 ft

Maximum or Minimum Values in Inequalities Questions

These questions are easy to identify: you'll see the word *maximum* or *minimum* in the question stem, and there will also be an x surrounded by $\leq$ or $<$ signs. The difference between $\leq$ and $<$ is *crucial*, so make sure you're paying attention! You might see a question like this:

What is the maximum value of $2x + x^2 - 4$ on the interval $-1 < x < 4$?

In this instance, maybe plugging in -1 will give you a maximum value. However, that value is NOT the correct answer, because it is not included in the range of values. The writers of the ISEE will almost certainly still include that value as an answer choice in order to trick you.

Example #1

What is the maximum value of $\frac{3x^2}{x+2}$ for $0 \leq x < 2$ if x is an integer?
(A)   1
(B)   2
(C)   3
(D)   4

You should work through this algebraically.

Plug in 0 first. $\frac{3(0)^2}{(0)+2} = \frac{0}{2} = 0$. Then, try 1.

$\frac{3(1)^2}{(1)+2} = \frac{3}{3} = 1$. Plugging in 2 results in an answer of 3. However, 2 is NOT included in the range of values. Therefore, the maximum possible value is 1. **The correct answer is (A).**

Example #2

What is the minimum value of $\frac{x^2}{x-3}$ for $-2 \leq x \leq 2$ if x is an integer?
(A)   -4
(B) $-1\frac{1}{3}$
(C) $-\frac{1}{2}$
(D)   0

Once again, we'll start by plugging in the smallest possible value for x, which is -2.

$\frac{(-2)^2}{(-2)-3} = -\frac{4}{5}$. Then, try 0. $\frac{(0)^2}{(0)-3} = -\frac{0}{3} = 0$.

Finally, try 2. $\frac{(2)^2}{(2)-3} = -\frac{4}{1} = -4$. **The correct answer is (A).**

Summary

How to recognize *maximum and minimum values in inequalities questions*:
1) The questions asks, "What is the maximum or minimum value of....?"
2) You see a variable (like x) surrounded by inequalities (for example, $-2 \leq x \leq 1$)

What you should keep in mind:
1) Double-check to see if the sign is $\leq$ or $<$. Circle the signs
2) Circle whether the question is asking for the *maximum* or the *minimum*
3) Plug in the smallest integer, the largest integer, and zero
4) Write down all your work to prevent careless mistakes

Practice Questions

1. What is the maximum value for y, if $y = x^2 + 1$ for $-2 \leq x \leq 1$?
   (A)   0
   (B)   1
   (C)   5
   (D)   7

2. What is the maximum value for y, if $y = x^2 - 1$ for $-3 < x < 2$?
   (A)   -1
   (B)   3
   (C)   7
   (D)   8

3. What is the maximum value for y, if $y = -x^2 + 1$ for $-2 \leq x \leq 1$?
   (A)   -3
   (B)   1
   (C)   3
   (D)   9

4. What is the minimum value for y, if $y = -2x^2 - 2$ for $-4 \leq x \leq 2$?
   (A)   -34
   (B)   -20
   (C)   -2
   (D)   20

5. What is the minimum value for y, if $y = x^2 + 2x$ for $-3 \leq x \leq 2$?
   (A)   -3
   (B)   -1
   (C)   0
   (D)   3

6. What is the maximum value for y, if $y = 3 - 3x - x^2$ for $-1 \leq x \leq 2$?
   (A)   -7
   (B)   -1
   (C)   3
   (D)   5

7. What is the maximum value for y, if $y = 2 - x - 2x^2$ for $-3 \leq x \leq 2$?
   (A)   -8
   (B)   1
   (C)   2
   (D)   4

8. What is the minimum value for y, if $y = 2 - x + x^2$ for $-1 \leq x \leq 3$?
   (A)   -2
   (B)   0
   (C)   2
   (D)   8

9. What is the minimum value for y, if $y = 1 - x^2$ for $-2 \leq x \leq 2$?
   (A)   -8
   (B)   -3
   (C)   1
   (D)   5

10. What is the minimum value for y if $y = \frac{x^2}{4} + 2$ for $-2 \leq x \leq 3$?
    (A)   0
    (B)   1
    (C)   2
    (D)   3

11. What is the maximum value for y if $y = \frac{x^2}{2} - 3$ for $-2 \leq x \leq 4$?
    (A)   -3
    (B)   0
    (C)   3
    (D)   5

Symbol Questions

Symbol questions present a variable surrounded by unusual symbols or shapes. Next to that variable will be an equation. Finally, next to that equation will be a number with the same symbols or shapes around it as the variable. It will look something like this:

$$\#n\# = 2n + 2........\#4\#$$

Replace the variable with the number and solve. In this instance, you'd replace the *n* in $2n + 2$ with 4, resulting in $2(4) + 2 = 10$. In questions with two variables, place close attention to their order. For example:

$$a@b = b - a.......2@3 = b - a.$$

In this example, $a = 2$ and $b = 3$, and the final answer is $3 - 2 = 1$.

Example #1
If $♪z♪ = 4z + 8$, what is the value of $♪6♪$?
(A)   4
(B)   6
(C)   16
(D)   32

Replace *z* with 6 in the equation. $4(6) + 8 = 32$.
The correct answer is (D).

Example #2
If $x@y$ is defined by $y^2 + x$, what is the value of $4@3$?
(A)   13
(B)   16
(C)   19
(D)   21

In symbol questions with two variables, you should always write down the value of each variable. It's very easy to mix them up if you try doing these in your head; the only way to ensure you don't make a mistake is to write down your work! Here, $x = 4$ and $y = 3$; $3^2 + 4 = 13$. **(A) is correct.** If you picked (C), you plugged in 3 for *x* and 4 for *y*.

Summary
How to recognize *symbol* questions:
   1) Unusual symbols such as ♪, #, @, $

What you should keep in mind:
   1) Double-check your work
   2) Don't mix up the order of the variables
   3) Write down the value of each variable to prevent careless mistakes

Practice Questions

1. If $a@b$ is defined by $b^3 - 2a$, what is the value of $3@2$?
   - (A) $\frac{1}{2}$
   - (B) 2
   - (C) 7
   - (D) 23

2. If $♪z♪ = \frac{3z - 12}{z}$, what is the value of $♪3♪$?
   - (A) -1
   - (B) 0
   - (C) 1
   - (D) 9

3. If $♪y♪ = \frac{12 - 6y}{y}$, what is the value of $♪\frac{1}{2}♪$?
   - (A) 1
   - (B) $\frac{3}{2}$
   - (C) 3
   - (D) 18

4. If $\#q\# = \frac{4q^2 - 5}{5}$, what is the value of $\#5\#$?
   - (A) 8
   - (B) 15
   - (C) 19
   - (D) 79

5. If $\$z\$ = \frac{z^5 + 3}{5}$, what is the value of $\$2\$$?
   - (A) 4
   - (B) 7
   - (C) 20
   - (D) $51\frac{1}{5}$

6. If $n* = 5n + 2$, what is the value of $6*$?
   - (A) 4
   - (B) 8
   - (C) 16
   - (D) 32

7. If $z* = 2z - 9$, what is the value of $15*$?
   - (A) 12
   - (B) 21
   - (C) 25
   - (D) 30

8. If $*y* = 12y^2$, what is the value of $*3*$?
   - (A) 108
   - (B) 120
   - (C) 132
   - (D) 144

9. If $c\%z$ is defined by $z^2 - c$, what is the value of $2\%4$?
   - (A) 0
   - (B) 7
   - (C) 14
   - (D) 21

10. If $e@g$ is defined by $g^2 - e$, what is the value of $3@5$?
    - (A) 4
    - (B) 22
    - (C) 25
    - (D) 30

11. If $b*a$ is defined by $a^2 - b$, what is the value of $3*4$?
    - (A) 5
    - (B) 8
    - (C) 13
    - (D) 20

Percent Change in Squares, Circles, and Triangles

Inputting your own numbers is an extremely useful strategy on these questions. You should pick numbers that are easy to work with when dealing with percents: 10 is generally a pretty safe choice.

Example #1
If the length of the base of a triangle is increased by 10 percent and the height is decreased by 10 percent, what is the percent decrease in the area of the triangle?

(A)   0%

(B)   .5%

(C)   1%

(D)   20%

Imagine a triangle with a height of 10 units and a base of 10 units. The equation for the area of a triangle is $\frac{1}{2} bh$, so the triangle's area is $\frac{1}{2}$ (10)(10) = 50 units. According to the question, the base increases by 10% to 11 units. The height decreases by 10% to 9 units. The area of the new triangle is $\frac{1}{2}$ (11)(9) = 49.5 units. Your first guess might be (B), but remember that the equation for percent change is ($\frac{change}{original}$) × 100. Here, it is ($\frac{.5}{50}$) × 100 = 1%, so **the correct answer is (C).**

The ISEE will give you answer choices that seem correct if you're not being careful; you'll notice that (A) is 10 – 10, which seems like an obvious choice, and (D) is 10 + 10, which could also trip you up if you're not paying attention!

Summary
How to recognize *percent change in squares, circles, and triangles* questions:
1) The questions mentions squares, circles, and triangles, and percent increase or decrease
2) The answer choices are all given as percents

What you should keep in mind:
1) For squares and rectangles, *A = (length)(width)*; for circles, *A = π (radius)²*; for triangles, $A = \frac{1}{2}$ *(base)(height)*
2) The formula for finding percent change is ($\frac{change}{original}$) × 100
3) Always start by making the length, width, height, and / or radius 10
4) Be VERY careful if the area increases from 10 to 20, 100 to 200, 100 to 400, etc. You might think that doubling from 10 to 20 means there was a 200% increase. Using the percent change formula, you'll see that $\frac{change}{original}$ × 100 = ($\frac{10}{10}$) × 100 = 100%

Practice Questions

1. If the length of the base of a triangle is increased by 20 percent and the height is decreased by 30 percent, what is the percent decrease in the area of the triangle?
   - (A)   8%
   - (B)   16%
   - (C)   20%
   - (D)   30%

2. If the length of the base of a triangle is decreased by 50 percent and the height is decreased by 20 percent, what is the percent decrease in the area of the triangle?
   - (A)   20%
   - (B)   30%
   - (C)   50%
   - (D)   60%

3. If the length of the base of a triangle is increased by 100 percent and the height is increased by 100 percent, what is the percent increase in the area of the triangle?
   - (A)   50%
   - (B)   100%
   - (C)   300%
   - (D)   400%

4. If the diameter of a circle is increased by 40%, what is the percent increase in the area of the circle?
   - (A)   40%
   - (B)   96%
   - (C)   100%
   - (D)   160%

5. If the diameter of a circle is decreased by 60%, what is the percent decrease in the area of the circle?
   - (A)   84%
   - (B)   60%
   - (C)   42%
   - (D)   20%

6. If the radius of a circle is increased by 25%, what is the percent increase in the area of the circle?
   - (A)   12.5%
   - (B)   56.25%
   - (C)   100%
   - (D)   156.25%

7. If the length of each side of a square is increased by 20%, what is the percent increase in the area of the square?
   - (A)   2%
   - (B)   20%
   - (C)   44%
   - (D)   100%

8. If the length of each side of a square is decreased by 90%, what is the percent decrease in the area of the square?
   - (A)   1%
   - (B)   9%
   - (C)   99%
   - (D)   100%

9. If the length of each side of a square is increased by 55%, what is the percent increase in the area of the square?
   - (A)   55%
   - (B)   140.25%
   - (C)   240.25%
   - (D)   300%

Net Cubes Questions

Net Cubes questions test spatial reasoning. You may be presented with an image of a cube and asked which of the four nets (unfolded cubes) below it could be folded up to create the cube. Alternatively, you may be presented with a net and asked which of the four folded cubes below it could have been created from the net.

To solve these questions, imagine folding the nets in your head and see which one would fold into the cube shown. You can also practice manipulating a real cube to help yourself gain a better understanding of how the nets might fold.

Example #1
A cube is shown below.

Which of the following could be a possible net of the cube?

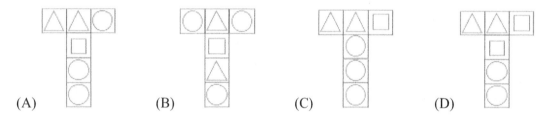

(A)   (B)   (C)   (D)

First, you should recognize that (D) only has two circles, and therefore cannot be correct. If (C) were folded into a cube, all three circles would line up in a row. The cube shown has circles on different sides, so (C) is also incorrect. **The correct answer is (A).**

How to recognize *net cubes questions:*
1) The question asks, "*Which of the following could be a possible net for the cube?*" or "*Which of the following could **not** be a possible net for the cube?*"
2) There is a picture of one cube and four nets, or four cubes and one net

What you should keep in mind:
1) Mentally fold each of the cubes in your head - can you find one that matches the folded cube?
2) Direction is very important for shapes like triangles. Which way does the tip of the triangle point? This will make a big difference in your answer
3) Color matters, as well. Sometimes certain sections of the net or cube will be shaded

Practice Questions

1. Which of the following could be a possible net of the cube?

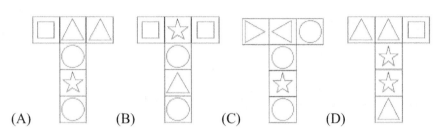

(A)   (B)   (C)   (D)

2. Which of the following could be a possible net of the cube?

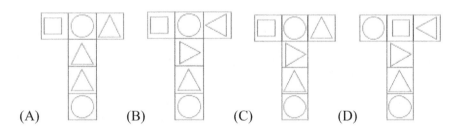

(A)   (B)   (C)   (D)

3. Which of the following could be a possible net of the cube?

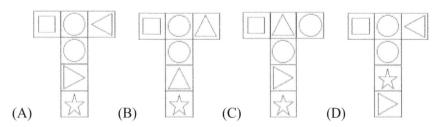

(A)   (B)   (C)   (D)

4. Which of the following could be a possible net of the cube?

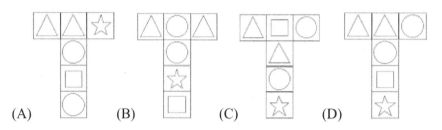

(A)   (B)   (C)   (D)

5. Which of the following cubes could have been created from the net?

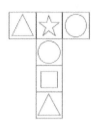

(A)   (B)   (C)   (D)

6. Which of the following cubes could have been created from the net?

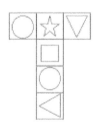

(A)   (B)   (C)   (D)

What is the value? Questions

What is the value? questions ask you to simplify a complicated expression that includes exponents and fractions.

Example #1
What is the value of the expression

$$\frac{2^3(8 + 16)}{2^5(2^3 + 2^2)} ?$$

(A)   0

(B) $\frac{1}{2}$

(C)   1

(D) $\frac{3}{2}$

Step 1: Rewrite the terms in the same base, if possible.

$$\frac{2^3(8 + 16)}{2^5(2^3 + 2^2)} = \frac{2^3(2^3 + 2^4)}{2^5(2^3 + 2^2)}$$

Step 2: Distribute all of the exponents and pull out like terms.

$$\frac{2^3(2^3 + 2^4)}{2^5(2^3 + 2^2)} = \frac{2^6 + 2^7}{2^8 + 2^7} = \frac{2^6(1 + 2)}{2^6(2^2 + 2)}$$

Step 3: Cancel like terms in the numerator and denominator.

$$\frac{2^6(1 + 2)}{2^6(2^2 + 2)} = \frac{(1 + 2)}{(2^2 + 2)}$$

Step 4: Simplify and solve

$$\frac{(1 + 2)}{(2^2 + 2)} = \frac{3}{4 + 2} = \frac{3}{6} = \frac{1}{2}$$

The correct answer is (B).

Summary
How to recognize *What is the value?* questions:
1) You see a complicated expression that contains fractions and exponents
2) The question asks, "What is the value?"

What you should keep in mind:
1) Convert as many terms to the same base as possible
2) You may need to play around with the distribution of exponents in order to find the best way to cross-cancel
3) Always double-check your work: there are many places to make mistakes in these questions!

Practice Questions

1. What is the value of the expression

$$\frac{4(4^2 + 4^3)}{16(4 + 8)}?$$

(A) $\frac{3}{5}$

(B) $\frac{5}{3}$

(C) 4

(D) 16

2. What is the value of the expression

$$\frac{2^5(16 + 8)}{4^3(4 + 4)}?$$

(A) 1

(B) $\frac{3}{2}$

(C) 2

(D) $\frac{5}{2}$

3. What is the value of the expression

$$\frac{6^2(6^2 + 36)}{6^3(6^3 + 6^3)}?$$

(A) 0

(B) $\frac{1}{36}$

(C) 1

(D) 6

4. What is the value of the expression

$$\frac{5(5^2 + 5^3)}{25(5 + 10)}?$$

(A) $\frac{1}{2}$

(B) 1

(C) 2

(D) 5

5. What is the value of the expression

$$\frac{2^5(4^2 + 8^2)}{16(2^3 + 2^6)}?$$

(A) 0

(B) $\frac{9}{20}$

(C) 1

(D) $\frac{20}{9}$

6. What is the value of the expression

$$\frac{2(2^4 + 2^3)}{8(4 + 16)}?$$

(A) $\frac{3}{10}$

(B) 1

(C) $\frac{4}{3}$

(D) $\frac{3}{2}$

7. What is the value of the expression

$$\frac{3^4(27 + 3^5)}{3^3(3^6 + 27)} ?$$

(A)   1

(B) $\frac{15}{14}$

(C) $\frac{9}{4}$

(D) $\frac{27}{10}$

8. What is the value of the expression

$$\frac{5^3(10 + 15)}{5^4(5^2 + 5)} ?$$

(A)   0

(B) $\frac{1}{8}$

(C) $\frac{1}{7}$

(D) $\frac{1}{6}$

Sum or Product of All Integers Questions

Sum or product of all integers questions are among the most conceptually difficult questions on the Upper Level ISEE. You should master all other QR question types before tackling these.

Example #1

If the sum of all integers from 1 to 900, inclusive, is x, then which expression represents the sum of all integers from 1 to 898, inclusive?

(A) $x - 1,799$
(B) $x + 1,799$
(C) $x - 899$
(D) $x + 899$

Approach these questions logically: will the sum of all integers from 1 to 898 be greater than or less than the sum of all integers from 1 to 900? Less, of course! You can already eliminate (B) and (D). Now, ask yourself exactly how much less it will be. The two integers that are not included in the second range that are included in the first range are 899 and 900. Therefore, if the sum of all integers from 1 to 900 is x, then the sum of all integers from 1 to 898 is $x - (899 + 900)$, or $x - 1,799$. **The correct answer is (A).**

Example #2

If the sum of all integers from 1 to 100, inclusive, is x, and the sum of all integers from 3 to 101, inclusive, is y, then what is $y - x$?

(A)   98
(B)   99
(C)   100
(D)   101

Example #2 requires more steps than Example #1, but the concept is essentially the same. You should note that in this question, you're being asked to solve an equation, rather than find one variable in terms of another. That's why you don't see any variables in the answer as you did in Example #1.

What is the difference between x and y? The range for y includes one new number (101) and excludes two of the numbers in x's range (1 and 2). Therefore, $y = x + 101 - 2 - 1$. You can then simplify this to $y = x + 98$. However, this doesn't match any of the answer choices! That's because you must now find the value of $y - x$. Once you've determined that $y = x + 98$, you can rewrite $y - x$ as $(x + 98) - x$. This simplifies to 98. **The correct answer is (A).**

Example #3

If the product of all the consecutive odd numbers from 1 to 19, inclusive, is c, then which of the following represents the product of all the consecutive odd numbers from 7 to 19, inclusive?

(A) $c - 36$

(B) $c + 36$

(C) $15c$

(D) $\frac{c}{15}$

There are two key differences between Example #3 and Examples #1 & #2: this question asks for the *product*, rather than the sum or the difference, and it asks about *consecutive odd integers*, rather than all integers in a given range.

Once again, think about this question logically. Will the product of all the consecutive odd integers from 7 to 19 be greater than or less than the product of all consecutive odd integers from 1 to 19? Less! You can eliminate (B) and (C).

$c = 1 \times 3 \times 5 \times 7 \times 9 \times 11 \times 13 \times 15 \times 17 \times 19$. The difference between c and the product of all the consecutive odd integers from 7 to 19 is that c contains $1 \times 3 \times 5$. You can divide c by $1 \times 3 \times 5$ in order to cancel those numbers out.

$$\frac{1 \times 3 \times 5 \times 7 \times 9 \times 11 \times 13 \times 15 \times 17 \times 19}{1 \times 3 \times 5} = \frac{c}{1 \times 3 \times 5} = \frac{c}{15}$$

The correct answer is (D).

Summary

How to recognize *sum or product of all integers* questions:

1)   The question asks you to find the sum, difference, product, or quotient of a range of integers

2)   You see "random" looking numbers in the answer choices: 1,799; 879, etc

What you should keep in mind:

1)   Think things through logically: will the value of the second expression be greater than or less than the value of the first expression? Use this to narrow down your answer choices

2)   Pay close attention to terms such as *even, odd, sum, difference, product*, and *consecutive*

3)   Do these questions last, and guess if necessary! If you can't figure one of these questions out in less than a minute, move on to something else

Practice Questions

1. If the sum of all integers from 1 to 500, inclusive, is x, then which expression represents the sum of all integers from 1 to 497, inclusive?
   (A)　　$x + 1,497$
   (B)　　$x + 498$
   (C)　　$x - 1,497$
   (D)　　$x - 498$

2. If the sum of all the odd numbers from 1 to 991, inclusive, is j, then which of the following represents the sum of all the odd numbers from 1 to 995, inclusive?
   (A)　　$j + 996$
   (B)　　$j - 996$
   (C)　　$j + 1,988$
   (D)　　$j - 1,988$

3. If the sum of all integers from 1 to 300, inclusive, is x, then which expression represents the sum of all integers from 1 to 302, inclusive?
   (A)　　$x - 301$
   (B)　　$x + 301$
   (C)　　$x - 603$
   (D)　　$x + 603$

4. If the sum of all the odd numbers from 1 to 55, inclusive, is y, then which of the following represents the sum of all the odd numbers from 1 to 51, inclusive?
   (A)　　$y + 108$
   (B)　　$y - 108$
   (C)　　$y + 51$
   (D)　　$y - 51$

5. If the sum of all the odd numbers from 1 to 99, inclusive, is b, then which of the following represents the sum of all the odd numbers from 1 to 93, inclusive?
   (A)　　$b + 97$
   (B)　　$b - 97$
   (C)　　$b + 291$
   (D)　　$b - 291$

6. If the sum of all the even numbers from 1 to 40, inclusive, is z, then which of the following represents the sum of all the even numbers from 1 to 46, inclusive?
   (A)　　$z + 46$
   (B)　　$z + 132$
   (C)　　$z - 46$
   (D)　　$z - 132$

7. If the sum of all integers from 1 to 50, inclusive, is n, then which expression represents the sum of all integers from 1 to 55, inclusive?
   (A)　　$n + 55$
   (B)　　$n + 265$
   (C)　　$n - 55$
   (D)　　$n - 265$

8. If the sum of all the even numbers from 1 to 84, inclusive, is q, then which of the following represents the sum of all the even numbers from 1 to 90, inclusive?
   (A)　　$q + 264$
   (B)　　$q - 90$
   (C)　　$q + 90$
   (D)　　$q - 264$

9. If the sum of all the odd numbers from 1 to 19, inclusive, is m, then which of the following represents the sum of all the odd numbers from 1 to 11, inclusive?
    (A) $m + 64$
    (B) $m - 64$
    (C) $m + 11$
    (D) $m - 11$

10. If the sum of all whole numbers from 10 to 30, inclusive, is p, and the sum of all whole numbers from 7 to 32, inclusive, is q, then what is $q - p$?
    (A)   81
    (B)   83
    (C)   85
    (D)   87

11. If the sum of all even consecutive integers from -8 to 8, inclusive, is d, and the sum of all even consecutive integers from -8 to 4, inclusive, is e, then what is $e - d$?
    (A)   -14
    (B) $d - 14$
    (C) $d + 14$
    (D)   14

12. If a is the sum of the consecutive odd numbers from 75 to 101, inclusive, and b is the sum of all the consecutive odd numbers from 73 to 105, inclusive, then what is the value of $b - a$?
    (A)   273
    (B)   277
    (C)   281
    (D)   285

13. If s is the sum of the consecutive even numbers from 10 to 44, inclusive, and t is the sum of all the consecutive even numbers from 12 to 46, inclusive, then what is the value of $s - t$?
    (A)   -36
    (B)   36
    (C) $s - 36$
    (D) $s + 36$

14. If y is the sum of the consecutive even numbers from 26 to 56, inclusive, and z is the sum of all the consecutive even numbers from 32 to 52, inclusive, then what is the value of $y - z$?
    (A)   -194
    (B) $z - 194$
    (C)   194
    (D) $z + 194$

15. If the product of all the integers from 9 to 25, inclusive, is x, then which of the following represents the product of all the integers from 11 to 25, inclusive?
    (A) $x - 9$
    (B) $x + 90$
    (C) $9x$
    (D) $\frac{x}{90}$

16. If the product of all the consecutive even numbers from 14 to 24, inclusive, is c, then which of the following represents the product of all the consecutive even numbers from 14 to 26, inclusive?
    (A) $c - 26$
    (B) $c + 26$
    (C) $26c$
    (D) $\frac{c}{26}$

Interpreting Graphs and Charts Questions

The ISEE contains many questions that will test your ability to analyze and interpret charts and graphs. When you encounter a chart or graph on the ISEE, we recommend that you spend a few seconds interpreting it before you even look at the question. It's always useful to know the title of the table or graph, what the x- and y-axes represent, what the units of each axis are, etc. There are a few types of charts and graphs that appear frequently:

1. *Time vs. distance graphs*

This graph compares the time (in hours) of Joffrey's bike ride vs. his distance from home (in miles). We can learn a lot from this graph. See how steep the line is from 0 to .25 hours? That must mean he traveled very quickly, since it only took him 15 minutes to ride 3 miles. It looks like he slows down from .25 hours to .75 hours, and he stops completely from .75 hours to 1 hour. At the end of the trip, he is not traveling negative miles per hour! The negatively sloped line indicates that he is getting closer and closer to home - he must have gotten tired and turned back!

2. *Mean, median, mode, and range graphs*

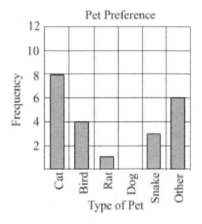

This graph shows the type of pet people own and compares that to how many people own each type of pet. It looks like most people prefer cats, while no one owns a dog. What else can we learn? Let's try lining these frequencies up from smallest to largest: 0 (dog), 1 (rat), 3 (snake), 4 (bird), 6 (other), 8 (cat). The range is 8, and the median is 3.5. There is no mode or mean, since you can't have an average of a type of animal. Don't forget to include dogs in your calculations!

3. *Time vs. temperature graphs*

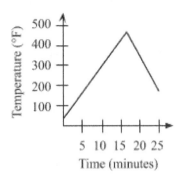

These graphs display the temperature of an object over time. In the graph to the left, we can see that the object started at around 50 degrees fahrenheit, and then heated up at a constant rate until it reached approximately 500 degree fahrenheit after 15 minutes. Then, the object started to cool down at a constant rate and reached 200 degrees fahrenheit after 25 minutes. We know the rate of temperature increase and decrease is constant because the lines are straight - if they were curved, this would not be the case!

4. *Mean, mean, mode, and range charts*

Number of pets	Number of students who own that many pets
1	5
2	7
3	3
4	4
5	1

These are probably the trickiest of any of the charts and graphs. To prevent yourself from making mistakes, it's a good idea to quickly write out all of the data: 1, 1, 1, 1, 1, 2, 2, 2, 2, 2, 2, 2, 3, 3, 3, 4, 4, 4, 4, 5. Doing this makes calculating the mean, median, mode, and range much simpler. For example, you can now see that the range is $5 - 1 = 4$, not $7 - 1 = 6$. Likewise, the median is 2 (not 4), the mode is 2, and the mean is 2.45.

Summary

What you should keep in mind when interpreting *charts and graphs*:
1) See what information you can learn from a chart or a graph before you look at the question
2) There is a lot of data to interpret in these questions; therefore, they are more time consuming than other questions on the test. You may want to leave them for the end and tackle the easier questions first

Practice Questions

Questions #1 - 3 refer to the graph below.

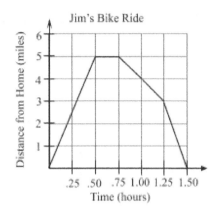

1. How quickly did Jim travel during the first 30 minutes of his bike ride?
    (A)   .5 miles / hour
    (B)   5 miles / hour
    (C)   10 miles / hour
    (D)   15 miles / hour

2. At one point, Jim stopped for a break. When did his break occur?
    (A)   0 - 10 minutes
    (B)   30 - 45 minutes
    (C)   30 - 60 minutes
    (D)   50 - 75 minutes

3. Assuming that Jim traveled in a straight line away from home and returned along the same route, what was the total distance he traveled after one hour?
    (A)   4 miles
    (B)   5 miles
    (C)   6 miles
    (D)   10 miles

Questions #4 - 6 refer to the graph below.

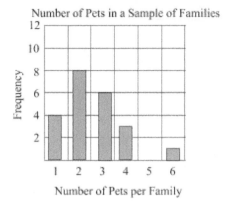

4. Which two measures were the same in the sample?
    (A)   median and range
    (B)   mode and range
    (C)   mean and median
    (D)   mode and median

5. What is the range of the data set?
    (A)   5
    (B)   6
    (C)   10
    (D)   12

6. What is the mean number of pets per family?
    (A)   2
    (B)   2.54
    (C)   3
    (D)   3.17

Henry placed a pizza in the oven. The graph below shows its temperature over time. Questions #7 - 8 refer to the graph.

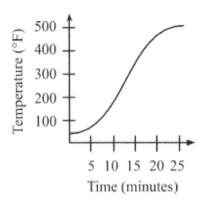

7. At what time interval did the heat of the pizza increase the fastest?
   (A)   0 - 2 minutes
   (B)   2 - 5 minutes
   (C)   10 - 15 minutes
   (D)   20 -25 minutes

8. What was the initial temperature of the pizza?
   (A)   0° F
   (B)   50° F
   (C)   100° F
   (D)   500° F

Gabe asked 28 students how many classes they are taking this semester. The table below shows the results of his survey.

Number of classes	Number of students who are taking that number of classes this semester
4	4
5	7
6	7
7	10

Questions #9 - 11 refer to the table.

9. What is the mode of the data?
   (A)   5
   (B)   6
   (C)   7
   (D)   10

10. What is the range of the data?
   (A)   3
   (B)   5
   (C)   6
   (D)   7

11. What is the median of the data?
   (A)   5
   (B)   5.5
   (C)   6
   (D)   7

Functions

Functions are another way of representing an equation. You're probably used to writing $y = 2x + 4$. Some questions, however, may rewrite that equation as $f(x) = 2x + 4$, and ask you to find $f(2)$. In this case, you must find the value of y when $x = 2$, so the final answer would be $f(2) = 2(2) + 4 = 8$. You can think of functions in terms of *input* vs. *output*. When you put a number in, what number comes out? While $f(x)$ is the most common notation for functions, you may see $g(x)$ or something similar.

Example #1
If $f(x) = 2x^2 + x + 1$, what is the value of $f(4)$?
(A)   4
(B)   12
(C)   13
(D)   37

$f(4) = 2(4)^2 + 4 + 1 = 37$. **The correct answer is (D).**

Example #2
If $f(x) = 2x + 1$ and $g(x) = x - 1$, for what value of x are $f(x)$ and $g(x)$ equal?
(A)   -3
(B)   -2
(C)   0
(D)   1

When $x = -2$, $f(-2) = 2(-2) + 1 = -3$. When $x = -2$, $g(-2) = -2 - 1 = -3$. **The correct answer is (B).**

You may see *composite functions* on the ISEE. Composite functions work the same way as regular functions, but there is one additional step. Instead of one function, there are two. They'll look like this: $f(g(x))$ or $(f \circ g)(x)$. You must first find the value of the first function for a certain value of x, and then you take that output from the first function and plug it into the second function. In composite functions, you always perform the inner function first and the outer function second.

Example #3
If $f(x) = 2x + 1$ and $g(x) = x - 1$, what is $(f \circ g)(2)$?
(A)   1
(B)   2
(C)   3
(D)   5

First, find $g(2)$. $g(2) = 2 - 1 = 1$. Then, take the 1 and plug it in to $f(x)$. $f(1) = 2(1) + 1 = 3$. **The correct answer is (C).**

You should also expect questions that require you to interpret graphs or charts of functions.

Example #4

x	f(x)	g(x)
-2	1	4
0	4	3
3	-2	2
5	6	6

In the table on the left, for what value of x are f(x) and g(x) equal?

(A)   0
(B)   3
(C)   5
(D)   6

Think again in terms of input vs. output: which value of x (input) results in the same value of y (output) for both f(x) and g(x)? **The correct answer is (C)**. Be careful not to choose (D)! Those two sixes are the y values that result when you plug in 5 to both equations. The question, however, asks for the value of x that will result in two equal outputs.

Example #5

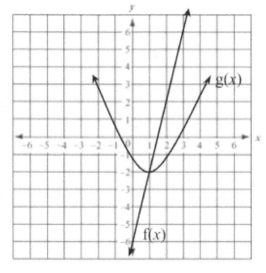

In the graph on the left, for what value of x are f(x) and g(x) equal?

(A)   -2
(B)   0
(C)   1
(D)   2

On this graph, you can see that f(x) and g(x) intersect at (1, -2). That means that when $x = 1$, f(x) and g(x) both equal -2. Because the question asks for an x value, **the answer is (C)**

Summary
How to recognize *functions* questions:
1) You see f(x) or g(x), or the question asks you to find the value of a function

What you should keep in mind:
1) You can think out functions as *input* vs. *output*
2) If the question shows f(2), plug 2 in for all the variables in the equation
3) When solving composite functions, work from the inner function to the outer function

Practice Questions

1. If $g(x) = x^2 - 2x + 3$, what is the value of $g(4)$?
   (A)   4
   (B)   8
   (C)   11
   (D)   16

2. In the table below, what is the maximum value of $f(x)$?

x	$f(x)$
2	2
3	8
4	7
5	4

   (A)   2
   (B)   5
   (C)   7
   (D)   8

3. If $f(x) = 2x - 3$ and $h(x) = 2x^2$, what is the value of $(f \circ h)(1)$?
   (A)   -1
   (B)   0
   (C)   1
   (D)   2

4. If $g(x) = 3x + 1$ and $f(x) = 2x + 1$, what is the value of $f(g(2))$?
   (A)   5
   (B)   7
   (C)   15
   (D)   16

5. If $f(x) = \frac{x + 7}{2}$, what is the value of $f(3)$?
   (A)   2
   (B)   5
   (C)   7
   (D)   10

6. In the table below, for which value of x are $f(x)$ and $g(x)$ equal?

x	$f(x)$	$g(x)$
-1	0	0
0	0	2
1	-4	1
2	5	4

   (A)   -1
   (B)   0
   (C)   1
   (D)   4

7. If $f(x) = 2x$ and $g(x) = x - 3$, for what value of x are $f(x)$ and $g(x)$ equal?
   (A)   -3
   (B)   0
   (C)   3
   (D)   6

8. In the graph below, what is the value of $f(x)$ when $x = 4$?

   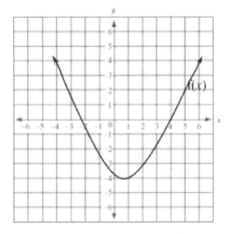

   (A)   -4
   (B)   0
   (C)   1
   (D)   4

Probability

Probability questions appear in both math sections of the ISEE. The questions will test the most basic principles of probability, but you need to pay very close attention to what each question is asking. Questions may have situations that include single-event probability or multi-event probability and situations that test replacement vs. non-replacement probability.

Example #1

A jar contains 3 black balls, 9 blue balls, and 5 yellow balls. If one ball is chosen at random and then removed from the jar, and a second ball is chosen at random, what is the probability that both balls will be black?

(A) $\frac{2}{17}$

(B) $\frac{3}{17}$

(C) $\frac{3}{17} \times \frac{2}{16}$

(D) $\frac{3}{17} \times \frac{3}{16}$

You should notice that the first ball is removed from the jar, not replaced. That means the first time a ball is removed, there are 17 balls total; the second time a ball is removed, there are 16. Therefore, the denominators are different and you can eliminate (A) and (B). Then, consider that if the first black ball is removed, there are only 2 black balls remaining. Note the difference between the second fractions in (C) and (D). Finally, the answer choices are all fractions, so you will not have to do any real calculations on this question. **The correct answer is (C).**

Example #2

Piper and Orion are playing a game using number cubes. Each player rolls two number cubes, numbered 1 through 6, and the sum of the numbers is recorded.

• Piper gets a point if her sum is a 5.
• Orion gets a point if his sum is either 5 or 6.

Who has a greater probability of receiving a point?

(A)   Piper
(B)   Orion
(C)   Piper and Orion have the same probability of earning a point
(D)   There is not enough information to determine the answer

This question is more of a brain teaser than a math question. You may be tempted to try to find the exact probability of rolling a 5: for example, the probability of rolling 1 and 4, or 2 and 3, or 4 and 1, or 3 and 2. However, this isn't necessary. Like Piper, Orion will receive a point if he rolls a 5. He also gets a point for rolling a 6. Therefore, Orion has a greater probability of receiving a point. **The correct answer is (B).**

Summary

How to recognize *probability* questions:
   1) You are asked to find the likelihood or probability of an event or series of events occurring

What you should keep in mind:
   1) You must determine if the question refers to single-event probability or multi-event probability
   2) You must determine if the question refers to replacement or non-replacement probability
   3) You probably won't have to do much math on these questions

Practice Questions

1. A bag contains 2 red marbles, 7 green marbles, 3 orange marbles, and 6 violet marbles. Anoush randomly removes 1 marble from the bag and keeps it. Paavo then randomly removes a marble from the bag. If the marble Anoush removed from the bag was violet, what is the probability that the marble Paavo removed was orange?

   (A) $\frac{3}{17}$

   (B) $\frac{3}{18}$

   (C) $\frac{6}{18} \times \frac{3}{17}$

   (D) $\frac{6}{18} \times \frac{3}{18}$

2. Simone and Porter are playing a game in which they draw colored dice from a bag. There are 18 colored dice in all: 4 are colored brown, 6 are colored red, and 8 are colored magenta. They then take turns drawing two dice at random. After the first die is drawn, it is placed back in the bag before the player draws a second die.

   • Simone earns a point if she draws two brown dice
   • Porter earns a point if he draws either two red dice or two magenta dice

   Who has the greater probability of earning a point?
   (A) Simone
   (B) Porter
   (C) Simone and Porter have the same probability of earning a point
   (D) There is not enough information to determine the answer

3. A spinner is divided into 15 equal sections: 4 are blue, 2 are orange, and 9 are pink. If the spinner is spun twice, what is the probability that both spins will land on a pink section?

   (A) $\frac{9}{15}$

   (B) $\frac{9}{15} \times \frac{8}{14}$

   (C) $\frac{9}{15} \times \frac{9}{14}$

   (D) $\frac{9}{15} \times \frac{9}{15}$

4. Mae and Lincoln are playing a game in which they draw crayons out of a jar. There are 3 black crayons, 4 blue crayons, 5 purple crayons, and 1 white crayon. They each draw two crayons at random (without replacement).

   • Mae wins a prize if she draws two purple crayons.
   • Lincoln wins a prize if he draws one white crayon and one black crayon (in any order)

   Who has the greater probability of winning a prize?
   (A) Mae
   (B) Lincoln
   (C) Mae and Lincoln have the same probability of earning a point
   (D) There is not enough information to determine the answer

5. A gumball machine contains 4 maroon gumballs, 2 blue gumballs, 7 green gumballs, and 6 red gumballs. When a gumball is purchased, it is selected at random and released from the machine. Rida buys a gumball and keeps it. Then Luc buys a gumball. If the gumball Rida bought was blue, what is the probability that the gumball Luc bought bought was red?

(A) $\frac{1}{3}$

(B) $\frac{6}{19}$

(C) $\frac{2}{19} \times \frac{6}{19}$

(D) $\frac{2}{19} \times \frac{6}{18}$

6. Lola and Dexter are playing a game in which they draw colored balls from a bag. There are 20 balls in all: 8 are red, 5 are yellow, 5 are blue, and 2 are rainbow. They then take turns drawing two balls at random (without replacement).

• Lola earns a point if she draws a blue ball and then a rainbow ball
• Dexter earns a point if he draws a rainbow ball and then a yellow ball

Who has the greater probability of earning a point?

(A)   Lola

(B)   Dexter

(C)   Lola and Dexter have the same probability of earning a point

(D)   There is not enough information to determine the answer

Objects Moving Together and Apart

These questions present a situation in which two objects move toward each other or move in the same direction and ask about finding an additional piece of information.

Example #1

Plane X departs Chicago's O'Hare Airport bound for JFK Airport in New York City, a distance of 825 miles. After Plane A has traveled 200 miles, Plane Y departs JFK bound for O'Hare. If the planes pass each other at 9:25 a.m. CST, which of the following would be needed to determine when Plane B left JFK, in Central Standard Time?

(A)   the speed of Plane X
(B)   the speed of Plane Y
(C)   the sum of the planes' speeds
(D)   the difference of the planes' speeds

You might be tempted to write out some complicated equation and try to find exactly when Plane B left JFK, when the two planes will cross paths, and when they will land. Don't bother! We know that the two planes are traveling toward each other along the same route. After Plane A has traveled 200 miles, the two planes will be 625 miles apart. Because we know this distance, in order to find the time Plane B leaves JFK we need to know how quickly the two planes are approaching each other. This rate is simply the sum of the speeds of the two planes. Therefore, **the correct answer is (C).**

Example #2

Josephina drives from Washington, DC bound for NYC. After she has traveled 100 miles, her mother begins to drive from Washington, DC along the same route, and she travels faster than Josephina. What additional piece of information would be needed to determine how long it will take Josephina's mother to pass Josephina?

(A)   Josephina's speed
(B)   the mother's speed
(C)   the sum of their speeds
(D)   the difference between their speeds

Once again, don't bother trying to do any actual math on this question. Because Josephina and her mother are traveling in the same direction and we know how far apart they were when Josephina's mother started driving, we only need to know the difference between their speeds to figure out when Josephina's mother will pass her daughter. The difference between their speeds tells us the distance that the mother gains over a period of time. **The correct answer is (D).**

Summary

How to recognize *objects moving together and apart* questions:

1) You are given a specific situation in which two objects move toward each other or in the same direction along the same route

What you should keep in mind:

1) In most cases, if the objects are headed toward each other you need to know the sum of their speeds; if they're moving away from each other, you need to know the difference of their speeds

Practice Questions

1. Boat A departs from Los Angeles headed to Beijing, a distance of about 6,200 miles. After Boat A has travelled 1,500 miles, Boat B departs from Beijing and heads for Los Angeles on the same route. What additional piece of information is needed to calculate how long Boat A has been at sea when it passes Boat B?

   (A)   the sum of the boats' speeds
   (B)   the difference between the boats' speeds
   (C)   the speed of cruise ship A
   (D)   the speed of cruise ship B

2. Leroy takes a train from Chicago to St. Louis, a distance of about 300 miles. When he has traveled 75 miles, Barack takes a train that travels the same route on a parallel track. If they pass each other at 1:30 p.m. CST, which of the following would be needed to determine when Leroy left Chicago, in Central Standard Time?

   (A)   Leroy's average speed
   (B)   Barack's average speed
   (C)   the sum of their speeds
   (D)   the difference between their speeds

3. Jimmy drives from Newark to Cincinnati. After he has traveled 50 miles, his friend Jeff begins to drive along the same route, and Jeff travels faster than Jimmy. What additional piece of information would be needed to determine how long it will take Jeff to pass Jimmy?

   (A)   Jimmy's speed
   (B)   Jeff's speed
   (C)   the sum of their speeds
   (D)   the difference between their speeds

4. Plane A flies from Shanghai toward Taipei, a distance of 430 miles. After Plane A has traveled 300 miles, Plane B departs Taipei bound for Shanghai. If the planes pass each other at 6:30 p.m. BST, which of the following would be needed to determine when Plane B left Taipei, in Beijing Standard Time?

   (A)   Plane A's speed
   (B)   Plane B's speed
   (C)   the sum of their speeds
   (D)   the difference between their speeds

Numbers and Operations

Numbers and operations questions test your understanding of numbers work. These questions usually include a lot of variables and seem very complicated, but most of them can be solved by plugging in your own numbers or using a bit of logic.

Example #1

If w is a factor of x and y is a factor of z, which statement must be true?

(A) xz is a multiple of wy
(B) w is a multiple of xz
(C) xz is a factor of wy
(D) x is a factor of wy

You might be inclined to skip this question because it looks headache-inducing, but plugging in your own numbers makes it a breeze.

Let's say that $w = 2$, $x = 4$, $y = 3$, and $z = 6$. These numbers fit the rules set by the original equation. Now, plug the numbers into the answer choices.

(A)   (4)(6) is a multiple of (2)(3)
(B)   (2) is a multiple of (4)(6)
(C)   (4)(6) is a factor of (2)(3)
(D)   (4) is a factor of (2)(3)

24 is a multiple of 6. All of the other choices are false. **(A) is the correct answer.**

Example #2

If a is a factor of 12 and b is a factor of 9, which is the least value that ab must be a factor of?

(A)   12
(B)   54
(C)   108
(D)   216

This question requires some logical thinking. The factors of 12 are 1, 2, 3, 4, 6, and 12. The factors of 9 are 1, 3, and 9. If $a = 4$ and $b = 3$, then their product would be 12. You might think that (A) is the correct answer. However, because a and b could be any of the factors of 12 and 9, and we are asked to find the least value that ab **must** be a factor of, we must choose the two largest factors of each number, which are 12 and 9. The product of 12 and 9 is 108, so **the correct answer is (C).**

Example #3

If m and n are prime numbers, what is the greatest common factor of $15m^3n^2$, $30m^2n^2$, and $45mn^4$?

(A) $5m^2n$
(B) $15mn^2$
(C) $15m^2n^2$
(D) $90m^3n^4$

Consider the coefficients first. The GCF of 15, 30, and 45 is 15, so you can eliminate (A) and (D). Then, you must find which term contains the fewest m's and which term contains the fewest n's. M appears only once in the last term, and n appears twice in the first and second terms, so **the correct answer is (B).**

Summary

How to recognize *numbers and operations questions*:
1) The question and answer choices contain lots of variables

What you should keep in mind:
1) Most of these questions can be solved by inputting your own numbers
2) Once you've selected an answer, think about whether it is logical!

Practice Questions

1. If a is a prime factor of 9, b is a prime factor of 78, and $a \neq b$, what is the least number that ab must be a factor of?
   (A)   6
   (B)   9
   (C)   39
   (D)   78

2. If x and y are prime numbers, what is the least common multiple of $2x^4y$, $6xy^3$, and $9xy^2$?
   (A) $12xy$
   (B) $12x^4y^2$
   (C) $18x^4y^3$
   (D) $54x^3y^3$

3. If f is a multiple of o and w is a factor of a, which of the following statements must be true?
   (A) ow is a multiple of af
   (B) o is a factor of w
   (C) af is a multiple of ow
   (D) a is a factor of o

4. If p and q are prime numbers, what is the greatest common factor of $9pq^3$, $18p^2q^2$ and $18pq$?
   (A) $9pq$
   (B) $9p^2q^3$
   (C) $18pq$
   (D) $18p^2q^3$

5. If h is an even integer, which of the following cannot be an integer?
   (A) $h + 1$
   (B) $h^2 + 2$
   (C) $\frac{h}{3}$
   (D) $\frac{h+1}{3}$

6. Which type of product could not result from the product of two irrational numbers?
   (A)   integer
   (B)   imaginary number
   (C)   irrational number
   (D)   rational number

7. If a is a factor of b and b is a factor of c, which statement must be true?
   (A) ab is a factor of c
   (B) c is a factor of ab
   (C) c is a factor of a
   (D) a is a factor of c

8. If d is the sum of the distinct prime factors of 12, and e is the sum of the distinct prime factors of 15, then what is $d - e$?
   (A)   -5
   (B)   -3
   (C)   3
   (D)   5

Answer Keys - Common ISEE Question Types:
Quantitative Reasoning

Applied Mean		**ax²+bx+c**		**Isolating Variables**	
1	B	1.	B	1.	C
2.	B	2.	B	2.	D
3.	C	3.	C	3.	D
4.	A	4.	B	4.	C
5.	C	5.	D	5.	C
6.	B	6.	A	6.	D
7.	A	7.	D	7.	A
8.	C	8.	D	8.	A
9.	C	9.	D	9.	B
10.	B	10.	B	10.	C
11.	B	11.	C		
12.	A	12.	C		
13.	A				
14.	C				
15.	D				
16.	B				

Maximizing and Minimizing the Area and Perimeter of Quadrilaterals		**Maximum or Minimum Values in Inequalities Questions**		**Symbol Questions**	
1.	B	1.	C	1.	B
2.	C	2.	B	2.	A
3.	D	3.	B	3.	D
4.	C	4.	A	4.	C
5.	D	5.	B	5.	B
6.	C	6.	D	6.	D
7.	A	7.	C	7.	B
8.	D	8.	C	8.	A
9.	D	9.	B	9.	C
10.	A	10.	C	10.	B
11.	D	11.	D	11.	C
12.	D				
13.	A				
14.	C				
15.	B				

Percent Change in Circles, Squares, and Rectangles

1.	B	4.	B	7.	C
2.	D	5.	A	8.	C
3.	C	6.	B	9.	B

Net cubes

1.   C
2.   B
3.   A
4.   D
5.   A
6.   C

Sum or Product of All Integers

1.   C
2.   C
3.   D
4.   B
5.   D
6.   B
7.   B
8.   A

Interpreting Graphs and Charts

1.   C
2.   B
3.   C
4.   D
5.   A
6.   B
7.   C
8.   B
9.   C
10.   A
11.   C

What is the Value?

1.   B
2.   B
3.   B
4.   C
5.   D
6.   A
7.   B
8.   D
9.   B
10.   D
11.   A
12.   C
13.   A
14.   C
15.   D
16.   C

Functions

1.   C
2.   D
3.   C
4.   C
5.   B
6.   A
7.   A
8.   B

Probability

1.   A
2.   B
3.   D
4.   A
5.   A
6.   C

Objects Moving Together and Apart

1.   A
2.   D
3.   D
4.   C

Numbers and Operations

1.   C
2.   C
3.   C
4.   A
5.   C
6.   B
7.   D
8.   B

Chapter 4

Mathematics Achievement
Question Types

Stem-and-Leaf Plots

Stem-and-leaf plots display large amounts of data in a concise manner. The plots look like this:

Stem	Leaf
4	0 0 0 0 1
5	3 3 5 5

The "stem" represents the tens place in a two-digit number; the "leaf" represents the ones / units place in that same two-digit number. The plot above contains the values 40, 40, 40, 40, 41, 53, 53, 55, and 55. You can see how each individual number has been split into two parts. Stem-and-leaf plot questions usually ask you to analyze the mean, median, mode, or range of a data set.

To find the **mean**, add up all the numbers and divide by the number of numbers. However, this can be time consuming. If you're running out of time, try eyeballing the plot and see if you can estimate the mean. This will at least help you eliminate some incorrect answers.

Identifying the **median** is trickier than you'd expect: it's very easy to lose track of which number falls exactly in the middle of the set. The best strategy for minimizing careless mistakes is to cross out numbers on each end of the plot and gradually move toward the center. The median of the plot below is **41**.

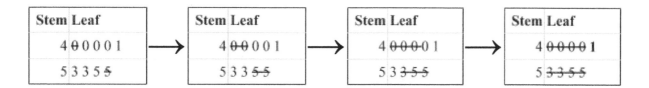

To find the **mode**, circle the number that shows up the most frequently in one row of the leaf portion of the chart. Once you've identified that number, make sure to add the stem portion back on!

Stem	Leaf
4	0 0 0 0 1
5	3 3 5 5

In the plot above, 0 appears four times in one row. However, the mode is **not** 0. The mode is **40**. If two numbers appear the same number of times, there is no mode.

Determining the **range** is simple: subtract the upper leftmost number from the bottom rightmost number. The range of the chart above is 55 – 40 = **15**.

Example #1

The stem-and-leaf plot below represents the ages of students who are taking a financial literacy course.

Stem	Leaf
2	2 2 5 7
3	2 5 7 8 9
4	2 2 2 5
5	4 5
6	4 7

Questions #1-3 refer to the chart above.

1. What is the median age in the class?
(A)   9
(B)   38
(C)   39
(D)   42

3. What is the mode of the data set?
(A)   2
(B)   22
(C)   25
(D)   42

2. What is the range of ages in the class?
(A)   5
(B)   22
(C)   45
(D)   67

The safest way to find the median is to slowly cross out numbers on each end of the range and carefully work your way toward the middle:

Stem	Leaf
2	~~2 2 5 7~~
3	~~2 5 7 8~~ 9
4	~~2 2 2 5~~
5	~~4 5~~
6	~~4 7~~

The median is 39, so **the correct answer for #1 is (C)**. Finding the range is easy: just subtract the top leftmost number from the bottom rightmost number. Don't make the mistake of thinking that it's 7 – 2! It's actually 67 – 22, so **the correct answer for #2 is (C)**.

Finally, we can see that the number that appears the most is 2. Since it appears in the row in which 4 is the stem, the mode is 42, and **the correct answer for #3 is (D).**

Summary

How to recognize *stem-and-leaf plot* questions:
1) You are shown a table that contains the words *stem* and *leaf*

What you should keep in mind:
1) The number in the stem matches up with every number in the corresponding leaf in order to form a series of numbers
2) Finding the median is trickier than you think

Practice Questions

Questions #1-3 refer to the stem-and-leaf plot below, which displays the scores of a math final.

Stem	Leaf
4	5
5	4 7 8
6	6 6 7 9
7	3 5 7 7 7
8	2 6
9	1 4 5

1. What is the range of scores on the test?
   (A)   0
   (B)   45
   (C)   50
   (D)   95

2. What is the mode of the data set?
   (A)   7
   (B)   66
   (C)   77
   (D)   95

3. What is the median score on the test?
   (A)   73
   (B)   74
   (C)   75
   (D)   77

Questions #4-6 refer to the stem-and-leaf plot below, which shows the number of students per class in 17 classrooms at a local high school.

Stem	Leaf
1	8 9 9 9 9
2	1 2 2 5 5 6 7 8 8 8 9
3	1

4. What is the range of the number of students per class?
   (A)   13
   (B)   18
   (C)   21
   (D)   31

5. What is the mode of the data set?
   (A)   8
   (B)   9
   (C)   19
   (D)   28

6. What is the median number of students per class?
   (A)   5
   (B)   22
   (C)   23
   (D)   25

Questions #7-9 refer to the stem-and-leaf plot below, which shows the results of a survey in which neighborhood residents were asked how many pets are in their households.

Stem	Leaf
0	1 1 1 1 1 2 2 2 2 3 3 3 3
1	0 0

7. What is the range of the number of pets per household?
   (A) 0
   (B) 1
   (C) 9
   (D) 10

8. How many pets does the household with the fewest number of pets have?
   (A) 0
   (B) 1
   (C) 2
   (D) 3

9. What is the mean number of pets per household?
   (A) 0
   (B) 1
   (C) 2
   (D) 3

Questions #10-12 refer to the stem-and-leaf plot below, which shows how many miles each member of the local track team ran over the weekend.

Stem	Leaf
0	0 4 4 4 5
1	1 1
2	0

10. What is the mode of the data?
    (A) 0
    (B) 1
    (C) 4
    (D) 11

11. How many miles did the student who ran the farthest run?
    (A) 0
    (B) 2
    (C) 11
    (D) 20

12. What is the range of the data?
    (A) 0
    (B) 5
    (C) 16
    (D) 20

Imaginary Numbers

Imaginary numbers will be unfamiliar to most students taking the Upper Level ISEE. You do **not** need a deep understanding of the concept in order to answer these questions correctly! A combination of memorizing a few pieces of information and using logic to eliminate wrong answer choices will suffice.

First, here's what you need to memorize:

$i = \sqrt{-1}$

$i^2 = -1$ because $\sqrt{-1} \times \sqrt{-1} = -1$

$i^3 = -i$ because $(\sqrt{-1} \times \sqrt{-1})(\sqrt{-1}) = (-1)(\sqrt{-1}) = -1(i) = -i$

$i^4 = 1$ because $\sqrt{-1} \times \sqrt{-1} \times \sqrt{-1} \times \sqrt{-1} = (-1)(-1) = 1$

Imaginary numbers are called *imaginary* because the value of any real number that is squared must be positive. $(1)^2 = 1$ **and** $(-1)^2 = 1$.

The question type you are most likely to see involves solving a simple algebraic expression that includes imaginary numbers.

Example #1

What is the solution set for $x^2 + 144 = 0$?

(A)   12
(B)   12i
(C) ± 12
(D) $\pm 12i$

Let's use logic to eliminate some of the incorrect answers. $12^2 = 144$, and $144 + 144 = 288$, so (A) and (C) are incorrect. Now you can use your memorized knowledge to check the remaining answers.

$(12i)^2 = 144i^2 = 144(-1) = -144$. $-144 + 144 = 0$, so (B) could be correct! However, you also need to check and see if $-12i$ will work.

$(-12i)^2 = 144i^2 = 144(-1) = -144$. $-12i$ is also a solution, so **the correct answer is (D).**

Example #2

What is the solution set for $2x^2 + 162 = 0$?

(A)   9
(B)   9i
(C) ± 9
(D) $\pm 9i$

This equation is easier to solve if you rearrange it first. Subtract 162 from both sides to get $2x^2 = -162$. Then, divide both sides by 2 to get $x^2 = -81$. Use logic to eliminate wrong answers: 9^2 and $(-9)^2$ both equal positive 81, and $81 + 81 = 162$, so (A) and (C) won't work.

$(9i)^2 = 81i^2 = 81(-1) = -81$.
$(-9i)^2 = 81i^2 = 81(-1) = -81$.

(D) is the correct answer.

You may be asked to find the value of something larger than i^4. The pattern for i repeats every 4 exponents ($i^4 = i^8 = i^{12}$; $i^3 = i^7 = i^{11}$, etc). With larger exponents, you must divide the exponent by 4 and find the remainder. The remainder corresponds to i, i^2, i^3, or i^4.

Example #3

Which of the following expressions is equivalent to i^{90}?

(A) i

(B)   -1

(C)   -i

(D)   1

$\frac{90}{4} = 22$ remainder 2. This means $i^{90} = i^2 = $ -1.

The correct answer is (B).

Example #4

Which of the following expressions is equivalent to i^{999}?

(A) i

(B)   -1

(C)   -i

(D)   1

$\frac{999}{4} = 249$ remainder 3. This means $i^{999} = i^3 = $ -i.

The correct answer is (C).

Finally, you may be asked to FOIL an expression that contains imaginary numbers. This process works exactly the same as it normally does, but the final step is converting i^2 to -1.

Example #5

Which of the following expressions is equivalent to $(2 + 3i)(1 - 2i)$?

(A) $8 - 7i$

(B) $3 + 6i$

(C) $8 - i$

(D) $3 + 4i$

FOIL: $2(1) + 2(-2i) + 3i(1) + 3i(-2i) =$
$2 - 4i + 3i - 6i^2 =$
$2 - i - 6(-1) =$
$2 - i + 6 =$
$8 - i$

The correct answer is (C).

Example #6

Which of the following expressions is equivalent to $(1 + 6i)(2 - 4i)$?

(A) $26 + 8i$

(B) $-22 + 8i$

(C) $-22 - 4i$

(D) $26 - 4i$

FOIL: $1(2) + 1(-4i) + 6i(2) + 6i(-4i) =$
$2 - 4i + 12i - 24i^2 =$
$2 + 8i - 24(-1) =$
$2 + 8i + 24 =$
$26 + 8i$

The correct answer is (A).

Summary

How to recognize *imaginary numbers* questions:
1) The answer choices contain an italicized i
2) Some of the answer choices contain a ± symbol

What you should keep in mind:
1) Use logic to eliminate answer choices
2) Memorizing the values of i, i^2, i^3, and i^4 will help you complete these questions

Practice Questions

1. What is the solution set for $x^2 + 64 = 0$?
   - (A) 8
   - (B) $8i$
   - (C) ± 8
   - (D) $\pm 8i$

2. What is the solution set for $x^2 + 100 = 0$?
   - (A) 10
   - (B) $10i$
   - (C) ± 10
   - (D) $\pm 10i$

3. What is the solution set for $x^2 = 81$?
   - (A) 9
   - (B) $9i$
   - (C) ± 9
   - (D) $\pm 9i$

4. What is the solution set for $x^2 + 4 = 0$?
   - (A) 2
   - (B) 4
   - (C) ± 2
   - (D) $\pm 2i$

5. What are all possible values such that $x^2 + 74 = 10$?
   - (A) ± 8
   - (B) $\pm 8i$
   - (C) 8
   - (D) $8i$

6. What are all possible values such that $x^2 + 40 = 24$?
   - (A) ± 4
   - (B) $\pm 4i$
   - (C) 4
   - (D) $4i$

7. What are all possible values such that $x^2 + 125 = 4$?
   - (A) $11i$
   - (B) $\pm 11i$
   - (C) 11
   - (D) ± 11

8. What is the solution set for $x^2 = 25$?
   - (A) ± 5
   - (B) $\pm 5i$
   - (C) 5
   - (D) $5i$

9. What is the solution set for $128 + 2x^2 = 0$?
   - (A) 8
   - (B) $\pm 8i$
   - (C) 64
   - (D) $\pm 64i$

10. What is the solution set for $32 + 2x^2 = 0$?
   - (A) 4
   - (B) ± 4
   - (C) $4i$
   - (D) $\pm 4i$

11. What is the solution set for $98 + 2x^2 = 0$?
   - (A) 7
   - (B) $7i$
   - (C) ± 7
   - (D) $\pm 7i$

12. What is the solution set for $-x^2 - 10 = 15$?
   - (A) ± 5
   - (B) $\pm 5i$
   - (C) 5
   - (D) $5i$

13. What is the solution set for $x^2 - 2 = 2$?
    (A) ± 2
    (B) $\pm 2i$
    (C)   2
    (D) $2i$

14. What is the solution set for
    $-x^2 - 11 = 70$?
    (A)   9
    (B) $9i$
    (C) ± 9
    (D) $\pm 9i$

15. What is the solution set for
    $-x^2 - 25 = 11$?
    (A) $6i$
    (B) $\pm 6i$
    (C)   6
    (D) ± 6

16. Which of the following expressions is
    equivalent to i^{45}?
    (A) i
    (B)   -1
    (C) $-i$
    (D)   1

17. Which of the following expressions is
    equivalent to i^{102}?
    (A) i
    (B)   -1
    (C) $-i$
    (D)   1

18. Which of the following expressions is
    equivalent to i^{16}?
    (A) i
    (B)   -1
    (C) $-i$
    (D)   1

19. Which of the following expressions is
    equivalent to $(1 + i)(1 - i)$?
    (A)   1
    (B)   2
    (C) $1 - i$
    (D) $1 + 2i$

20. Which of the following expressions is
    equivalent to $(6 + 2i)(2 - 4i)$?
    (A) $24 - 8i$
    (B) $24 + 8i$
    (C) $20 + 20i$
    (D) $20 - 20i$

21. Which of the following expressions is
    equivalent to $(2 + 3i)(1 - 2i)$?
    (A) $8 + i$
    (B) $8 - i$
    (C) $2 + 6i$
    (D) $2 - 6i$

Equivalent Exponents

Equivalent exponents questions require you to use your knowledge of exponent properties to simplify an expression. Memorizing a few rules will help you master these questions.

1. When a coefficient and a variable are under a root, the root applies to each term separately. For example, $\sqrt{64x^{16}} = \sqrt{64}\sqrt{x^{16}}$

2. To simplify a term like $\sqrt{x^{16}}$, you do **not** take the square root of 16. $\sqrt{x^{16}} = (x^{16})^{1/2} = x^{8}$

Example #1

Which expression is equivalent to $\sqrt{4s^{12}}$?

(A) $2s^{3}$
(B) $2s^{6}$
(C) $4s^{3}$
(D) $4s^{6}$

$\sqrt{4} = 2$, so you can eliminate (C) and (D).
$\sqrt{s^{12}} = (s^{12})^{1/2} = s^{6}$. **The correct answer is (B).**

Example #2

Which expression is equivalent $[(3x^{4})(4x^{3})]^{2}$?

(A) $49x^{9}$
(B) $49x^{14}$
(C) $144x^{9}$
(D) $144x^{14}$

Remember the order of operations. You must solve what's inside the parentheses first.
$(3x^{4})(4x^{3}) = 12x^{7}$. $(12x^{7})^{2} = (12)^{2}(x^{7})^{2} = 144x^{14}$.
The correct answer is (D).

Summary

How to recognize *equivalent exponents* questions:
  1) The question asks for an "equivalent expression"
  2) The question or multiple choice answers contain complicated expressions filled with variables and exponents

What you should keep in mind:
  1) A square root applies to each term separately: $\sqrt{64x^{16}} = \sqrt{64}\sqrt{x^{16}}$
  2) The square root of an exponent will always be equal to one half of the exponent: $\sqrt{x^{100}} = x^{50}$, $\sqrt{x^{30}} = x^{15}$, $\sqrt{x^{64}} = x^{32}$, etc.

Practice Questions

1. Which expression is equivalent to

    $\sqrt{64x^{16}}$?

    (A) $4x^4$
    (B) $4x^8$
    (C) $8x^8$
    (D) $16x^4$

2. Which expression is equivalent to

    $\sqrt{25y^{50}}$?

    (A) $5y^5$
    (B) $5y^{25}$
    (C) $5y^{100}$
    (D) $50y^{25}$

3. Which expression is equivalent to

    $\sqrt{81z^2}$?

    (A) $9z$
    (B) $9z^2$
    (C) $81z$
    (D) $81z^2$

4. Which expression is equivalent to

    $\sqrt{2x^4}$?

    (A) $\sqrt{2}x^2$
    (B) $\sqrt{2}x^4$
    (C) $2x^2$
    (D) $2x^4$

5. Which expression is equivalent to
    $[(x^2)(x^2)]^2$?
    (A) x^4
    (B) x^8
    (C) x^{12}
    (D) x^{16}

6. Which expression is equivalent to
    $[(3b)(3b^2)]^2$?
    (A) $6b^6$
    (B) $9b^5$
    (C) $81b^5$
    (D) $81b^6$

7. Which expression is equivalent to
    $[(g^2)(4g)]^3$?
    (A) $4g^6$
    (B) $16g^9$
    (C) $64g^9$
    (D) $128g^6$

8. Which expression is equivalent to
    $[(4x^2)(2x^2)]^2$?
    (A) $8x^6$
    (B) $8x^8$
    (C) $16x^6$
    (D) $64x^8$

9. Which expression is equivalent to

    $\dfrac{\sqrt{4p^2}}{4p^2}$?

    (A) 1

    (B) $\dfrac{1}{p^2}$

    (C) $\dfrac{p}{p^2}$

    (D) $\dfrac{1}{2p}$

10. Which expression is equivalent to

$\dfrac{\sqrt{100x^8}}{\sqrt{25x^4}}$?

(A) $2x^2$
(B) $2x^4$
(C) $5x^2$
(D) $10x^4$

11. Which expression is equivalent to $4x^4$?

(A) $\sqrt{8x^2}$

(B) $\sqrt{8x^8}$

(C) $\sqrt{16x^8}$

(D) $\sqrt{16x^{16}}$

12. Which expression is equivalent to $5q^{32}$?

(A) $\sqrt{10q^{64}}$

(B) $\sqrt{25q^{64}}$

(C) $\sqrt{25q^{128}}$

(D) $\sqrt{50q^{64}}$

13. Which expression is equivalent to s^{32}?

(A) $\sqrt{2s^{64}}$

(B) $\sqrt{10s^{64}}$

(C) $\dfrac{\sqrt{s^{64}}}{\sqrt{s^{32}}}$

(D) $\dfrac{\sqrt{10s^{80}}}{\sqrt{10s^{16}}}$

14. Which expression is equivalent to $4t^4$?

(A) $\sqrt{8t^8}$

(B) $\sqrt{16t^8}$

(C) $\dfrac{\sqrt{32t^8}}{\sqrt{16t^4}}$

(D) $\dfrac{\sqrt{16t^{12}}}{\sqrt{8t^8}}$

Matrix Addition and Subtraction

Matrix addition and subtraction questions are among the easiest on the Upper Level ISEE. They only require that you are comfortable with addition and subtraction!

Example #1
What is the result of the expression

$$\begin{bmatrix} 2 & 3 \\ 4 & 5 \end{bmatrix} + \begin{bmatrix} 1 & 2 \\ 3 & 4 \end{bmatrix} ?$$

(A) $\begin{bmatrix} 1 & 2 \\ 3 & 4 \end{bmatrix}$

(B) $\begin{bmatrix} 2 & 3 \\ 4 & 5 \end{bmatrix}$

(C) $\begin{bmatrix} 3 & 5 \\ 7 & 9 \end{bmatrix}$

(D) $\begin{bmatrix} 21 & 32 \\ 43 & 54 \end{bmatrix}$

All you need to do is note whether you are being asked to add or subtract, and then match the corresponding numbers in each matrix.

In this example, you'll find that $2 + 1 = 3$; $3 + 2 = 5$; $4 + 3 = 7$; and $5 + 4 = 9$. These sums should then be placed in their respective spaces within the matrix. **The correct answer is (C).**

Summary
How to recognize *matrix addition and subtraction* questions:
1) You see a pair of strange-looking boxes with a (+) or (−) sign in the middle

What you should keep in mind:
1) Add or subtract the numbers that fall in the same position in each matrix
2) These questions tend to show up at the end of the MA section - make sure you reach the end of the section so you can get this easy point!

Practice Questions

1. What is the result of the expression

$$\begin{bmatrix} 4 & 4 \\ 4 & 4 \end{bmatrix} + \begin{bmatrix} 5 & 5 \\ 5 & 5 \end{bmatrix} ?$$

(A) $\begin{bmatrix} 1 & 1 \\ 1 & 1 \end{bmatrix}$

(B) $\begin{bmatrix} 9 & 9 \\ 9 & 9 \end{bmatrix}$

(C) $\begin{bmatrix} 5 & 4 \\ 5 & 4 \end{bmatrix}$

(D) $\begin{bmatrix} 4 & 5 \\ 4 & 5 \end{bmatrix}$

2. What is the result of the expression

$$\begin{bmatrix} 6 & 2 \\ 4 & 7 \end{bmatrix} - \begin{bmatrix} 1 & 2 \\ 2 & 6 \end{bmatrix} ?$$

(A) $\begin{bmatrix} 5 & 0 \\ 2 & 1 \end{bmatrix}$

(B) $\begin{bmatrix} 7 & 4 \\ 6 & 13 \end{bmatrix}$

(C) $\begin{bmatrix} 6 & 2 \\ 4 & 7 \end{bmatrix}$

(D) $\begin{bmatrix} 61 & 22 \\ 42 & 76 \end{bmatrix}$

3. What is the result of the expression

$$\begin{bmatrix} 9 & 9 \\ 8 & 8 \end{bmatrix} - \begin{bmatrix} 3 & 2 \\ 3 & 2 \end{bmatrix} ?$$

(A) $\begin{bmatrix} 1 & 2 \\ 3 & 4 \end{bmatrix}$

(B) $\begin{bmatrix} 6 & 7 \\ 5 & 6 \end{bmatrix}$

(C) $\begin{bmatrix} 3 & 5 \\ 7 & 9 \end{bmatrix}$

(D) $\begin{bmatrix} 21 & 32 \\ 43 & 54 \end{bmatrix}$

4. What is the result of the expression

$$\begin{bmatrix} 4 & 7 \\ 4 & 4 \end{bmatrix} + \begin{bmatrix} 3 & 2 \\ 0 & 5 \end{bmatrix} ?$$

(A) $\begin{bmatrix} 7 & 9 \\ 4 & 8 \end{bmatrix}$

(B) $\begin{bmatrix} 7 & 8 \\ 4 & 9 \end{bmatrix}$

(C) $\begin{bmatrix} 7 & 9 \\ 5 & 9 \end{bmatrix}$

(D) $\begin{bmatrix} 7 & 9 \\ 4 & 9 \end{bmatrix}$

Expected Values

Expected values basically tell you the likelihood of the occurrence of a particular scenario over a long period of time. These questions look confusing, but they're very easy. All you have to do is find the product of the numbers in each row, then add all of those products together.

Example #1

The table below shows the probability distribution of a random variable X.

X	$P(X)$
0	0.2
1	0.1
2	0.2
3	0.5

What is the expected value of X?
(A)   0.1
(B)   0.2
(C)   1.1
(D)   2.0

Multiply straight across each row, then add all of those products together. In Example #1, your work will look like this: $(0 \times 0.2) + (1 \times 0.1) + (2 \times 0.2) + (3 \times 0.5) = 2.0$. **The correct answer is (D).**

Summary

How to recognize *expected values* questions:
1) You are presented with a chart that contains two columns and several rows
2) The question asks you to find the **expected value** of a variable, number, or situation

What you should keep in mind:
1) Be careful when multiplying decimals and fractions. Double check your work!
2) Don't add all the numbers in the column on the right before you find the products of the rows
3) Just because your answer doesn't seem to make sense doesn't mean it is incorrect. For example, if the "expected number of red socks" that you pick from a sock drawer is 1.6, you might wonder how you could pick .6 socks. Again, because expected values tell us the likelihood of an occurrence over time, it ends up being more like an average than an exact number

Practice Questions

1. Z is a discrete random variable. The table below defines a probability distribution for Z.

Z	$P(Z)$
0	0.7
1	0.9
2	0.4

What is the expected value of Z?
(A)   1.7
(B)   2.0
(C)   2.7
(D)   3.0

2. A is a discrete random variable. The table below defines a probability distribution for A.

A	$P(A)$
0	$\frac{6}{7}$
1	$\frac{4}{5}$
2	$\frac{2}{3}$
3	$\frac{3}{15}$

What is the expected value of A?

(A) $\frac{2}{3}$

(B) $\frac{6}{15}$

(C)   1

(D) $\frac{41}{15}$

3. Amy randomly guesses on 2 multiple choice questions that each have 5 possible answers. The table below shows the possible outcomes and the probabilities of each outcome.

Number of Correct Answers	Probability
0	$\frac{16}{25}$
1	$\frac{4}{25}$
2	$\frac{1}{25}$

What is the expected number of correct answers?

(A) $\frac{5}{25}$

(B) $\frac{6}{25}$

(C) $\frac{21}{25}$

(D) $\frac{25}{25}$

4. A drawer contains 6 socks: 3 red, 2 green, and 1 blue. 2 socks are drawn, without replacement, from the drawer at random. The table shows the possible outcomes and the probability of each outcome.

Number of green socks selected	Probability
0	$\frac{2}{3}$
1	$\frac{1}{3}$
2	$\frac{1}{15}$

What is the expected number of green socks?

(A) $\frac{1}{15}$

(B) $\frac{4}{15}$

(C) $\frac{6}{15}$

(D) $\frac{7}{15}$

5. The table below shows the probability of rolling each number on a fair 6-sided die.

Number Rolled	Probability
1	$\frac{1}{6}$
2	$\frac{1}{6}$
3	$\frac{1}{6}$
4	$\frac{1}{6}$
5	$\frac{1}{6}$
6	$\frac{1}{6}$

What is the expected value of the number rolled?

(A) $\frac{1}{6}$

(B)   1

(C)   3

(D) $\frac{7}{2}$

Box-and-Whisker Plots

Box-and-whisker plots are another unusual way of representing data.

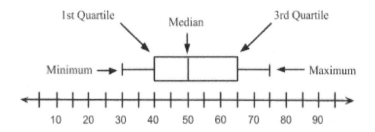

Box-and-whisker questions will most often ask you to find the range or median of a data set.

Range: the ends of the "whiskers" that stick out of the box represent the maximum and minimum values of the data set.

Median: the vertical line that cuts the box into two pieces represents the median.

Quartiles: You can see that the plot is split into four distinct sections. These are called "quartiles." Each quartile contains one-fourth of the data points in the total data set. Therefore, if there are 36 data points in the plot above, 9 of them fall between 30 and 40, 9 of them fall between 40 and 50, etc. The most difficult box-and-whisker questions pertain to quartiles.

Example #1
Questions #1-3 refer to the plot below.

Mr. Kleine gave his students a difficult math test. The box-and-whisker plot represents the scores received by the 16 students in his class.

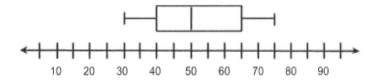

1. What is the range of the scores?
(A)   30
(B)   40
(C)   45
(D)   75

2. What is the median score?
(A)   30
(B)   40
(C)   50
(D)   65

3. How many students scored between 30 and 65 on the test?

(A)   4
(B)   12
(C)   35
(D)   50

To find the range, subtract the minimum number from the maximum number. In the plot above, **the range would be 75 − 30 = (C) 45.**

The median is represented by the vertical line that splits the box into two pieces. **The median of this plot is (C) 50.**

Scores ranging from 30 to 65 encompass three quartiles of this plot (the left whisker and both pieces of the box). Therefore, three quarters of the 16 students who took the test fall within this range. **The correct answer is (B).**

Summary

How to recognize *box-and-whisker plot* questions:
1) The question contains a box-and-whisker plot!

What you should keep in mind:
1) The median is represented by the vertical line that cuts the box into two pieces
2) The ends of the whiskers represent the largest and smallest data points. You can use this information to find the range
3) Box-and-whisker plots contain four quartiles. One quarter of the total number of data points fall within each quartile

Practice Questions

Questions #1-3 refer to the plot below.

The box-and-whisker plot represents the annual snowfall, in inches, in Toronto over the past 20 years.

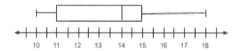

1. What is the median of the data?
    (A)   10
    (B)   11
    (C)   13
    (D)   14

2. What is the range of the data?
    (A)   8
    (B)   10
    (C)   14
    (D)   18

3. For how many years did Toronto experience more than 15 inches of snowfall?
    (A)   5
    (B)   10
    (C)   15
    (D)   20

Questions #4-6 refer to the plot below.

The box-and-whisker plot represents the length of all of Desta's workouts over the course of a month (in minutes).

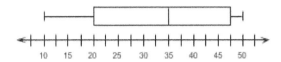

4. What was the median length of Desta's workouts?
    (A)   10 minutes
    (B)   20 minutes
    (C)   35 minutes
    (D)   50 minutes

6. What is the range of the data?
    (A)   10
    (B)   20
    (C)   35
    (D)   40

5. How long was Desta's longest workout?
    (A)   35 minutes
    (B)   47.50 minutes
    (C)   50 minutes
    (D)   60 minutes

Questions #7-9 refer to the plot below.

The box-and-whisker plot below represents the results of a very difficult math test taken by the 16 students in Mr. Yarbrough's math class.

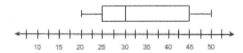

7. What was the lowest score in the class?
    (A)   20
    (B)   25
    (C)   30
    (D)   45

9. What is the range of the scores?
    (A)   20
    (B)   25
    (C)   30
    (D)   35

8. How many students scored above a 30 on the test?
    (A)   4
    (B)   8
    (C)   12
    (D)   16

Unit Conversion

There are a lot of places to make mistakes on *unit conversion* questions, but they're quite easy once you've practiced them!

Example #1

There are 1.61 kilometers in 1 mile. If a plane flies 450 miles in 1 hour, how many kilometers does it fly in 35 seconds?

(A) $\dfrac{60 \times 35}{1.61 \times 450 \times 60}$

(B) $\dfrac{60 \times 60 \times 35}{1.61 \times 450}$

(C) $\dfrac{1.61 \times 60 \times 35}{60 \times 450}$

(D) $\dfrac{1.61 \times 450 \times 35}{60 \times 60}$

The first thing you should notice here is that the answers do NOT require that you do any actual calculations. Don't bother trying to do multiplication on these questions - it's a waste of time.

Setting up the equation is more complicated, but you can follow the exact same method every single time. Take the first piece of information the question gives you ("there are 1.61 kilometers in 1 mile") and represent it as a fraction:

$$\frac{1.61 \; kilometers}{1 \; mile}$$

If the question gives you any other terms, you should include those as well:

$$\frac{1.61 \; kilometers}{1 \; mile} \times \frac{450 \; miles}{1 \; hour}$$

Make sure that you write the fractions so that like terms will cancel out. For example, you should **not** write:

$$\frac{1.61 \; kilometers}{1 \; mile} \times \frac{1 \; hour}{450 \; miles}$$

If you have all of your miles in the denominator, they will not cancel out!

Now that you've written in everything the question has provided for you, you'll have to start thinking critically. What are the units you have to end up in? How can you convert from what you have to what you need? In this case, we're going to want an answer in *kilometers*. That means that every other unit of measurement will have to cancel out. Let's convert from hours, which are the units we have now, to seconds:

$$\frac{1.61 \; kilometers}{1 \; mile} \times \frac{450 \; miles}{1 \; hour} \times \frac{1 \; hour}{60 \; minutes} \times \frac{1 \; minute}{60 \; seconds}$$

So far, three of our units will cancel out: miles, hours, and minutes. We're left with kilometers and seconds. Our final task is to cancel out the seconds so we're left with only kilometers. To do that, we'll need to multiply by the 35 seconds that are given in the question:

$$\frac{1.61 \; kilometers}{1 \; mile} \times \frac{450 \; miles}{1 \; hour} \times \frac{1 \; hour}{60 \; minutes} \times \frac{1 \; minute}{60 \; seconds} \times \frac{35 \; seconds}{1}$$

The correct answer is (D).

Example #2

There are 3.281 feet in 1 meter. Violet runs 100 feet in 8 seconds. If she continues jogging at a constant rate, how many minutes will it take her to jog 17 meters?

(A) $\dfrac{3.281 \times 17}{100 \times 60 \times 8}$

(B) $\dfrac{3.281 \times 8 \times 17}{100 \times 60}$

(C) $\dfrac{100 \times 60 \times 17}{3.281 \times 8}$

(D) $\dfrac{100 \times 17}{3.281 \times 60 \times 17}$

Once again, let's create fractions out of the information given in the question:

$$\frac{3.281 \; feet}{1 \; meter} \times \frac{8 \; seconds}{100 \; feet}$$

You may have noticed that we put feet on the bottom of the second fraction instead of on the top. How can you tell which units go on top and which units go on bottom? That depends on the first fraction. Because feet were on top in the first fraction, they must go on the bottom of the second fraction so that they cancel out.

Our target units are minutes and meters. So far, feet cancel out, leaving us with meters and seconds. Now, we just have to convert seconds to minutes:

$$\frac{3.281 \; feet}{1 \; meter} \times \frac{8 \; seconds}{100 \; feet} \times \frac{1 \; minute}{60 \; seconds}$$

Finally, add in a fraction that includes 17 meters so that meters will cancel out:

$$\frac{3.281 \text{ } feet}{1 \text{ } meter} \times \frac{8 \text{ } seconds}{100 \text{ } feet} \times \frac{1 \text{ } minute}{60 \text{ } seconds} \times \frac{17 \text{ } meters}{1}$$

The correct answer is (B).

Summary

How to recognize *unit conversion* questions:

1) You are given a rate in feet per second (or miles per hour, kilometers per day, etc) and asked to convert into other units

What you should keep in mind:

1) First, write out as fractions the rates that are given to you
2) Then, determine what units you have and what units you need
3) Finally, choose one unit type that you want to convert (e.g., from seconds to hours) and add in new fractions as necessary. Ensure that units will cancel out

Practice Questions

1. There are 3.281 feet in 1 meter. If a turtle travels 10 feet in 1 hour, how many minutes does it take the turtle to go 10 meters?

    (A) $\dfrac{3.281 \times 10}{10 \times 60}$

    (B) $\dfrac{3.281 \times 60}{10 \times 10}$

    (C) $\dfrac{3.281 \times 60 \times 10}{10}$

    (D) $\dfrac{60 \times 10}{10 \times 3.281}$

2. There are 5,280 feet in 1 mile. There are .305 meters in 1 foot. A car drives at 1,000 meters per minute. Which expression is equal to the car's speed in miles per hour?

    (A) $\dfrac{.305 \times 1,000 \times 5,280}{60}$

    (B) $\dfrac{5,280 \times 60 \times 1,000}{.305}$

    (C) $\dfrac{5,280 \times 60}{1,000 \times .305}$

    (D) $\dfrac{1,000 \times 60}{.305 \times 5,280}$

3. There are .621 miles in a kilometer. If Alec walks 5 km in 56 minutes, what is his pace in miles per hour?

(A) $\dfrac{60}{56 \times 5 \times .621}$

(B) $\dfrac{56 \times 60}{.621 \times 5}$

(C) $\dfrac{56 \times 60 \times 5}{.621}$

(D) $\dfrac{.621 \times 5 \times 60}{56}$

4. There are 3.281 feet in 1 meter. Steve jogs 250 feet in 20 seconds. If he continues jogging at a constant rate, how many minutes will it take him to jog 10 meters?

(A) $\dfrac{10 \times 3.281 \times 20}{250 \times 60}$

(B) $\dfrac{3.281 \times 60 \times 20}{10 \times 250}$

(C) $\dfrac{20 \times 10}{3.281 \times 60 \times 250}$

(D) $\dfrac{3.281}{20 \times 60 \times 10 \times 250}$

5. There are .621 miles in a kilometer. If a horse runs 20 kilometers in 45 minutes, how quickly did it run in miles per minute?

(A) $\dfrac{.621 \times 45}{20}$

(B) $\dfrac{.621 \times 20}{45}$

(C) $\dfrac{.621 \times 20 \times 60}{45}$

(D) $\dfrac{20 \times 45}{.621}$

6. A bus drives 96 feet per second. How many feet will it travel in 2 hours?

(A) $\dfrac{96 \times 60}{2 \times 60}$

(B) $\dfrac{96 \times 2}{60 \times 60}$

(C) $\dfrac{96 \times 60 \times 60 \times 2}{1}$

(D) $\dfrac{1}{96 \times 60 \times 60 \times 2}$

7. There are 5,280 feet in 1 mile. There are .305 meters in 1 foot. A man runs 2 meters per second. Which expression is equal to the man's speed in miles per hour?

(A) $\dfrac{5,280 \times 60 \times 60 \times 2}{.305}$

(B) $\dfrac{5,280 \times 60 \times 2}{.305 \times 60}$

(C) $\dfrac{2 \times 5,280 \times .305}{60 \times 60}$

(D) $\dfrac{2 \times 60 \times 60}{.305 \times 5,280}$

Shaded Regions

Shaded region questions test your knowledge of area and perimeter, as well as your ability to pay attention to what the question asks! These questions are pretty simple, but it's easy to make careless mistakes.

Example #1

The area of the shaded region is 200 cm².

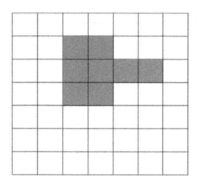

What is the length of one side of each square?

(A)   1 cm

(B)   5 cm

(C)   25 cm

(D)   50 cm

If the total area of the shaded region is 200 cm², then the area of each square is 25 cm². Because we know that the lengths of the sides of a square are all equal, we know that each side must be 5 cm. **The correct answer is (B).**

Summary

What you should keep in mind:

1) Area of squares and rectangles = length × width

2) Perimeter = the sum of the lengths of all sides of a shape

3) Although these questions aren't that difficult, you can be sure that the answers will be designed to trick you. You should circle or underline words like **area, perimeter, total, one side, shaded, unshaded**, etc

Practice Questions

1. The perimeter of the shaded region below is 48 cm.

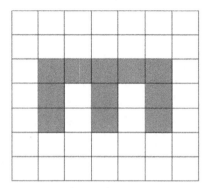

What is the area of the shaded region?
(A)   24 cm^2
(B)   34 cm^2
(C)   44 cm^2
(D)   54 cm^2

2. The area of the shaded region below is 81 in^2.

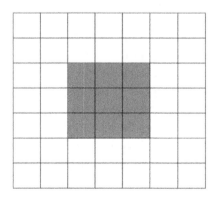

What is the perimeter of the shaded region?
(A)   3 in
(B)   9 in
(C)   12 in
(D)   36 in

3. The length of each side of the squares in the table below is 9 meters.

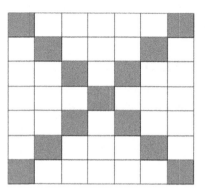

What is the area of the shaded region?
(A)   39 m^2
(B)   117 m^2
(C)   468 m^2
(D)   1,053 m^2

4. The area of the shaded region below is 96 ft^2.

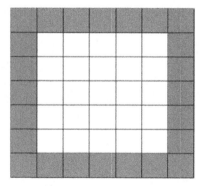

What is the perimeter of the unshaded region?
(A)   20 ft
(B)   40 ft
(C)   56 ft
(D)   100 ft

Inscribed Shape Geometry

Inscribed shape questions combine knowledge of circles, squares, rectangles, and triangles into more difficult questions. In order to answer these questions, you must be familiar with the equations for area, perimeter, and circumference, and you must know the difference between the radius and the diameter of a circle.

Example #1

In the figure below, a circle is inscribed in a square. The area of the circle is 25π cm^2. What is the area of the square?

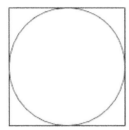

(A)   40 cm^2

(B)   75 cm^2

(C)   100 cm^2

(D)   125 cm^2

The equation for the area of a circle is πr^2, so the radius of this circle is 5. The radius of the circle is equal to half the length of one of the sides of the square, so each side of the square is equal to 10 cm. Therefore, the area of the square is 100 cm^2. **The correct answer is (C).**

Example #2

In the figure below, a circle is inscribed in a square. The circumference of the circle is 12π inches. What is the area of the shaded region?

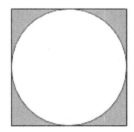

(A) $(12 - 36\pi)$ in^2

(B) $(144 - 12\pi)$ in^2

(C) $(144 - 36\pi)$ in^2

(D)   136 in^2

If the circumference of the circle is 12π inches, then the radius of the circle must be 6 inches (because circumference $= 2\pi r$). Doubling the radius gives us the length of one side of the square, which is 12 inches. To find the area of the shaded region, we must subtract the area of the circle from the area of the square. The area of the square is 144 in^2, and the area of the circle is 36π in^2. Therefore, **the correct answer is (C).**

Summary

What you should keep in mind:
1) Area of squares and rectangles = length × width
2) Area of triangles = $\frac{base \; x \; height}{2}$
3) Area of circles = πr^2
4) Circumference = $2\pi r$
5) You should circle key words: is the question asking you to find perimeter, radius, area, etc?
6) If the figure is given to you, you should label it; if there is no figure given, you should draw one!

Practice Questions

1. In the figure below, a circle is inscribed in a square. The area of the circle is 36π cm². What is the area of the square?

    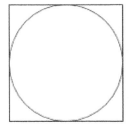

    (A)   64 cm²
    (B)   81 cm²
    (C)   100 cm²
    (D)   144 cm²

2. A circle is inscribed in a square. The area of the circle is 100π cm². What is the perimeter of the square?
    (A)   20 cm
    (B)   80 cm
    (C)   100 cm
    (D)   400 cm

3. In the figure below, a circle is inscribed in a square. The area of the circle is 121π cm². What is the perimeter of the square?

    (A)   22 cm
    (B)   75 cm
    (C)   88 cm
    (D)   484 cm

4. A circle is inscribed in a square. The circumference of the circle is 8π ft. What is the area of the square?
    (A)   64 ft²
    (B)   81 ft²
    (C)   100 ft²
    (D)   144 ft²

5. A circle is inscribed in a square. The circumference of the circle is 24π inches. What is the area of the square?
    (A)   24 in²
    (B)   96 in²
    (C)   216 in²
    (D)   576 in²

6. A square is inscribed in a circle. The area of the square is 64 square inches. What is the area of the circle?
    (A) 16π in²
    (B) 32π in²
    (C) 48π in²
    (D) 64π in²

7. In the figure below, a square is inscribed in a circle. The area of the square is 36 square inches. What is the area of the circle?

    (A) 18π in²
    (B) 32π in²
    (C) 36π in²
    (D) 48π in²

8. In the figure below, a circle is inscribed in a square. The radius of the circle is 7 yards. What is the area of the shaded region?

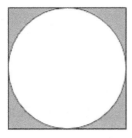

(A) $(49 - 7\pi)$ yd^2
(B) $(49\pi - 7)$ yd^2
(C) $(196 - 49\pi)$ yd^2
(D) $(196\pi - 49)$ yd^2

9. In the figure below, a circle is inscribed in a square. The area of the square is 64 square units. What is the area of the shaded region?

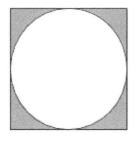

(A) $(64 - 4\pi)$ square units
(B) $(64 - 8\pi)$ square units
(C) $(64 - 16\pi)$ square units
(D) $(64 - 36\pi)$ square units

10. In the figure below, a triangle is inscribed in a square. The length of one side of the square is 6 square units. What is the area of the shaded region?

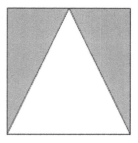

(A)   6 square units
(B)   18 square units
(C)   24 square units
(D)   36 square units

11. In the figure below, a triangle is inscribed in a circle. The base of the triangle is also the diameter of the circle. The circle has a radius of 8 inches. What is the area of the shaded region?

(A) $(16\pi - 64)$ square units
(B) $(16\pi - 128)$ square units
(C) $(64\pi - 64)$ square units
(D) $(64\pi - 128)$ square units

Right Angle Trigonometry

Most students don't cover *right angle trigonometry* until 11th grade. However, don't let that worry you: not only will there be at most one or two trigonometry questions on the ISEE, the topic is tested at a very superficial level. Having a basic understanding of a few key terms will allow you to answer these questions correctly.

Trigonometry is the study of the relationship between the angles and side lengths of triangles. The three trigonometric ratios that you will need to memorize are *sine*, *cosine*, and *tangent*. Each of these ratios measures the relationship between different sides of a triangle. You can remember them by using the mnemonic **SOHCAHTOA**: **S**ine = **O**pposite over **H**ypotenuse, **C**osine = **A**djacent over **H**ypotenuse, and **T**angent = **O**pposite over **A**djacent. Take a look at the triangles below to get a sense of what this means:

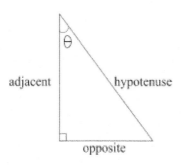

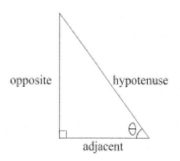

In this triangle, the reference angle is represented by the Greek letter *theta* (θ). The side across from the reference angle is the opposite side. The longest, diagonal side is always called the hypotenuse. The remaining side, which is next to angle *theta*, is called the adjacent side.

In this triangle, the location of the reference angle has changed - it's now on the bottom-right side of the triangle. Therefore, the opposite and adjacent sides are in different locations than they were in the first figure. The hypotenuse remains the same.

The two triangles above should make it clear that the opposite and adjacent sides of the triangle depend on the location of the reference angle. So, how does this all relate to SOHCAHTOA? Let's take a look at another triangle:

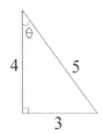

Now it's possible to find actual values for sine, cosine, and tangent. Sine of theta = $\frac{3}{5}$ (opposite over hypotenuse); cosine of theta = $\frac{4}{5}$ (adjacent over hypotenuse); and tangent of theta = $\frac{3}{4}$ (opposite over adjacent).

Example #1

In the triangle below, what is $\tan\theta$?

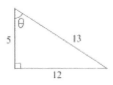

(A) $\frac{5}{13}$

(B) $\frac{5}{12}$

(C) $\frac{12}{13}$

(D) $\frac{12}{5}$

Tangent = TOA = $\frac{opposite}{adjacent}$. The length of the side opposite θ is 12, while the length of the side adjacent to θ is 5. Therefore, $\tan\theta = \frac{12}{5}$.

The correct answer is (D).

Bonus: $\sin\theta = \frac{12}{13}$ and $\cos\theta = \frac{5}{13}$. Can you see why?

Let's also try two examples in which the measure of θ is given.

Example #2

In the triangle below, what is the value of x?

(A) $17\sin40°$

(B) $\frac{\sin40°}{17}$

(C) $17\tan40°$

(D) $\frac{17}{\cos40°}$

This example is a bit more difficult because it requires rearranging an expression. First, you should note that we have been given opposite (x) and hypotenuse (17). Which trig identity uses those two sides? If you guessed sine, you're correct! Let's take the information we have and plug it into the equation: $\sin40° = \frac{x}{17}$.
Multiplying both sides by 17 gives us
$17\sin40° = x$. **The correct answer is (A).**

Example #3

In the triangle below, what is the value of x?

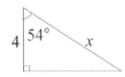

(A) $4\cos54°$

(B) $4\sin54°$

(C) $\dfrac{4}{\cos54°}$

(D) $\dfrac{4}{\tan54°}$

Here, we are given adjacent and hypotenuse, which means we should use cosine (CAH): $\cos54° = \dfrac{4}{x}$. Multiplying by x on both sides gives us $x\cos54° = 4$. Then, dividing by $\cos54°$ on both sides gives us $x = \dfrac{4}{\cos54°}$. **The correct answer is (C)**.

Summary

How to recognize *right angle trigonometry* questions:

1) The question or the answer choices mention *sine*, *cosine*, or *tangent*
2) The question displays a right triangle and gives some angle or side length measurements

What you should keep in mind:

1) **SOHCAHTOA**: **S**ine = **O**pposite over **H**ypotenuse, **C**osine = **A**djacent over **H**ypotenuse, and **T**angent = **O**pposite over **A**djacent

Practice Questions

1. In the figure below, $\overline{NP} = 5$ and $\overline{NO} = 13$. What is the length of $\overline{PO}$?

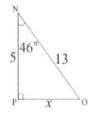

     (A) $13\cos46°$

     (B) $13\sin46°$

     (C) $\dfrac{13}{\tan46°}$

     (D) $\dfrac{13}{\cos46°}$

2. In the figure below, $\overline{AB} = 3$ and $\overline{AC} = 4$. What is the length of $\overline{BC}$?

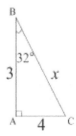

     (A) $4\cos32°$

     (B) $3\cos32°$

     (C) $\dfrac{4}{\tan32°}$

     (D) $\dfrac{3}{\cos32°}$

3. In the figure below, $\overline{YZ}$ = 12. What is the length of $\overline{XZ}$?

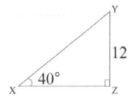

(A) $\frac{12}{tan40°}$

(B) $\frac{12}{cos40°}$

(C)   13cos46°

(D)   13cos46°

4. In the figure below, $\overline{ED}$ = 12 and $\overline{EF}$ = 15. What is the length of $\overline{DF}$?

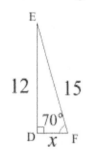

(A)   15sin20°

(B)   15cos20°

(C) $\frac{15}{tan20°}$

(D) $\frac{15}{sin20°}$

5. In the figure below, $\overline{RQ}$ = 8 and ∠QRS = 38°. What is the length of $\overline{QS}$?

(A) $\frac{8}{sin38°}$

(B) $\frac{8}{tan38°}$

(C)   8tan38°

(D)   8cos38°

6. In the figure below, $\overline{ST}$ = 50 and ∠STU = 47°. What is the length of $\overline{TU}$?

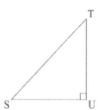

(A) $\frac{50}{sin47°}$

(B) $\frac{50}{cos47°}$

(C)   50tan47°

(D)   50cos47°

7. In the figure below, $\overline{YZ} = 10$ and
    $\angle YXZ = 36°$. What is the length of
    $\overline{XY}$?

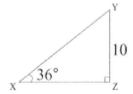

(A) $\dfrac{36}{cos36°}$

(B) $\dfrac{10}{cos54°}$

(C) $10tan36°$

(D) $10cos54°$

8. In the figure below, $\overline{AB} = 7$ and
    $\angle ABC = 30°$. What is the length of
    $\overline{AC}$?

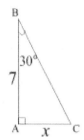

(A) $\dfrac{7}{tan60°}$

(B) $\dfrac{7}{tan30°}$

(C) $7cos30°$

(D) $7cos60°$

Surveys

Survey questions on the ISEE require an understanding of the basics of surveying a representative sample. A representative sample accurately reflects the population being sampled.

For example, if you want to know the average number of hours that students in your school spend each week doing homework, would you survey the students at another school to get an answer? Of course not - you'll need information from the students in your own school in order to answer that question. Likewise, if you want to know the average number of hours that students in your school spend each week on homework, interviewing students who are in the school library at 6:00pm on a Wednesday isn't going to be helpful, because you aren't surveying a representative sample of the student population.

Example #1
Xerxes is planning a survey to try to determine the average number of hours students at her school spend playing sports. Which sample of students will give her the most reliable information about the students in her school?

(A)   Her friends
(B)   A random sample of members of the soccer team
(C)   All members of every sports team in the school
(D)   A random sample of students in the school

Think logically: should Xerxes ask her friends (some of whom may not even attend her school) about the amount of time they spend playing sports? That doesn't make sense, so (A) is incorrect. (B) and (C) seem more promising, but the question asks about students in the school. Therefore, both (B) and (C) are too specific. Asking a random sample of members of the soccer team will give you a good idea of the number of hours students on the soccer team spend playing sports; asking every member of every sports team in the school how many hours they spend playing sports will tell you *exactly* how long students on sports teams spend playing sports. But! What about all the students in the school who don't play sports at all? The results of the survey will be skewed if you only survey students who are on sports teams. Therefore, **the correct answer is (D).** This survey will include both students who play sports and students who do not play sports, and will therefore give a representative sample of the school as a whole.

Summary
How to recognize *survey* questions:
1) The question asks about a sample or survey
2) The question asks you to determine which answer gives the most reliable response rate

What you should keep in mind:
1) Think about these questions logically: based on what the surveyor wants to know, which group of people does it make sense to survey?
2) Try to choose the answer choice that contains specific details that most closely match up with the details mentioned in the question stem

Practice Questions

1. Beatrix is planning a survey to determine the favorite candidate for the upcoming senior class president election. Only seniors can vote in the election. Which sample will give her the most reliable sample?
   (A) Her friends and family
   (B) A random sample of all students in the school
   (C) A random sample of seniors at the school
   (D) All the students who attend a student government meeting

2. A candy bar company wants to determine which candy bar is the most popular at a certain college. Which survey would yield the most reliable data?
   (A) A random sample of students surveyed on the way to class
   (B) All the students in the cafeteria at lunchtime
   (C) A random sample of students in a Health and Nutrition class
   (D) All the students in the Student Union at 3:00pm on a Saturday

3. Ajax is planning a survey to gather information on the average educational attainment of the residents of his town. Which sample will give him the most reliable information?
   (A) A random door-to-door sample of the residents of his town
   (B) His friends and family
   (C) Students at the local community college
   (D) A random sample of people at the library

4. Grayson is planning a survey about the study habits of the students in his Spanish class. Which sample will give him the most reliable information?
   (A) His friends in Spanish class
   (B) A random sample of students in his Spanish class
   (C) A random sample of students in his school
   (D) All the students in the school's various language programs

5. Penelope is planning a survey to determine the average number of minutes the teachers at her school spend brushing their teeth each week. Which sample of teachers will give her the most reliable information about teachers at her school?
   (A) All of her own teachers
   (B) A random sample of teachers in the lunchroom during lunch
   (C) All the math teachers
   (D) A random sample of all the teachers in the school

Volume and Surface Area

Volume and surface area questions test your ability to solve algebraic expressions. The equations for volume are always given, and you can often solve these questions by working backwards.

Example #1

The formula for the surface area of a sphere is $SA = 4\pi r^2$, where r is the radius of the sphere. A sphere has a surface area of 100π in^2. What is the radius of this sphere?

(A)   5 in
(B)   10 in
(C)   20 in
(D)   25 in

First, let's solve algebraically. Fill in the equation with all the information we know:

$$SA = 4\pi r^2$$

$$100\pi \text{ in}^2 = 4\pi r^2$$

$$\frac{100\pi}{4\pi} = r^2$$

$$25 = r^2$$

$$\pm 5 = r$$

The length of a radius cannot be negative. **The correct answer is (A).** You could also solve this question by working backwards. Try (B) first: $4\pi(10)^2 = 400\pi$. This answer is much too big, since the question tells us $SA = 100\pi$. Therefore, (A) must be the correct answer.

Example #2

The formula for the volume of a cone is $V = \frac{1}{3}\pi r^2 h$, where r is the radius of the base and h is the height. A cone has a radius of 3 cm and a volume of 12π cm^3. What is the height of this cone?

(A)   2 cm
(B)   3 cm
(C)   4 cm
(D)   12 cm

Once again, let's solve this algebraically:

$$V = \frac{1}{3}\pi r^2 h$$

$$12\pi \text{ cm}^3 = \frac{1}{3}\pi(3)^2 h$$

$$12\pi \text{ cm}^3 = \frac{1}{3}\pi(9)h$$

$$12\pi \text{ cm}^3 = 3\pi h$$

$$\frac{12\pi}{3\pi} = h$$

$$4 = h$$

The correct answer is (C). Like Example #1, this question could also be solved by working backwards.

Summary

How to recognize *volume and surface area* questions:
1) The question includes a picture of a 3D shape
2) There is a complicated equation and you are asked to solve for surface area, volume, radius, etc

What you should keep in mind:
1) You can often work backwards on these questions
2) When solving algebraically, first carefully input the given information into the equation

Practice Questions

1. The formula for the volume of a cone is $V = \frac{1}{3}\pi r^2 h$, where r is the radius of the base and h is the height. A cone has a height of 6 ft and a volume of 50π ft^3. What is the radius of the base of this cone?
   (A)   4 ft
   (B)   5 ft
   (C)   6 ft
   (D)   7 ft

2. The formula for the volume of a sphere is $V = \frac{4}{3}\pi r^3$. If the volume of a sphere is 36π in^3, what is the radius of the sphere?
   (A)   3 in
   (B)   4 in
   (C)   5 in
   (D)   6 in

3. The formula for the surface area of a cylinder is $SA = 2\pi r^2 + 2\pi rh$, where r is the radius of the base and h is the height. A cylinder has a radius of 3 inches and a surface area of 48π square inches. What is the height of the cylinder?
   (A)   2 in
   (B)   3 in
   (C)   4 in
   (D)   5 in

4. The formula for the surface area of a cube is $SA = 6s^2$ and the formula for the volume of a cube is $V = s^3$, where s is the length of one side of the cube. If a cube has a surface area of 24 cm^2, what is its volume?
   (A)   2 cm^3
   (B)   8 cm^3
   (C)   16 cm^3
   (D)   20 cm^3

5. The formula for the volume of a sphere is $V = \frac{4}{3}\pi r^3$. If the radius of the sphere is 6 mm, what is the volume of the sphere?
   (A) 36π mm^3
   (B) 48π mm^3
   (C) 124π mm^3
   (D) 288π mm^3

6. The formula for the surface area of a cylinder is $SA = 2\pi r^2 + 2\pi rh$, where r is the radius of the base and h is the height. A cylinder has a height of 4 inches and a surface area of 120π square inches. What is the radius of the cylinder?
   (A)   4 in
   (B)   5 in
   (C)   6 in
   (D)   7 in

7. The formula for the surface area of a cube is $SA = 6s^2$ and the formula for the volume of a cube is $V = s^3$, where s is the length of one side of the cube. If a cube has a volume of 64 in^3, what is its surface area?
   (A)   48 in^2
   (B)   96 in^2
   (C)   108 in^2
   (D)   144 in^2

8. The formula for the volume of a cone is $V = \frac{1}{3}\pi r^2 h$, where r is the radius of the base and h is the height. A cone has a height of 3 ft and a volume of 48π ft^3. What is the radius of the base?
   (A)   4 ft
   (B)   8 ft
   (C)   12 ft
   (D)   16 ft

Sequences

In mathematics, *sequences* are strings of numbers that follow a particular pattern.

In an arithmetic sequence, you add or subtract a certain number from the previous term to get the next term:

$$3, 6, 9, 12, 15$$

In the 5-term sequence above, you can see that 3 is added to each term to get the next term. The difference between each of the terms is constant.

In geometric sequences, you multiply or divide the previous term by a certain number in order to get the next term:

$$4, -16, 48, -144, 432$$

This one is more complicated. You can see that the numbers get bigger, although they alternate between positive and negative numbers. That means the multiplier must be a negative number. In this case, the multiplier is -3.

The ISEE will usually ask you to match a sequence of numbers to the correct equation. They will ask about the nth term of a sequence. For example, if the second term in a sequence is 5, you could say "when $n = 2$, the expression is equal to 5."

Example #1

The first five terms of a sequence are 5, 6, 7, 8, and 9. Which expression represents the nth term of this sequence?

(A) $5x$

(B) $2x + 3$

(C) $x + 4$

(D) $3x - 2$

In this sequence, the first term is 5. That means when $n = 1$, the sequence is equal to 5. When $n = 2$, the sequence is equal to 6. So, when we plug 1 into the sequence, 5 comes out; plugging 2 into the sequence results in 6, and so on. Look at (A): plugging in 1 does result in 5, so you might think this is the correct answer. But, when you plug in 2, it results in 10. This isn't correct! The same thing happens with (B): plugging in 1 results in 5, but plugging in 2 results in 7. Not until you reach (C) do you find an expression that matches the sequence exactly. **(C) is the correct answer.**

Summary

How to recognize *sequence* questions:

1) You're asked to find the nth term of a sequence

What you should keep in mind:

1) When $n = 1$ matches a sequence given in the multiple choice, this doesn't necessarily mean you've found the correct sequence. Test out the first few terms to make sure it's the right one.

Practice Questions

1. The first five terms of a sequence are 5, 7, 9, 11, and 13. Which expression represents the nth term of this sequence?
   - (A) $5x$
   - (B) $x + 4$
   - (C) $2x + 3$
   - (D) $6x - 1$

2.
3. The first five terms of a sequence are 1, 4, 7, 10, and 13. Which expression represents the nth term of this sequence?
   - (A) x^2
   - (B) $3x - 2$
   - (C) $x + 1$
   - (D) $4x - 3$

4. The first five terms of a sequence are 2, 5, 10, 17, and 26. Which expression represents the nth term of this sequence?
   - (A) $2x$
   - (B) $3(x - 4)$
   - (C) $3x - 1$
   - (D) $x^2 + 1$

5. The first five terms of a sequence are 0, 1, 2, 3, and 4. Which expression represents the nth term of this sequence?
   - (A) $x - 1$
   - (B) $x + 1$
   - (C) $2x + 1$
   - (D) x

Working backwards in *Mathematics Achievement*

The Mathematics Achievement section contains many questions that can be solved by *working backwards*. As you may recall from the Math Strategies section in Part II, working backwards involves using the given answer choices to answer a question. Let's take a look at a variety of MA questions that can be solved using this strategy. Many of these questions would be overly complicated or difficult if you tried to solve them mathematically, but they become very simple when you try working backwards!

Example #1

If $(1.90 + 3.10)x = x$, then what is the value of x?

(A)   0

(B) $\frac{1}{5}$

(C)   1

(D)   5

If you plug in 0, you get $5(0) = 0$. This is true, so **the correct answer is (A).** If you plug in $\frac{1}{5}$ you get $5(\frac{1}{5}) = \frac{1}{5}$, which simplifies to $1 = \frac{1}{5}$. Plugging in 1 gives you $5(1) = 1$, which is also not true. Finally, (D) gives you $5(5) = 5$.

Example #2

For what value of y is the equation $\frac{y+1}{1+y} = 0$ true?

(A)   -1

(B)   0

(C)   All real numbers

(D)   There are no values for y that would make the equation true.

On questions involving fractions, it is critical that you remember that $\frac{0}{0}$ is **not** equal to 0; it is *undefined*. Keeping that in mind, let's start with (A). $\frac{-1+1}{1+(-1)} = \frac{0}{0} =$ undefined. Don't fall for this answer choice! If (A) doesn't work, then clearly (C) does not work, either. Now, try (B): $\frac{0+1}{1+0} = \frac{1}{1} = 1$. This doesn't work, so **the correct answer must be (D).**

Example #3

Ben and Jerry are working on a group essay. Ben writes 3 pages in the amount of time that it takes Jerry to write 2 pages. Yesterday, they wrote a total of 20 pages together. How many pages did Ben write?

(A)   2

(B)   3

(C)   8

(D)   12

Start with either (B) or (C). If Ben wrote 3 pages, then Jerry would have written 2 pages. That's a total of 5 pages, not 20. (B) is incorrect. By default, we can also eliminate (A) since we need *more* pages, not *fewer* pages. And, since it seems like we need a lot more pages, let's skip directly to (D). If Ben wrote 12 pages, then Jerry would have written 8 pages, which is 20 pages total. **(D) is correct.**

Example #4

If $2z - 2 = za - a$ and $z \neq 1$, what is the value of a?

(A)   -2

(B)   -1

(C)   1

(D)   2

On this question, it looks like the answer is most likely 2 or -2. Start with (D). $z(2) - 2 = 2z - 2$, which matches the original equation. **Choice (D) is correct.**

Example #5

For what value(s) of x does $\dfrac{x^2 - 81}{(x+5)(x-8)} = 0$?

(A) $x = 9$ only

(B) $x = -5$ and $x = 8$

(C) $x = -9$ and $x = 9$

(D) $x = -9$, $x = -5$, $x = 8$, and $x = 9$

Start with (A). $\dfrac{9^2 - 81}{(9+5)(9-8)} = \dfrac{0}{(14)(1)} = 0$. This answer works! But, you're not done yet. You can safely eliminate (B), since it doesn't include 9 as an option. But what about (C)?

$\dfrac{(-9)^2 - 81}{(-9+5)(-9-8)} = \dfrac{81 - 81}{(-4)(-17)} = \dfrac{0}{68} = 0$. This also works. So, **the correct answer is (C)**. If you plug in -5 or 8, you'll end up with a 0 in the denominator, which leads to an answer that is undefined.

Summary

How to recognize *working backwards* questions:

1) The answer choices are all numbers
2) It seems like you might need to create a complicated equation in order to solve the question
3) There is a lot of algebra involved in the question
4) Even in cases where all of the above is true of a question, you can't necessarily work backwards!

What you should keep in mind:

1) To save time, pick (B) or (C) first. Since the answer choices are generally arranged in order from smallest to largest, if (B) ends up being too small, this means you'll also be able to eliminate (A)
2) It takes a lot of practice to master this strategy. Don't worry if you feel like you aren't quite getting it yet!

Practice Questions

1. You ask a friend how old they are, and they say, "If you multiply my age by 24 and subtract the square of my age, the result is 128." How old is your friend?
   (A)   13
   (B)   16
   (C)   24
   (D)   36

2. There are 40 boys and girls in Mr. Stein's economics class. $\frac{2}{3}$ of the boys and $\frac{1}{2}$ of the girls did their homework, and twice as many boys as girls did their homework. How many girls did their homework?
   (A)   8
   (B)   16
   (C)   20
   (D)   24

3. If $6b - 6 = bx - x$ and $b \neq 1$, what is the value of x?
   (A)   -6
   (B)   -1
   (C)   1
   (D)   6

4. For what value(s) of x does
   $$\frac{x^2 - 4}{(x + 2)(x - 2)} = 0?$$
   (A) $x = 0$ only
   (B) $x = 2$ only
   (C) $x = -2$ and $x = 2$
   (D)   There are no values for x that would make the equation true.

5. If $3x + 2 = 7(x - 2)$, then $x = ?$
   (A)   -2
   (B)   0
   (C)   2
   (D)   4

6. The cost of a music streaming membership is a one time fee of $15, plus a monthly fee of $12. Pam wrote a $171 check to pay for her membership for a certain number of months, including the one time fee. How many months of membership did she pay for?
   (A)   9
   (B)   11
   (C)   13
   (D)   15

7. Two machines make cars on an assembly line. Machine X makes 4 times the number of cars as Machine Y. This week, the machines together will make 10 cars. How many cars did Machine Y make?
   (A)   1
   (B)   2
   (C)   5
   (D)   8

8. A rectangular room that is 6 feet longer than it is wide has an area of 187 square feet. How many feet wide is the room?
   (A)   10
   (B)   11
   (C)   17
   (D)   18

9. If $(8.55 + 1.45)p = (6.20 + 3.8)p$, then what is the value of p?

(A)   0

(B) $\dfrac{1}{10}$

(C)   1

(D)   all real numbers

10. For what value of q is the equation $\dfrac{q + 4}{4 - q} = 0$ true?

(A)   -4

(B)   0

(C)   4

(D)   There are no values for q that would make the equation true.

11. For what value(s) of x does $\dfrac{x^2 - 49}{(x + 7)(x - 3)} = 0$?

(A) $x = 7$ only

(B) $x = -7$ and $x = 7$

(C) $x = -7$ and $x = 3$

(D) $x = -7$, $x = 3$, and $x = 7$

12. If $(2.25 + 2.75)k = k$, then what is the value of k?

(A)   0

(B) $\dfrac{1}{5}$

(C)   1

(D)   5

13. For what value of a is the equation $\dfrac{a + 1}{a - 1} = 0$ true?

(A)   -1

(B)   0

(C)   1

(D)   There are no values for a that would make the equation true.

14. Hermione and Ron are brewing potions in their potions class. Hermione brews potions 8 times as fast as Ron. At the end of the class, they have brewed a total of 36 potions. How many potions did Hermione brew?

(A)   1

(B)   4

(C)   8

(D)   32

Answer Keys - Common ISEE Question Types
Mathematics Achievement

Stem-and-Leaf Plots

1. C
2. C
3. B
4. A
5. C
6. D
7. C
8. B
9. D
10. C
11. D
12. D

Imaginary Numbers

1. D
2. D
3. C
4. D
5. B
6. B
7. B
8. A
9. B
10. D
11. D
12. B
13. A
14. D
15. B
16. A
17. B
18. D
19. B
20. D
21. B

Equivalent Exponents

1. C
2. B
3. A
4. A
5. B
6. D
7. C
8. D
9. D
10. A
11. C
12. B
13. D
14. B

Matrix Addition and Subtraction

1. B
2. A
3. B
4. D

Expected Values

1. A
2. D
3. B
4. D
5. D

Box-and-Whisker Plots

1. D
2. A
3. A
4. C
5. C
6. D
7. A
8. B
9. C

Unit Conversion

1. C
2. D
3. D
4. A
5. B
6. C
7. D

Shaded Regions

1. C
2. D
3. D
4. B

Inscribed Shape Geometry

1. D
2. B
3. C
4. A
5. D
6. B
7. A
8. C
9. C
10. B
11. C

Right Angle Trigonometry

1. B
2. D
3. A
4. A
5. C
6. D
7. B
8. A

Surveys

1. C
2. A
3. A
4. B
5. D

Volume and Surface Area

1. B
2. A
3. D
4. A
5. D
6. C
7. B
8. A

Sequences

1. C
2. B
3. D
4. A

Backsolving

1. B
2. A
3. D
4. D
5. D
6. C
7. B
8. B
9. D
10. A
11. A
12. A
13. A
14. D

Part V
Putting It All Together

Putting It All Together

This section is designed to help you practice recognizing question types and to help you identify how to solve questions. In the space provided under each question, you should write the type of question, the difficulties the question may present, and how to solve the question. On the following page, the same questions are presented alone. You should then complete the questions within the given time limit.

Example

A student was trying to calculate the mean of his test scores. He did not know what he had scored on each of the first 3 tests but knew that the sum of his scores was 240. If the student scored a 92 on his fourth test, then what was the mean of all four scores?

(A)   80
(B)   83
(C)   92
(D)   332

Applied Mean. Time consuming question; easy to make careless mistakes. Set up the equation for averages, fill in the info you know, and solve. If you're running out of time, you can eliminate answer choices that seem too extreme. The correct answer is (B).

Practice Set #1

1. $-9 - (-23) =$
      (A)   -32
      (B)   -14
      (C)   14
      (D)   32

2.   If a is a factor of b and e is a factor of f, which statement must be true?
      (A) bf is a multiple of ae
      (B) a is a multiple of bf
      (C) bf is a factor of ae
      (D) b is a factor of ae

3.   A jar contains 4 black balls, 8 red balls, and 2 yellow balls. If one ball is chosen at random and then removed from the jar, and a second ball is chosen at random, what is the probability that both balls will be black?

      (A) $\frac{3}{14}$

      (B) $\frac{4}{14}$

      (C) $\frac{4}{14} \times \frac{3}{13}$

      (D) $\frac{4}{14} \times \frac{4}{13}$

4.   If $f(x) = 3x + 2$ and $g(x) = 2x - 1$, what is $(f \circ g)(3)$?
      (A)   1
      (B)   5
      (C)   11
      (D)   17

5. $\dfrac{6x\sqrt{16x^4}}{3\sqrt{4x^6}} =$

      (A)   4
      (B)   8
      (C) $2x$
      (D) $10x$

6.   The area of the shaded region is 72 m^2.

      What is the length of one side of each square?
      (A)   3 m
      (B)   8 m
      (C)   9 m
      (D)   10 m

Mini Quiz #1
Questions: 6
Time Limit: 5 minutes

1.   -9 – (-23) =
      (A)   -32
      (B)   -14
      (C)   14
      (D)   32

2.   If a is a factor of b and e is a factor of f, which statement must be true?
      (A) bf is a multiple of ae
      (B) a is a multiple of bf
      (C) bf is a factor of ae
      (D) b is a factor of ae

3.   A jar contains 4 black balls, 8 red balls, and 2 yellow balls. If one ball is chosen at random and then removed from the jar, and a second ball is chosen at random, what is the probability that both balls will be black?

      (A) $\frac{3}{14}$

      (B) $\frac{4}{14}$

      (C) $\frac{4}{14} \times \frac{3}{13}$

      (D) $\frac{4}{14} \times \frac{4}{13}$

4.   If f(x) = 3x + 2 and g(x) = 2x – 1, what is (f ∘ g)(3)?
      (A)   1
      (B)   5
      (C)   11
      (D)   17

5. $\dfrac{6x\sqrt{16x^4}}{3\sqrt{4x^6}} =$

      (A)   4
      (B)   8
      (C) $2x$
      (D) $10x$

6.   The area of the shaded region is 72 m^2.

      What is the length of one side of each square?
      (A)   3 m
      (B)   8 m
      (C)   9 m
      (D)   10 m

Practice Set #2

1. A rectangle has an area of 56 in². If the length and the width of the rectangle are measured in whole inches, what is the least possible perimeter of the rectangle?

   (A) 7 in
   (B) 15 in
   (C) 30 in
   (D) 56 in

2. If $x@y$ is defined by $y^2 + 2x$, what is the value of $2@3$?

   (A) 10
   (B) 13
   (C) 20
   (D) 24

3. In the figure below, lines M and N are parallel. If $a = 55°$ and $b = 50°$, what is the value of c?

   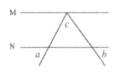

   (A) 65°
   (B) 75°
   (C) 180°
   (D) Cannot be determined

4. If the product of all the integers from 4 to 10, inclusive, is a, then which of the following represents the product of all the integers from 2 to 10, inclusive?

   (A) $a + 6$
   (B) $5a$
   (C) $6a$
   (D) $\frac{a}{6}$

5. If $\frac{ab}{4} = 15$, then which expression is equal to b?

   (A) $60 - a$
   (B) $60 + a$
   (C) $60a$
   (D) $\frac{60}{a}$

6. If the length of the base of a triangle is increased by 10 percent and the height is decreased by 40 percent, what is the percent decrease in the area of the triangle?

   (A) 17%
   (B) 34%
   (C) 46%
   (D) 50%

Mini Quiz #2
Questions: 6
Time Limit: 5 minutes

1.   A rectangle has an area of 56 in². If the length and the width of the rectangle are measured in whole inches, what is the least possible perimeter of the rectangle?
(A)   7 in
(B)   15 in
(C)   30 in
(D)   56 in

2.   If $x@y$ is defined by $y^2 + 2x$, what is the value of $2@3$?
(A)   10
(B)   14
(C)   20
(D)   24

3.   In the figure below, lines M and N are parallel. If $a = 55°$ and $b = 50°$, what is the value of c?

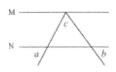

(A)   65°
(B)   75°
(C)   180°
(D)   Cannot be determined

4.   If the product of all the integers from 4 to 9, inclusive, is z, then which of the following represents the product of all the integers from 2 to 10, inclusive?
(A) $z + 15$
(B) $15z$
(C) $60z$
(D) $\frac{z}{60}$

5.   If $\frac{ab}{4} = 15$, then which expression is equal to b?

(A) $60 - a$
(B) $60 + a$
(C) $60a$
(D) $\frac{60}{a}$

6.   If the length of the base of a triangle is increased by 10 percent and the height is decreased by 40 percent, what is the percent decrease in the area of the triangle?
(A)   17%
(B)   34%
(C)   46%
(D)   50%

Practice Set #3

1. How many ways can first place and second place prizes be awarded to nine people?
    (A)   17
    (B)   18
    (C)   72
    (D)   81

2. The stem-and-leaf plot below represents the ages of students who are taking a GED course.

Stem	Leaf
2	2 2 5 7
3	2 5 7 8 9
4	2 2 2 5
5	4 5
6	4 7

    What is the mode age in the class?
    (A)   9
    (B)   38
    (C)   39
    (D)   42

3. $0.999 \div 0.009 =$
    (A)   1.11
    (B)   11.1
    (C)   111
    (D)   1,110

4. If $(x + n)^2 = x^2 - 4x + b$, what is the value of b?
    (A)   -4
    (B)   -2
    (C)   2
    (D)   4

5. Plane D departs Austin's Bergstrom Airport bound for Denver International Airport, a distance of 900 miles. After Plane D has traveled 300 miles, Plane E departs Denver bound for Austin. If the planes pass each other at 3:25 p.m. CST, which of the following would be needed to determine when Plane D left Austin, in Central Standard Time?

    (A)   the sum of the planes' speeds
    (B)   the difference of the planes' speeds
    (C)   the speed of plane D
    (D)   the speed of plane E

6. $\frac{x}{8} - 5 = -4$
    (A)   1
    (B)   3
    (C)   5
    (D)   8

Mini Quiz #3
Questions: 6
Time Limit: 5 minutes

1. How many ways can first place and second place prizes be awarded to nine people?
   (A) 17
   (B) 18
   (C) 72
   (D) 81

2. The stem-and-leaf plot below represents the ages of students who are taking a GED course.

Stem	Leaf
2	2 2 5 7
3	2 5 7 8 9
4	2 2 2 5
5	4 5
6	4 7

   What is the mode age in the class?
   (A) 9
   (B) 38
   (C) 39
   (D) 42

3. $0.999 \div 0.009 =$
   (A) 1.11
   (B) 11.1
   (C) 111
   (D) 1,110

4. If $(x + n)^2 = x^2 - 4x + b$, what is the value of b?
   (A) -4
   (B) -2
   (C) 2
   (D) 4

5. Plane D departs Austin's Bergstrom Airport bound for Denver International Airport, a distance of 900 miles. After Plane D has traveled 300 miles, Plane E departs Denver bound for Austin. If the planes pass each other at 3:25 p.m. CST, which of the following would be needed to determine when Plane D left Austin, in Central Standard Time?

   (A) the sum of the planes' speeds
   (B) the difference of the planes' speeds
   (C) the speed of plane D
   (D) the speed of plane E

6. $\frac{x}{8} - 5 = -4$
   (A) 1
   (B) 3
   (C) 5
   (D) 8

Practice Set #4

1. The table below shows the probability distribution of a random variable X.

X	$P(X)$
0	0.4
1	0.3
2	0.1
3	0.2

What is the expected value of X?
(A) 1.0
(B) 1.1
(C) 1.4
(D) 1.9

2. What is the maximum value of $\frac{2x^2}{x+2}$ for $-1 \leq x < 2$ if x is an integer?
(A) -1
(B) 0
(C) 1
(D) 2

3. $4 + (2 \times 1)^3 \div (16 \div 4) =$
(A) 3
(B) 6
(C) 9
(D) 12

4. In the figure below, a circle is inscribed in a square. The circumference of the circle is 16π inches. What is the area of the shaded region?

(A) $(256 - 64\pi)\,\text{in}^2$
(B) $(256 - 32\pi)\,\text{in}^2$
(C) $(64 - 64\pi)\,\text{in}^2$
(D) $256\,\text{in}^2$

5. $x^2 - 6x - 55 =$
(A) $(x + 5)(x + 11)$
(B) $(x + 55)(x - 1)$
(C) $(x + 5)(x - 11)$
(D) $(x + 1)(x - 55)$

6. There are 63 animals in the zoo, and the ratio of turtles to zebras to kangaroos is 3 : 1 : 5. How many kangaroos are there in the zoo?
(A) 5
(B) 7
(C) 21
(D) 35

Mini Quiz #4
Questions: 6
Time Limit: 5 minutes

1. The table below shows the probability distribution of a random variable X.

X	$P(X)$
0	0.4
1	0.3
2	0.1
3	0.2

   What is the expected value of X?
   (A) 1.0
   (B) 1.1
   (C) 1.4
   (D) 1.9

2. What is the maximum value of $\frac{2x^2}{x+2}$ for $-1 \leq x < 2$ if x is an integer?
   (A) -1
   (B) 0
   (C) 1
   (D) 2

3. $4 + (2 \times 1)^3 \div (16 \div 4) =$
   (A) 3
   (B) 6
   (C) 9
   (D) 12

4. In the figure below, a circle is inscribed in a square. The circumference of the circle is 16π inches. What is the area of the shaded region?

   (A) $(256 - 64\pi)\,\text{in}^2$
   (B) $(256 - 32\pi)\,\text{in}^2$
   (C) $(64 - 64\pi)\,\text{in}^2$
   (D) $256\,\text{in}^2$

5. $x^2 - 6x - 55 =$
   (A) $(x+5)(x+11)$
   (B) $(x+55)(x-1)$
   (C) $(x+5)(x-11)$
   (D) $(x+1)(x-55)$

6. There are 63 animals in the zoo, and the ratio of turtles to zebras to kangaroos is $3:1:5$. How many kangaroos are there in the zoo?
   (A) 5
   (B) 7
   (C) 21
   (D) 35

Practice Set #5

1. If the mean of three different positive integers is 21, what is the greatest possible value of one of the integers?
    (A)   21
    (B)   60
    (C)   61
    (D)   63

    _____

    _____

2. What is the least common multiple of 14 and 21?
    (A)   7
    (B)   21
    (C)   42
    (D)   294

    _____

    _____

3. The first five terms of a sequence are 0, 3, 8, 15, and 24. Which expression represents the nth term of this sequence?
    (A) $2x + 4$
    (B) $x - 1$
    (C) $-x + 1$
    (D) $x^2 - 1$

    _____

    _____

4. There are 1.61 kilometers in 1 mile. If a plane flies 550 miles in 1 hour, how many kilometers does it fly in 40 seconds?

    (A) $\dfrac{60 \times 40}{1.61 \times 550 \times 60}$

    (B) $\dfrac{60 \times 60 \times 40}{1.61 \times 550}$

    (C) $\dfrac{1.61 \times 60 \times 40}{60 \times 550}$

    (D) $\dfrac{1.61 \times 550 \times 40}{60 \times 60}$

    _____

    _____

5. Mr. Kleine gave his students a difficult math test. The box-and-whisker plot represents the scores received by the 8 students in his class.

    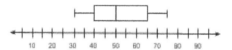

    How many students scored 50 or higher on the test?
    (A)   2
    (B)   4
    (C)   6
    (D)   8

    _____

    _____

Mini Quiz #5
Questions: 5
Time Limit: 4 minutes

1. If the mean of three different positive integers is 21, what is the greatest possible value of one of the integers?
   (A) 21
   (B) 60
   (C) 61
   (D) 63

2. What is the least common multiple of 14 and 21?
   (A) 7
   (B) 21
   (C) 42
   (D) 294

3. The first five terms of a sequence are 0, 3, 8, 15, and 24. Which expression represents the nth term of this sequence?
   (A) $2x + 4$
   (B) $x - 1$
   (C) $-x + 1$
   (D) $x^2 - 1$

4. There are 1.61 kilometers in 1 mile. If a plane flies 550 miles in 1 hour, how many kilometers does it fly in 40 seconds?

   (A) $\dfrac{60 \times 40}{1.61 \times 550 \times 60}$

   (B) $\dfrac{60 \times 60 \times 40}{1.61 \times 550}$

   (C) $\dfrac{1.61 \times 60 \times 40}{60 \times 550}$

   (D) $\dfrac{1.61 \times 550 \times 40}{60 \times 60}$

5. Mr. Kleine gave his students a difficult math test. The box-and-whisker plot represents the scores received by the 8 students in his class.

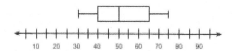

   How many students scored 50 or higher on the test?
   (A) 2
   (B) 4
   (C) 6
   (D) 8

Practice Set #6

1. What is the solution set for
    $2x^2 + 98 = 0$?
    (A)   7
    (B) $7i$
    (C) ± 7
    (D) $\pm 7i$

2. The formula for the volume of a cone is
    $V = \frac{1}{3}\pi r^2 h$, where r is the radius of the
    base and h is the height. A cone has a
    height of 6 cm and a volume of 50π cm^3.
    What is the radius of this cone?
    (A)   3 cm
    (B)   5 cm
    (C)   15 cm
    (D)   25 cm

3. What is the value of the expression

    $\dfrac{2^3(8+16)}{2^5(2^3+2^2)}$?

    (A)   0
    (B) $\frac{1}{2}$
    (C)   1
    (D) $\frac{3}{2}$

4. In the triangle below, what is the length
    of x?

    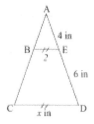

    (A)   3 in
    (B)   5 in
    (C)   7 in
    (D)   10 in

5. $-2 < \dfrac{-x-2}{3} \le 1$
    (A) $4 \le x < -5$
    (B) $4 < x \le -5$
    (C) $-5 < x \le 4$
    (D) $-5 \le x < 4$

6. A car drives 30 miles in three hours.
    How many miles does the car travel in
    2.5 hours?
    (A)   10
    (B)   15
    (C)   20
    (D)   25

Mini Quiz #6
Questions: 6
Time Limit: 5 minutes

1.   What is the solution set for
        $2x^2 + 98 = 0$?
        (A)   7
        (B) $7i$
        (C) ± 7
        (D) $\pm 7i$

2.   The formula for the volume of a cone is
        $V = \frac{1}{3}\pi r^2 h$, where r is the radius of the
        base and h is the height. A cone has a
        height of 6 cm and a volume of 50π cm³.
        What is the radius of this cone?
        (A)   3 cm
        (B)   5 cm
        (C)   15 cm
        (D)   25 cm

3.   What is the value of the expression
        $\frac{2^3(8+16)}{2^5(2^3+2^2)}$?

        (A)   0
        (B) $\frac{1}{2}$
        (C)   1
        (D) $\frac{3}{2}$

4.   In the triangle below, what is the length
        of x?

        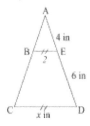

        (A)   3 in
        (B)   5 in
        (C)   7 in
        (D)   10 in

5. $-2 < \frac{-x-2}{3} \le 1$
        (A) $4 \le x < -5$
        (B) $4 < x \le -5$
        (C) $-5 < x \le 4$
        (D) $-5 \le x < 4$

6.   A car drives 30 miles in three hours.
        How many miles does the car travel in
        2.5 hours?
        (A)   10
        (B)   15
        (C)   20
        (D)   25

Practice Set #7

1. $(2.44 \times 10^2) + (1.22 \times 10^5) =$
   (A) 1.22×10^3
   (B) 3.66×10^3
   (C) 1.22244×10^5
   (D) 3.66×10^7

2.   A student is trying to determine the average number of hours students at her school spend playing video games. Which sample of students will give her the most reliable information about the students in her school?

   (A)   Her friends
   (B)   A random sample of members of the video game club
   (C)   All of the boys in the school
   (D)   A random sample of students in the school

3.   A line has a point at (2, 2) and its y-intercept is -6. What is the equation of the line?
   (A) $y = 4x - 6$
   (B) $y = 4x - 5$
   (C) $y = -2x + 1$
   (D) $y = 3x + 4$

4.   Which expression is equivalent to $[(2x^4)(3x^5)]^2$?
   (A) $6x^{11}$
   (B) $6x^{18}$
   (C) $36x^{11}$
   (D) $36x^{18}$

5.   In the triangle below, what is the value of x?

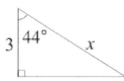

   (A) $3\cos44°$
   (B) $3\sin44°$
   (C) $\dfrac{3}{cos44°}$
   (D) $\dfrac{3}{tan44°}$

6.   A circle is inscribed in a square. Each side of the square is 12 units. What is the area of the circle?
   (A) 6π
   (B) 36π
   (C) 72π
   (D) 144π

Mini Quiz #7
Questions: 6
Time Limit: 5 minutes

1. $(2.44 \times 10^2) + (1.22 \times 10^5) =$
    (A) 1.22×10^3
    (B) 3.66×10^3
    (C) 1.22244×10^5
    (D) 3.66×10^7

2. A student is trying to determine the average number of hours students at her school spend playing video games. Which sample of students will give her the most reliable information about the students in her school?

    (A) Her friends
    (B) A random sample of members of the video game club
    (C) All of the boys in the school
    (D) A random sample of students in the school

3. A line has a point at (2, 2) and its y-intercept is -6. What is the equation of the line?
    (A) $y = 4x - 6$
    (B) $y = 4x - 5$
    (C) $y = -2x + 1$
    (D) $y = 3x + 4$

4. Which expression is equivalent to $[(2x^4)(3x^5)]^2$?
    (A) $6x^{11}$
    (B) $6x^{18}$
    (C) $36x^{11}$
    (D) $36x^{18}$

5. In the triangle below, what is the value of x?

    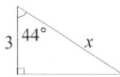

    (A) $3\cos44°$
    (B) $3\sin44°$
    (C) $\dfrac{3}{\cos44°}$
    (D) $\dfrac{3}{\tan44°}$

6. A circle is inscribed in a square. Each side of the square is 12 units. What is the area of the circle?
    (A) 6π
    (B) 36π
    (C) 72π
    (D) 144π

Practice Set #8

1. Jori has two more candy bars than Sonja, and Sonja has half as many candy bars as Jefferson. If j is the number of candy bars that Jori has, then in terms of j, how many candy bars does Jefferson have?
   (A) $j + 2$
   (B) $2j$
   (C) $2j - 2$
   (D) $2j - 4$

2. If there is no waste, how many square feet of carpeting are required to cover a rectangular floor that is 12 yards by 24 yards? (1 yard = 3 feet)
   (A) 32
   (B) 288
   (C) 2,592
   (D) 4,248

3. The price of a \$19.00 entree increases 15%. What is the new price?
   (A) \$2.85
   (B) \$19.15
   (C) \$21.85
   (D) \$285.00

4. $2^{-6} \times 4^3 =$
   (A) 1
   (B) 6^{-6}
   (C) 8^{-3}
   (D) 8^{-18}

5. What is the result of the expression
$$\begin{bmatrix} 2 & 3 \\ 4 & 5 \end{bmatrix} + \begin{bmatrix} 1 & 2 \\ 3 & 4 \end{bmatrix}?$$

   (A) $\begin{bmatrix} 1 & 2 \\ 3 & 4 \end{bmatrix}$

   (B) $\begin{bmatrix} 2 & 3 \\ 4 & 5 \end{bmatrix}$

   (C) $\begin{bmatrix} 3 & 5 \\ 7 & 9 \end{bmatrix}$

   (D) $\begin{bmatrix} 21 & 32 \\ 43 & 54 \end{bmatrix}$

Mini Quiz #8
Questions: 5
Time Limit: 4 minutes

1. Jori has two more candy bars than
    Sonja, and Sonja has half as many
    candy bars as Jefferson. If j is the
    number of candy bars that Jori has, then
    in terms of j, how many candy bars does
    Jefferson have?
    (A) $j + 2$
    (B) $2j$
    (C) $2j - 2$
    (D) $2j - 4$

2. If there is no waste, how many square
    feet of carpeting are required to cover a
    rectangular floor that is 12 yards by 24
    yards? (1 yard = 3 feet)
    (A)   32
    (B)   288
    (C)   2,592
    (D)   4,248

3. The price of a $19.00 entree increases
    15%. What is the new price?
    (A) $2.85
    (B) $19.15
    (C) $21.85
    (D) $285.00

4. $2^{-6} \times 4^3 =$
    (A)   1
    (B) 6^{-6}
    (C) 8^{-3}
    (D) 8^{-18}

5. What is the result of the expression

    $\begin{bmatrix} 2 & 3 \\ 4 & 5 \end{bmatrix} + \begin{bmatrix} 1 & 2 \\ 3 & 4 \end{bmatrix}$?

    (A) $\begin{bmatrix} 1 & 2 \\ 3 & 4 \end{bmatrix}$

    (B) $\begin{bmatrix} 2 & 3 \\ 4 & 5 \end{bmatrix}$

    (C) $\begin{bmatrix} 3 & 5 \\ 7 & 9 \end{bmatrix}$

    (D) $\begin{bmatrix} 21 & 32 \\ 43 & 54 \end{bmatrix}$

Answer Keys - Putting It All Together

Practice Set #1

1.   (C) Negative numbers. Is the number becoming more negative or less negative?

2.   (A) Choose your own numbers. Try not to use 1 because it could mess up your answer. Write everything down rather than trying to do it in your head.

3.   (C) Non-replacement probability. Denominator will change in the second event. In this case, the numerator will also change, because you're picking the same item twice.

4.   (D) Functions. This is a composite function. Work inward to outward. Think about input vs. output. Double-check your algebra to make sure there are no careless mistakes.

5.   (A) Radicals. Be very careful with your algebra. The square root of an exponent = one half of that exponent($\sqrt{x^8} = (x^8)^{1/2} = x^4$).You can only cancel division and multiplication, not addition and subtraction.

6.   (A) Finding the area and perimeter of shapes. Circle the key words, and beware of misleading answer choices.

Practice Set #2

1.   (C) Maximizing and minimizing the area and perimeter of quadrilaterals. For maximum area, the shape should be as square as possible; for minimum area, the shape should be as flat as possible. For maximum perimeter, the shape should be as flat as possible; for minimum area, the shape should be as square as possible. Draw a picture to avoid careless mistakes. Circle key words in the question stem. What are you supposed to find?

2.   (B) Symbol question. Write down the value of x and y so you don't get them mixed up. Be careful about which variables you replace.

3.   (B) Angles and parallel lines. Lines have 180°. Write the value of the angles on the figure. Vertical angles are congruent.

4.   (C) Sum or product of all integers. Think logically: will the answer be larger or smaller than the given range? How much larger or smaller will it be?

5.   (D) Isolating variables. You can plug in your own numbers, but this can be time consuming and confusing. It's best to do these algebraically. Anything you do to one side of the equation must be done to the other side. Double-check your work to avoid careless mistakes.

6.   (B) Percent increase and decrease in squares, rectangles, and triangles. Plug in your own numbers. Using 10 for the base and height of the triangle will make things easy. The original triangle will have an area of 50; the new triangle will have an area of 33. Percent means 100, so you need to change these numbers to 100 and 66 to see the actual decrease.

Practice Set #3

1.   (C) Permutations and combinations. Figure out if it's a permutation or a combination. Make a figure with two spaces so you can visualize the question. Put a 9 in the first spot and an 8 in the second spot, then multiply.

2.   (D) Stem-and-leaf charts; mean, median, mode, and range. Mode means most. Find the number that appears the most times in the "leaf" section of the chart. Then, combine that number with its stem to get 42.

3.   (C) Decimals. Move the decimal in each number over the same number of spaces until there are no longer any decimals remaining. $0.999 \div 0.009 = 999 \div 9$. Think logically: will the answer be very large or very small?

4.   (D) $ax^2 + bx + c$. FOIL $(x + n)^2$ and then compare it to $x^2 - 4x + b$.

5.   (A) Objects moving together and apart. If the objects move toward one another, you need the sum of their speeds. If they are moving in the same direction, you need the difference of their speeds.

6.   (D) Basic algebra. Anything you do to one side of the equation must be done to the other. You can work backwards on these questions if you're having trouble solving. Double-check your answer choice at the end to make sure there are no careless mistakes.

Practice Set #4

1.   (B) Expected values. Multiply horizontally, then add up all the products. Be careful not to make any mistakes when multiplying and adding decimals. The "expected value" may not make logical sense, but that doesn't mean you've done anything wrong.

2.   (D) Maximum and minimum values of inequalities. Circle the inequalities - are they inclusive or exclusive? Circle "minimum" or "maximum." Plug in the smallest possible integer, the largest possible integer, and zero. Double check your work.

3.   (B) PEMDAS. Parentheses come first, then exponents. Then, multiply and divide from left to right. Finally, add and subtract from left to right. Double-check your work: it's very easy to make mistakes on these questions.

4.   (A) Inscribed shape geometry. Find the area of the smaller shape and subtract it from the area of the bigger shape. Guesstimate: how much of the total area is taken up by the shaded region?

5.   (C) FOIL and reverse FOIL. You need to find two numbers that multiply to c and add to b. Plugging in a number works well in these questions. 1 will usually do the trick.

6.   (D) Ratios. Be careful about the order of the ratio and what each number corresponds to. Add up the integers, and divide the total number of objects by that sum in order to find the multiplier. Then, multiply each individual number by the multiplier to find the actual number of each object.

Practice Set #5

1.   (B) Mean, median, mode, and range. Circle key words: positive, different, and integers. The three numbers must add up to 63. The two smaller numbers could be 1 and 2, which means the largest number could be 60.

2.   (C) Least common multiple. Working backwards works well on these questions. Do 14 and 21 both go into 7 or 21? No. Do they both go into 42? Yes.

3.   (D) Sequences. Plug in 1, 2, and 3 into each equation until you find the one where input matches output. Beware of trick answers in which plugging in 1 works, but plugging in 2 or 3 does not.

4.   (D) Unit conversion. Think logically: will the answer be very big or very small? Set up your fractions so that everything cancels out.

5.   (B) Box-and-whisker plots. The line in the middle of the box represents the median. The range can be found by subtracting the value of the leftmost whisker from the value of the rightmost whisker. Each quartile contains 25% of the data points. 50 and above contains two quartiles, or 50% of the 8 data points.

Practice Set #6

1.   (D) Imaginary numbers. Use logic: $2x^2$ must equal -98, so x^2 must equal -49. All real numbers are positive when squared, so (A) and (C) won't work.

2.   (B) Volume and 3D shapes. Try working backwards on a question like this. Plugging in 5 for r results in a volume of 50π cm^3, so (B) must be correct.

3.   (B) *What is the value?* questions. When possible, convert everything to the same base. Here, you can pull out 2^6 on the top and the bottom and cancel those. Simplify what's left over.

4.   (B) Similar triangles. The ratio between the triangles is 4 : 10, not 4 : 6.

5.   (D) Multi-part inequalities. These work the same way as regular inequalities. Remember that when you divide or multiply by a negative number, you must flip the inequalities.

6.   (D) Rates. Set up a ratio and cross multiply. Convert units when necessary. Ask yourself whether your answer makes sense: it shouldn't be that much less than 30.

Practice Set #7

1.   (C) Scientific notation. When adding and subtracting, always convert to standard notation, add or subtract those numbers, and then convert back to scientific notation. Think logically: if a small number is added to a huge number, it is unlikely that the exponent next to 10 will increase.

2.   (D) Samples. Circle the target group in the question: *students in the school*. To get a representative sample, you must interview a random sample of all students in the school.

3.   (A) Slope and the standard equation of a line. Set up as much of the equation as you can: $y = mx - 6$. Plug in 2 for x and y and solve for m: $2 = 2m - 6$.

4.   (D) Equivalent exponents. Remember your rules for exponents. You can try plugging in 1 to see if that will help you eliminate any answers. Once you've gotten to $(6x^9)^2$, remember that the squared applies to each part of the expression within the parentheses.

5.   (C) Right angle trigonometry. Always remember *SOHCAHTOA*. Set up the equation and rearrange as necessary. If you don't find your answer the first time, try finding the value of the missing angle and then solving.

6.   (B) Inscribed shape geometry. Draw out the shape to help you visualize. The radius of the circle will be one half the length of one side of the square.

Practice Set #8

1.   (A) Converting words into math. Write everything down to prevent careless mistakes. You can work backwards on this question. If Jori has 6 candy bars, then Sonja has 4 candy bars and Jefferson has 8 candy bars. $j = 6$, and $j + 2 = 8$.

2.   (C) Unit conversion. Think logically: there are 3 feet in 1 yard, so the final answer must be greater than 12×24. This allows you to eliminate (A) and (B). Then, convert to feet by multiplying each of the measurements by 3.

3.   (C) Percents and percent change. Think logically: you can probably solve this question without doing any math at all. You know the price has increased, so you can eliminate (A). (B) is a trick answer.

4.   (D) Laws of exponents. $2^{-6} \times 4^3 = 2^{-6} \times (2^2)^3 = 2^{-6} \times 2^6 = 2^0 = 1$.

5.   (C) Matrix addition and subtraction. Circle the addition or subtraction sign so you don't forget which operation to do. Then, add the numbers in the corresponding locations of each matrix.

Part VI
Upper Level ISEE
Math Practice Tests

Chapter 5

Quantitative Reasoning
Practice Test #1

Section 2
Quantitative Reasoning

| 32 Questions | Time: 30 minutes |

This section is divided into two parts that contain two different types of questions. As soon as you have completed Part One, answer the questions in Part Two. You may write in your test booklet. For each answer you select, remember to fill in the corresponding circle on your answer document.

Any figures that accompany the questions in this section may be assumed to be drawn as accurately as possible EXCEPT when it is stated that a particular figure is not drawn to scale. Letters such as x, y, and n stand for real numbers.

Part One - Word Problems

Each question in Part One consists of a word problem followed by four answer choices. You may write in your test booklet; however, you may be able to solve many of these problems in your head. Next, look at the four answer choices given and select the best answer.

EXAMPLE 1:   <u>Sample Answer</u>

What is the value of the expression $4 + (2 \times 8) \div (1 + 3)$?

(A)   0
(B)   4
(C)   8
(D)   16

The correct answer is 8, so circle C is darkened.

Part Two — Quantitative Comparisons

All questions in Part Two are quantitative comparisons between the quantities shown in Column A and Column B. Using the information given in each question, compare the quantity in Column A to the quantity in Column B, and choose one of these four answer choices:

(A) The quantity in Column A is greater.
(B) The quantity in Column B is greater.
(C) The two quantities are equal.
(D) The relationship cannot be determined from the information given.

EXAMPLE 2:

Column A	Column B	Sample Answer
30% of 60	40% of 40	● Ⓑ Ⓒ Ⓓ

The quantity in Column A (18) is greater than the quantity in Column B (16), so circle A is darkened.

EXAMPLE 3:

y is any integer

Column A	Column B	Sample Answer
$-y^2$	y	Ⓐ Ⓑ Ⓒ ●

Since y can be any integer (including zero or negative numbers), there is not enough information given to determine the relationship, so circle D is darkened.

Practice Test #1

Part One - Word Problems

Directions: Choose the best answer from the four choices given.

1. A triangle is shown below. $\overline{BE}$ is parallel to $\overline{CD}$.

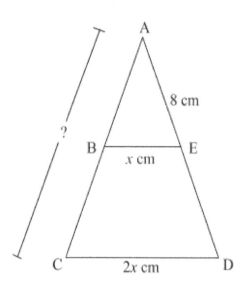

What is the length of side $\overline{AC}$?

(A)   8 cm
(B)   8x cm
(C)   16 cm
(D)   16x cm

2. If the sum of all integers from 55 to 65, inclusive, is x, then which expression represents the sum of all integers from 55 to 67, inclusive?

(A) $x + 133$
(B) $x - 133$
(C) $x + 66$
(D) $x - 66$

3. If $2y + 4x = 8$, then which expression is equal to y?

(A) $4 + 2x$

(B) $4 - 2x$

(C) $2 - \frac{1}{2}x$

(D) $2 + \frac{1}{2}x$

4. Meredith was trying to calculate the mean of her test scores. She did not know what she had scored on each of the first 3 tests but knew that the sum of her scores was 240. If Meredith scored a 90 on her fourth test, then what was the mean score for all four tests?

(A)   79.25
(B)   82.50
(C)   85.75
(D)   100.00

5. If the length of the base of a triangle is increased by 20 percent and the height is decreased by 40 percent, what is the percent decrease in the area of the triangle?

(A)   8%
(B)   20%
(C)   28%
(D)   30%

Practice Test #1

6. Davis puts a frozen pizza in a hot (450°F) oven to cook for 15 minutes, then takes the pizza out of the oven to cool. Which graph best represents what happens to the temperature of the pizza?

    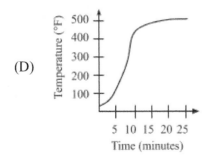

7. If #*q*# = 6*q* – 4, what is the value of #3#?

    (A)   2
    (B)   3
    (C)   10
    (D)   14

8. A rectangle has an area of 65 square inches. If the length and the width of the rectangle are measured in whole inches, what is the greatest possible perimeter of the rectangle?

    (A)   36 inches
    (B)   65 inches
    (C)   130 inches
    (D)   132 inches

9. Weishun and Olivia are playing a game using number cubes. Each player rolls two cubes, numbered 1 to 6, and the sum of the numbers is recorded.

    - Weishun receives a point if her sum is 3 or 5.
    - Olivia receives a point if her sum is 3.

    Who has a greater probability of receiving a point?

    (A)   Weishun
    (B)   Olivia
    (C)   They have the same probability of receiving a point
    (D)   There is not enough information to determine the answer

Practice Test #1

10. A cube is shown.

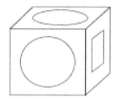

Which figure is a possible net for the cube?

(A)

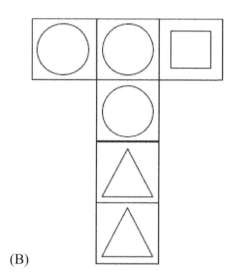

(B)

(C)

(D)

11. The graph shows the distance Joffrey was from home as a function of time during his bike ride.

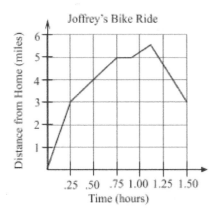

At one point during his ride, Joffrey stopped at the store to buy an ice cream cone. How far from Joffrey's home was the store?

(A)   2 miles
(B)   3 miles
(C)   4 miles
(D)   5 miles

12. What is the value of the expression

$$\frac{2^5(4^2 + 8^2)}{16(2^3 + 2^6)}?$$

(A) $\frac{1}{4}$

(B)   1

(C) $\frac{20}{9}$

(D) $\frac{33}{6}$

13. Jermaine surveys a group of his classmates to find out what animals they prefer as pets. He makes a bar graph of his findings but does not finish it.

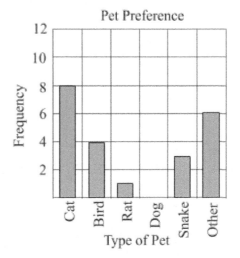

If the mean number of students who chose each pet is 5, how many students chose dogs?

(A)   4
(B)   6
(C)   8
(D)   10

14. If f(x) = 2x and g(x) = x^3, which inequality is true?

(A) $g(-2) < f(-2) < g(-.5) < f(-.5)$
(B) $f(-2) < g(-2) < f(-.5) < g(-.5)$
(C) $g(-2) < g(-.5) < f(-2) < f(-.5)$
(D) $g(-2) < f(-2) < f(-.5) < g(-.5)$

Practice Test #1

15. Mr. Rymer gave his 20 students a math test. He then calculated the mean, median, mode, and range of the test scores. The table gives the value of each of these statistical measures.

STATISTICAL MEASURES

Measure	Value
Mean	68
Median	65
Mode	71
Range	50

Due to the relatively low scores on the test, Mr. Rymer decided to add 10 points to each student's test score, and then he recalculated the values of each measure. Which of the measures changed the least?

(A) mean
(B) median
(C) mode
(D) range

16. If b is a positive integer and $(x + 4)^2 = x^2 + bx + 16$, what is the value of b?

(A) 2
(B) 4
(C) 6
(D) 8

17. What is the maximum value for y, if x is an integer and $y = \frac{2x^2}{x+1}$ for $-3 \le x \le 1$?

(A) -9
(B) 0
(C) 1
(D) 8

18. Peter and Becky drive in separate cars, each at a constant speed, on the same highway and starting from the same location. Peter drives faster than Becky. When Peter started driving, Becky had already driven 30 miles. Which one piece of additional information, in miles per hour, would be needed to determine how long, in hours, Peter had been driving when he caught up to Becky?

(A) Peter's speed
(B) Becky's speed
(C) the sum of Peter and Becky's speeds
(D) the difference of Peter and Becky's speeds

Practice Test #1

Part Two - Quantitative Comparisons

Directions: Using the information given in each question, compare the quantity in Column A to the quantity in Column B. All questions in Part Two have these answer choices:

    (A) The quantity in Column A is greater.
    (B) The quantity in Column B is greater.
    (C) The two quantities are equal.
    (D) The relationship cannot be determined from the information given.

Column A	Column B
19. $4x + 4$	$4(x + 4)$

The product of 3 consecutive odd integers is 105.

Column A	Column B
20. The least of the 3 consecutive integers	5

Column A	Column B
21. $7 + 4 \times (2 + 6)$	39

Column A	Column B
22. $(a + b)(a^2 + b^2)$	$a^3 + b^3$

A drawer contains 6 t-shirts: 2 black t-shirts and 4 white t-shirts. One t-shirt is selected at random and replaced. Then a second t-shirt is selected.

Column A	Column B
23. The probability that both t-shirts selected are white	The probability that the first t-shirt selected is black

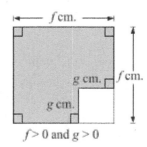

$f > 0$ and $g > 0$

Note: Figure not drawn to scale.

Column A	Column B
24. $f^2 + fg - g^2$ centimeters^2	Area of the shaded region

Practice Test #1

A fair, 6-sided die, numbered 1 to 6, is rolled, and a coin is tossed.

Column A	Column B
25. If a number greater than 4 is rolled on the die, the probability of the coin landing heads up	If a number greater than 2 is rolled on the die, the probability of the coin landing tails up

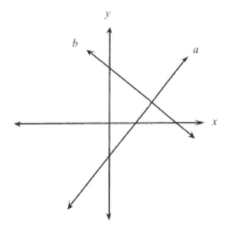

Line *a* is the graph of $y = 2x - 2$.
Line *b* is perpendicular to line *a*.

Column A	Column B
26. The slope of line *b*	-2

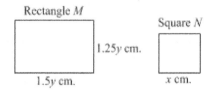

Note: Figures not drawn to scale.

Column A	Column B
27. The area of Square *N*	The area of Rectangle *M*

Amalia had $1,000 in her stock portfolio in 2015. In 2016, her holdings were 20% higher than they were in 2015. In 2017, her holdings were 10% lower than they were in 2016.

Column A	Column B
28. $1,050	The value of Amalia's holdings in 2017

Winnie's piggy bank contains $1.75 in nickels and pennies, and there are twice as many pennies as nickels. (Note: 1 nickel = $.05; 1 penny = $.01)

Column A	Column B
29. The total value of the nickels	$1.20

Practice Test #1

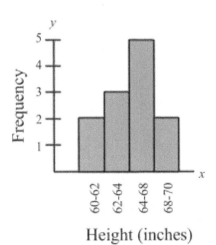

Height (inches)

The histogram shows the heights of the students in Ms. Bennet's 9th grade science class.

Column A	Column B
30. The range of heights	The mean height

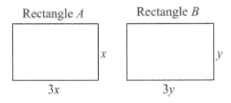

Note: Figures not drawn to scale.

The perimeter of Rectangle A is 40 ft. The area of Rectangle B is 48 ft^2.

Column A	Column B
31. x	y

The area of a rectangle is 72 cm^2.

Column A	Column B
32. 146 cm	The perimeter of the rectangle

Chapter 6

Mathematics Achievement Practice Test #1

Section 4
Mathematics Achievement

42 Questions

Time: 30 minutes

Each question is followed by four suggested answers. Read each question and then decide which one of the four suggested answers is best.

Find the row of spaces on your answer document that has the same number as the question. In this row, mark the space having the same letter as the answer you have chosen. You may write in your test booklet.

EXAMPLE 1:

Sample Answer

If n is a nonnegative integer and $(x + 10)(x - 10) = x^2 - n$, what is the value of n?

(A)   0
(B)   10
(C)   100
(D)   1,000

The correct answer is 100, so circle C is darkened.

STOP. Do not go on until told to do so.

STOP

Practice Test #1

1. If $(2.45 + 2.55)x = x$, then what is the value of x?

    (A)   0
    (B) $\frac{1}{5}$
    (C)   1
    (D)   5

2. Which value is NOT equal to $\frac{1}{6}$?

    (A) $\frac{1.5}{9}$
    (B) $\frac{\frac{5}{6}}{3}$
    (C)   .166666667
    (D)   .16

3. For what value(s) of y does $\dfrac{y^2 - 16}{(y - 6)(y + 10)} = 0$?

    (A) $y = 4$ only
    (B) $y = -4$ and $y = 4$
    (C) $y = 6$ and $y = -10$
    (D) $y = -10$, $y = -4$, $y = 4$, and $y = 6$

4. A sandwich shop offers 7 possible toppings on its sandwiches. Joanna decides to choose 4 of those toppings to put on her sandwich. How many combinations of 4 toppings are possible from the 7 toppings offered?

    (A)   24
    (B)   35
    (C)   276
    (D)   840

5. A school has 6 classrooms, labeled A through F. The bar graph below shows the number of students in each classroom.

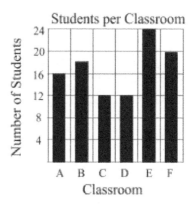

    What is the mean number of students per classroom?

    (A)   12
    (B)   15
    (C)   17
    (D)   20

6. Malik is planning a survey to try to determine the average number of hours that students in his school spend on homework each week. Which sample of students will give him the most reliable information about the students in his school?

    (A)   all of the students in the cafeteria during lunch
    (B)   a random sample of the students in his statistics class
    (C)   a random sample of all the students in the school
    (D)   his friends

7. The area of each grid square shown is 9 in^2.

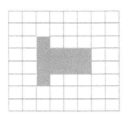

What is the area of the shaded region?

(A)   70 in^2
(B)   80 in^2
(C)   85 in^2
(D)   90 in^2

8. There are .305 meters in 1 foot. There are 5,280 feet in 1 mile. A car drives at 13 meters per second. What is the car's speed, in miles per hour?

(A) $\dfrac{13 \times 60 \times 60}{5,280 \times .305}$

(B) $\dfrac{13 \times 60 \times 60 \times .305}{5,280}$

(C) $\dfrac{13 \times 5,280}{.305 \times 60 \times 60}$

(D) $\dfrac{13 \times 60 \times 60 \times 5,280}{.305}$

9. Which expression is equivalent to the expression $(x + 4)(x - 5)$?

(A) $x^2 - 20$
(B) $x^2 - 1$
(C) $x^2 - x - 20$
(D) $x^2 + x - 20$

10. Rosa had a mean score of 94 on her first four math tests. What is the lowest score she can possibly get on her fifth and final test while still finishing with a mean score of at least 80 on all her tests?

(A)   24
(B)   30
(C)   36
(D)   42

11. For what value of z is the equation $\dfrac{z + 8}{8 + z} = 0$ true?

(A)   -8
(B)   0
(C)   8
(D)   There are no values for z that would make the equation true.

12. What is the value of the numerical expression $4.5 \times 10^3 + 3.2 \times 10^4$?

(A) 1.44×10^3
(B) 3.65×10^4
(C) 7.7×10^4
(D) 7.7×10^7

13. If $9x + 9x = yx + xy$ and $x \neq 1$, what is the value of y?

(A)   -9
(B)   -1
(C)   1
(D)   9

Practice Test #1

14. The box-and-whisker plot below represents the annual precipitation, in inches, in New York City over the past 50 years.

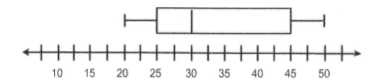

What is the median of the data?

(A) 20
(B) 25
(C) 30
(D) 45

15. Khaleesi wrote down the number of times each of her classmates was absent over the course of a month.

Number of Absences	Number of Students Absent That Many Times
0	9
1	6
2	5
3	4
4	1

What is the median of the data?

(A) 0
(B) 1
(C) 2
(D) 9

16. What type of number could result from the product of two integers?

(A) complex number
(B) composite number
(C) irrational number
(D) imaginary number

17. Which is the most reasonable unit to use when measuring the weight of a coffee cup?

(A) grams
(B) inches
(C) pounds
(D) milliliters

18. What is the value of the numerical expression $\sqrt{36 + 64}$?

(A) 4
(B) 10
(C) 14
(D) 50

Practice Test #1

19. The graph shows the number of miles Betty rode her bike each day for five days.

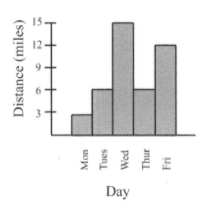

What was the median number of miles Betty rode per day?

(A)   3
(B)   6
(C)   9
(D)   12

20. The diameter of the circle shown is 16 ft, and the circle is tangent to the sides of the square in which it is inscribed. What is the area of the shaded region?

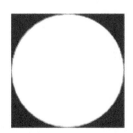

(A) $(64 - 16\pi)$ ft^2
(B) $(64 - 32\pi)$ ft^2
(C) $(256 - 64\pi)$ ft^2
(D) $(256 - 128\pi)$ ft^2

21. Point (2, 9) is on a circle with a center (-3, -3). What is the radius of the circle?

(A)   5 grid units
(B)   10 grid units
(C)   12 grid units
(D)   13 grid units

22. If a and b are prime numbers, what is the least common multiple of $4a$, $5ab$, and $2b^2$?

(A) $5ab$
(B) $5ab^2$
(C) $10ab^2$
(D) $20ab^2$

23. Which expression is equivalent to the expression $5n^3m^6 - 7n^6m^3 - (3n^6m^3 - 4n^3m^6)$?

(A) $2n^3m^6 - 11n^6m^3$
(B) $2n^3m^6 - 3n^6m^3$
(C) $9n^3m^6 - 4n^6m^3$
(D) $9n^3m^6 - 10n^6m^3$

24. A bag contains 7 red jelly beans, 4 black jelly beans, 5 yellow jelly beans, and 9 blue jelly beans. Isaac randomly takes one jelly bean from the bag and eats it. His friend Glen then randomly takes a jelly bean from the bag. If the jelly bean Isaac ate was blue, what is the probability that Glen chose a red jelly bean?

(A) $\frac{7}{24}$
(B) $\frac{7}{25}$
(C) $\frac{9}{25} \times \frac{7}{25}$
(D) $\frac{9}{25} \times \frac{7}{24}$

Practice Test #1

25. Which describes all values of x for which $|\,2x + 4\,| \geq 10$?

    (A) $x \geq 3$

    (B) $x \leq -7$

    (C) $x \geq 3$ or $x \leq -7$

    (D) $x \leq 3$ or $x \geq -7$

26. Dan writes his essays twice as fast as Kerry. Yesterday, Dan and Kerry wrote a total of 24 pages of their essays. How many pages did Kerry write yesterday?

    (A)   6

    (B)   8

    (C)   12

    (D)   16

27. A box that is 9 feet tall casts a shadow that is 3 feet long. What is the height of a box that casts a shadow that is 2 feet long?

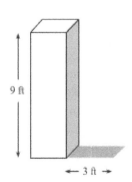

9 ft

← 3 ft →

    (A)   2 feet

    (B)   3 feet

    (C)   5 feet

    (D)   6 feet

28. Which expression is equivalent to the expression $\sqrt{36x^{36}}$?

    (A) $6x^6$

    (B) $6x^{18}$

    (C) $18x^6$

    (D) $18x^{18}$

29. Which numerical expression does NOT represent an integer?

    (A) $\sqrt{16 - 9}$

    (B) $\sqrt{16} \times \sqrt{9}$

    (C) $\sqrt{9} - \sqrt{16}$

    (D) $\sqrt{16 \times 9}$

30. Triangle XYZ is shown below. What is the measure, in degrees, of m?

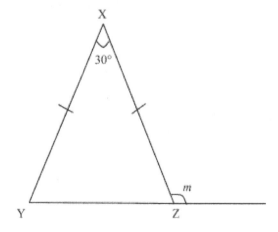

    (A)   75

    (B)   85

    (C)   95

    (D)   105

Practice Test #1

31. Andrea's closet contains 3 black shirts, 4 green shirts, and 9 white shirts. If Andrea chooses one shirt at random, puts it in the hamper at the end of the day, and chooses another shirt at random the following day, what is the probability that she will choose a black shirt and then a green shirt?

(A) $\frac{3}{16}$

(B) $\frac{4}{15}$

(C) $\frac{3}{16} \times \frac{4}{16}$

(D) $\frac{3}{16} \times \frac{4}{15}$

32. The graph of a line is shown.

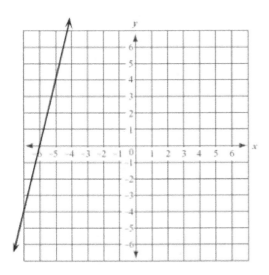

What is the slope of the line?

(A) -6
(B) -4
(C) 4
(D) 6

33. A spinner is divided into four equal portions. Three portions are black, and one portion is white. Jolene spins the spinner three times. The table below shows the possible outcomes and the probability of each outcome.

Number of spins that land on white	Probability
0	$\frac{27}{64}$
1	$\frac{1}{4}$
2	$\frac{1}{16}$
3	$\frac{1}{64}$

What is the number of spins expected to land on white?

(A) 0

(B) $\frac{1}{64}$

(C) $\frac{27}{64}$

(D) 1

34. The formula for the surface area of a right cylinder is $SA = 2\pi rh + 2\pi r^2$, where r is the radius of the cylinder and h is the height of the cylinder. A cylinder has a surface area of 42π in^2 and a height of 4 inches. What is the radius of this cylinder?

(A) 1 in
(B) 3 in
(C) 4 in
(D) 9 in

Practice Test #1

35. The stem-and-leaf plot shown represents the heights, in inches, of students in Ms. Bell's class.

HEIGHT

Stem	Leaf
5	1 4 7 7
6	2 5 6 6 8
7	0 1 2 4

What is the range of heights?

(A)   23
(B)   51
(C)   56
(D)   74

36. The height of the cylinder shown is 4 times its radius. The formula for finding the volume of a cylinder is $V = \pi r^2 h$, where r is the radius of the cylinder and h is the height of the cylinder.

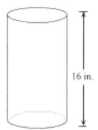

16 in.

If the height of the cylinder is 16 inches, what is its volume?

(A) 16π inches^3
(B) 64π inches^3
(C) 128π inches^3
(D) 256π inches^3

37. Which graph represents the solution set of the inequality $-2 \leq 4x - 2 \leq 18$?

(A)

(B)

(C)

(D)

Practice Test #1

38. The solution set of which inequality is shown on the number line below?

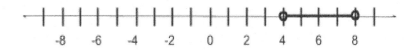

(A) $\left| \frac{x}{2} - 3 \right| < 1$

(B) $\left| \frac{x}{2} + 3 \right| < 1$

(C) $\left| \frac{x}{2} - 3 \right| > 1$

(D) $\left| \frac{x}{2} + 3 \right| > 1$

39. The grid shows two vertices of an isosceles triangle.

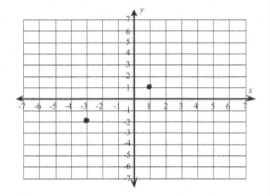

Which could NOT be the coordinates of the third vertex of the isosceles triangle?

(A) (5, -2)

(B) (-7, 1)

(C) (-3, 4)

(D) (3, -2)

40. Triangle ABC is shown. The length of $\overline{AC}$ is 10 in. The measure of angle ABC is 35°.

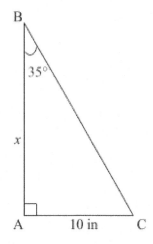

The value of which expression is equal to the length of side $\overline{AB}$?

(A) $\frac{10}{\tan 35°}$

(B) $\frac{\tan 35°}{10}$

(C) $\frac{10}{\sin 35°}$

(D) $\frac{\sin 35°}{10}$

Practice Test #1

41. What is the result of the expression

$$\begin{bmatrix} 1 & 2 \\ 3 & 4 \end{bmatrix} + \begin{bmatrix} 1 & 2 \\ 3 & 4 \end{bmatrix} ?$$

(A) $\begin{bmatrix} 1 & 2 \\ 3 & 4 \end{bmatrix}$

(B) $\begin{bmatrix} 1 & 4 \\ 9 & 16 \end{bmatrix}$

(C) $\begin{bmatrix} 2 & 4 \\ 6 & 8 \end{bmatrix}$

(D) $\begin{bmatrix} 0 & 0 \\ 0 & 0 \end{bmatrix}$

42. What is the solution set for $x^2 + 100 = 0$?

(A)   10

(B) $10i$

(C) ± 10

(D) $\pm 10i$

Chapter 7

Quantitative Reasoning
Practice Test #2

Section 2
Quantitative Reasoning

| 32 Questions | | Time: 30 minutes |

This section is divided into two parts that contain two different types of questions. As soon as you have completed Part One, answer the questions in Part Two. You may write in your test booklet. For each answer you select, remember to fill in the corresponding circle on your answer document.

Any figures that accompany the questions in this section may be assumed to be drawn as accurately as possible EXCEPT when it is stated that a particular figure is not drawn to scale. Letters such as x, y, and n stand for real numbers.

Part One - Word Problems

Each question in Part One consists of a word problem followed by four answer choices. You may write in your test booklet; however, you may be able to solve many of these problems in your head. Next, look at the four answer choices given and select the best answer.

EXAMPLE 1:   <u>Sample Answer</u>

                                                          (A) (B) ● (D)

       What is the value of the expression $4 + (2 \times 8) \div (1 + 3)$?

       (A)   0
       (B)   4
       (C)   8
       (D)   16

       The correct answer is 8, so circle C is darkened.

                                          Go on to the next page. ⟶

Part Two — Quantitative Comparisons

All questions in Part Two are quantitative comparisons between the quantities shown in Column A and Column B. Using the information given in each question, compare the quantity in Column A to the quantity in Column B, and choose one of these four answer choices:

    (A) The quantity in Column A is greater.
    (B) The quantity in Column B is greater.
    (C) The two quantities are equal.
    (D) The relationship cannot be determined from the information given.

EXAMPLE 2:   <u>Column A</u>   <u>Column B</u>   <u>Sample Answer</u>

           30% of 60   40% of 40   ● Ⓑ Ⓒ Ⓓ

The quantity in Column A (18) is greater than the quantity in Column B (16), so circle A is darkened.

EXAMPLE 3: y is any integer

         <u>Column A</u>   <u>Column B</u>   <u>Sample Answer</u>

           $-y^2$ y Ⓐ Ⓑ Ⓒ ●

Since y can be any integer (including zero or negative numbers), there is not enough information given to determine the relationship, so circle D is darkened.

Practice Test #2

Part One - Word Problems

Directions: Choose the best answer from the four choices given

1. What is the value of the expression

   $$\frac{5^3(5^2+5^3)}{25(15+10)} \ ?$$

   (A)   5
   (B)   25
   (C)   30
   (D)   60

2. The students in Mr. Potter's class recently took a test, and the range of the test scores was 30 points. Mr. Potter gave 10 extra credit points to the highest scoring student in the class. What was the new range of the test scores?

   (A)   10
   (B)   20
   (C)   30
   (D)   40

3. If x is the sum of all the consecutive even integers from 10 to 30, inclusive, and y is the sum of all the consecutive even integers from 14 to 34, inclusive, then what is the value of $y - x$?

   (A)   24
   (B)   34
   (C)   44
   (D)   54

4. If the radius of a circle is increased by 10%, what is the percent increase in the area of the circle?

   (A)   10%
   (B)   21%
   (C)   32%
   (D)   43%

5. If n is a nonnegative integer and $(x + 11)(x - 11) = x^2 - n$, what is the value of n?

   (A)   0
   (B)   11
   (C)   22
   (D)   121

6. In a two-dimensional plane, lines are drawn through a given point, A, such that the measure of each non-overlapping angle formed about point A is 15°. How many different lines are there?

   (A)   6
   (B)   12
   (C)   18
   (D)   24

Practice Test #2

7. If x is an integer, what is the maximum value of $x^2 + 2x - 4$ on the interval $-1 < x < 4$?

    (A)   -1
    (B)   4
    (C)   11
    (D)   20

8. If w is a multiple of x and y is a factor of z, which of the following must be true?

    (A) xy is a factor of wz

    (B) wz is a factor of xy

    (C) $\frac{w}{z}$ is a multiple of $\frac{x}{y}$

    (D) $\frac{x}{y}$ is a multiple of $\frac{w}{z}$

9. If $\sqrt{2x + y} + 4 = 6$, then which expression is equal to y?

    (A) $y = 4 - 2x$
    (B) $y = 36 - 2x$
    (C) $y = 4 + 2x$
    (D) $y = 20 - 2x$

10. At their family reunion, the Ower family took a total of 273 pictures. The family members took an average of 13 pictures each. How many people are in the Ower family?

    (A)   18
    (B)   19
    (C)   20
    (D)   21

11. The graph below shows Vincent's distance from home as a function of time during a drive he took this weekend.

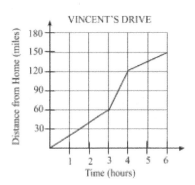

During what time interval was Vincent driving the fastest?

    (A)   0 to 1.5 hours
    (B)   1.5 to 3 hours
    (C)   3 to 4 hours
    (D)   4 to 5 hours

12. Plane A flies from Los Angeles to New York City, a distance of about 2,500 miles. After Plane A has traveled 500 miles, Plane B departs from New York City and flies to Los Angeles on the same route. What one additional piece of information is needed to calculate how long Plane B has been flying when it passes Plane A?

    (A)   The difference between the speeds of Plane A and Plane B

    (B)   The sum of the speeds of Plane A and Plane B

    (C)   The speed of Plane A

    (D)   The speed of Plane B

Practice Test #2

13. A device is shown below.

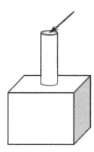

If water is poured at a constant rate into the opening at the top of the cylinder, which of the graphs best demonstrates what happens to the depth of the water in the device over time?

(A)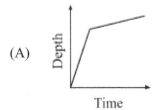

(B)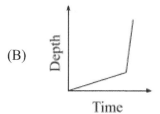

(C)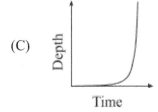

(D)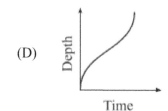

14. The formula for the volume of a right rectangular pyramid is $\frac{lwh}{3}$, where l = length, w = width, and h = height. The volume of Pyramid A is 3 times the volume of Pyramid B. Which of the following statements could be true?

(A)   The width and length of Pyramid A are 6 times the width and length of Pyramid B, and the height of Pyramid A is 2 times the height of Pyramid B.

(B)   The width and height of Pyramid A are the same as the width and height of Pyramid B, and the length of Pyramid A is 3 times the length of Pyramid B.

(C)   The length, width, and height of Pyramid A are 6 times the length, width, and height of Pyramid B.

(D)   The length of Pyramid B is $\frac{1}{3}$ the length of Pyramid A, and the width and height of Pyramid B are 3 times the width and height of Pyramid A.

Practice Test #2

15. Triangles *ABC* and *DEF* are similar.

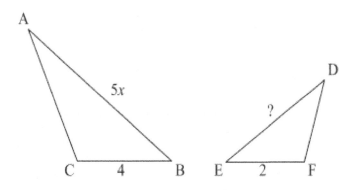

The length of $\overline{BC}$ = 4, the length of $\overline{EF}$ = 2, and the length of $\overline{AB}$ = 5x. What is the length of $\overline{DE}$?

(A)   2.5
(B)   10
(C)   2.5x
(D)   10x

16. A farmer needs to fence off her square pigpen, which has an area of 64 ft². How many feet of fencing must she buy to construct her fence?

(A)   8 ft
(B)   16 ft
(C)   32 ft
(D)   64 ft

17. If $4x^2 + 4y^2 = 52$ and $8xy = 48$, what is the value of $(2x + 2y)^2$?

(A)   6
(B)   18
(C)   100
(D)   2,496

18. If $@r@ = \frac{3r^2 - 5}{5}$, then what is the value of $@2@$?

(A) $\frac{5}{7}$
(B)   1
(C) $\frac{7}{5}$
(D)   2

Practice Test #2

Part Two - Quantitative Comparisons

Directions: Using the information given in each question, compare the quantity in Column A to the quantity in Column B. All questions in Part Two have these answer choices:

(A) The quantity in Column A is greater.
(B) The quantity in Column B is greater.
(C) The two quantities are equal.
(D) The relationship cannot be determined from the information given.

	Column A	Column B
19.	x^2	x^4

	Column A	Column B
20.	The measure of an interior angle of an equilateral triangle	The measure of an interior angle of a square

	Column A	Column B
21.	5% of 10	10% of 5

384 is the product of 4 consecutive even integers

	Column A	Column B
22.	10	The greatest of the four consecutive even integers

	Column A	Column B
23.	$4 + (2 \times 3)^2 - 10$	31

The volume of a rectangular prism is 50 cm³. The height of the prism is 2 and the length of the prism is equal to its width.

	Column A	Column B
24.	The product of the prism's length and height	10

A bag contains 2 pennies, 8 nickels, and 10 quarters.

	Column A	Column B
25.	The probability of choosing a penny	The probability of choosing a nickel, placing it back in the bag, and then choosing a quarter

Practice Test #2

Column A	Column B
26. The sum of the even integers from 100 to 200, inclusive	The sum of all integers from 1 to 100, inclusive

Column A	Column B
27. $\left(\frac{1}{4}\right)^2$	$\left(\frac{1}{4}\right)^{-\frac{1}{2}}$

$$(x + 6)(x - 3) = 0$$

Column A	Column B
28. x	2

A rectangle has a perimeter of 32

Column A	Column B
29. The greatest possible area of the rectangle	60

In May, apples cost \$3 per pound. In June, the price dropped by 20%. In July, apples were 10% more expensive than they were in June.

Column A	Column B
30. \$2.64	The price of a pound of apples in June

$$\frac{x}{9} = 3$$

Column A	Column B
31. x	30

Column A	Column B
32. 16^3	2^{10}

Chapter 8

Mathematics Achievement
Practice Test #2

Section 4
Mathematics Achievement

42 Questions	Time: 30 minutes

Each question is followed by four suggested answers. Read each question and then decide which one of the four suggested answers is best.

Find the row of spaces on your answer document that has the same number as the question. In this row, mark the space having the same letter as the answer you have chosen. You may write in your test booklet.

EXAMPLE 1:
Sample Answer

If n is a nonnegative integer and $(x + 10)(x - 10) = x^2 - n$, what is the value of n?

(A) 0
(B) 10
(C) 100
(D) 1,000

The correct answer is 100, so circle C is darkened.

STOP. Do not go on
until told to do so. **STOP**

Practice Test #2

1. The price of a notebook increased from $1.25 to $1.75. What was the percent increase in price?

   (A) 25%
   (B) 40%
   (C) 50%
   (D) 60%

2. For what value of x is the equation $\frac{x+4}{x-4} = 0$ true?

   (A) $x = 4$ only
   (B) $x = -4$ only
   (C) $x = 4$ and $x = -4$
   (D) There are no values for x that would make the equation true.

3. Aisha wrote down how many pets each of her classmates owns.

Number of Pets	Number of Students Who Own That Number of Pets
0	6
1	8
2	5
3	3
4	2

   What is the mode of the data?

   (A) 0
   (B) 1
   (C) 6
   (D) 8

4. What is the value of the numerical expression $\frac{6.0 \times 10^6}{1.5 \times 10^2}$?

   (A) 4.0×10^3
   (B) 4.5×10^3
   (C) 4.0×10^4
   (D) 4.5×10^4

5. Which expression is equivalent to the following expression?

   $$3a^7b^2 - 3b^4a^5 - (7a^7b^2 + 5b^4a^5)$$

   (A) $-4a^7b^2 - 8b^4a^5$
   (B) $-4a^7b^2 + 2b^4a^5$
   (C) $11a^7b^2 + 2b^4a^5$
   (D) $11a^7b^2 - 8b^4a^5$

6. What is 45% of 60?

   (A) 15
   (B) 27
   (C) 45
   (D) 87

7. 6 students volunteer for a beach cleanup, but their teacher decides he will only allow 3 of them to participate. How many combinations of 3 students are possible from the 6 total volunteers?

   (A) 6
   (B) 20
   (C) 60
   (D) 80

Practice Test #2

8. For what value(s) of y does

$$\frac{y^2 - 64}{(y - 8)(y + 4)} = 0?$$

   (A) $y = -8$ only
   (B) $y = -8$ and $y = 8$
   (C) $y = 8$ and $y = -4$
   (D) $y = -8$, $y = -4$, and $y = 8$

9. What are the prime factors of 30?

   (A) 1, 2, 3, 5, 6, 10, 15, and 30
   (B) 1, 2, 3, and 5
   (C) 2, 3, and 5
   (D) 3 and 5

10. The perimeter of the shaded region is 96 centimeters.

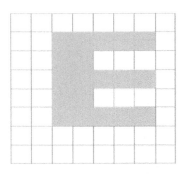

What is the area of the shaded region?

   (A) 19 cm^2
   (B) 48 cm^2
   (C) 171 cm^2
   (D) 192 cm^2

11. $$\frac{5x^4 y^3 z^{10}}{30 x^6 y^2 z^4} =$$

   (A) $\dfrac{5x^2 yz^6}{6}$

   (B) $\dfrac{yz^6}{6x^2}$

   (C) $\dfrac{x^2 yz^6}{6}$

   (D) $\dfrac{x^{24} y^6 z^{40}}{6}$

12. Triangle ABC is similar to Triangle XYZ. The length of $\overline{BC}$ is 7 cm, and the length of $\overline{YZ}$ is 10.5 cm. If the length of $\overline{XY}$ is 6 cm, what is the length of $\overline{AB}$?

   (A) 2 cm
   (B) 4 cm
   (C) 9 cm
   (D) 10 cm

13. Bessie got an average score of 82 on her six algebra tests this year. Her teacher is going to drop her lowest score, which is 37, before calculating her final average grade. What will be Bessie's final algebra grade?

   (A) 80
   (B) 85
   (C) 89
   (D) 91

Practice Test #2

14. There are .301 meters in 1 foot. A space shuttle flies at 3,250 meters per second. Which expression is equal to the number of feet the space shuttle drives in 1 hour?

(A) $\dfrac{3{,}250 \times 60 \times 60}{.301}$

(B) $\dfrac{3{,}250 \times 60}{.301 \times 60}$

(C) $\dfrac{3{,}250}{.301 \times 60 \times 60}$

(D) $\dfrac{3{,}250 \times .301}{60 \times 60}$

15. Which value is equivalent to $\frac{1}{9}$?

(A) $\frac{1.5}{18}$
(B) .11
(C) .111112
(D) .12

16. The surface area of the cube below is 96 in².

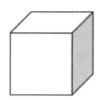

What is the cube's volume?

(A) 16 in³
(B) 32 in³
(C) 64 in³
(D) 128 in³

17. In the figure below, a square is inscribed in a circle. The area of the square is 100 square inches. What is the area of the circle?

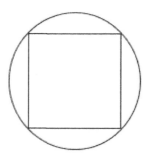

(A) 20π in²
(B) 30π in²
(C) 40π in²
(D) 50π in²

18. Ahmed made a chart of his friends' favorite foods.

Favorite Food	Number of Students
Pizza	15
Hamburger	10
Hot Dog	7
Lasagna	3
Sandwich	5

A circle graph is made using the data. What is the central angle of the portion of the graph representing sandwiches?

(A) 45°
(B) 90°
(C) 100°
(D) 120°

Practice Test #2

19. The box-and-whisker plot below represents the test scores of 40 students who took a science test.

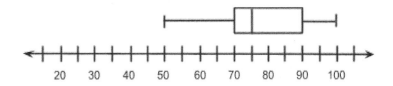

How many students scored between 50 and 75 on the science test?

(A)   10
(B)   20
(C)   30
(D)   40

20. What is the solution set to the inequality $-6 \leq 3x - 3 \leq 6$?

(A) $-6 \geq x \geq 6$
(B) $-3 \leq x \leq 9$
(C) $-1 \geq x \geq 3$
(D) $-1 \leq x \leq 3$

21. A drawer contains 4 pairs of black socks, 6 pairs of white socks, 2 pairs of red socks, and 3 pairs of gray socks. If Emil takes 2 pairs of socks out of the drawer, what is the probability that both pairs will be red?

(A) $\frac{4}{14}$
(B) $\frac{4}{15}$
(C) $\frac{2}{15} \times \frac{1}{14}$
(D) $\frac{2}{15} \times \frac{1}{15}$

22. If $(3.44 + 2.56) = 2x$, then what is the value of x?

(A)   0
(B)   2
(C)   3
(D)   6

23. In the diagram below, line x is parallel to line y.

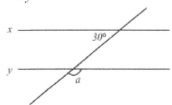

What is the measure of $2a$?

(A)   60°
(B)   100°
(C)   150°
(D)   300°

Practice Test #2

24. Which is the most reasonable unit to use when measuring the length of a car?

    (A) centimeters
    (B) kilograms
    (C) inches
    (D) feet

25. The ratio of adults to children at a school event is 1:3. If there are 428 people at the event, how many children are there?

    (A) 107
    (B) 142
    (C) 225
    (D) 321

26. A cylinder that is 4 feet tall casts a shadow that is 14 feet long. What is the height of a cylinder that casts a shadow that is 24.5 feet long?

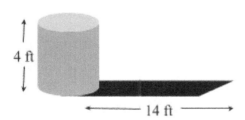

    (A) 6 feet
    (B) 7 feet
    (C) 8 feet
    (D) 9 feet

27. What is the value of the numerical expression $\sqrt{81} + 144$?

    (A) 15
    (B) 21
    (C) 108
    (D) 225

28. Which expression is equivalent to the expression $(2x + 2)(x - 4)$?

    (A) $x^2 - 6x - 8$
    (B) $2x^2 - 6x + 8$
    (C) $2x^2 + 6x - 8$
    (D) $2x^2 - 6x - 8$

29. The stem-and-leaf plot shown represents the scores on a recent test.

SCORES

Stem	Leaf
6	2 9 9
7	4 4 6 7 8
8	1 2 5 5 8 8
9	0 0 3 4 5

What is the median of the data?

    (A) 2
    (B) 4
    (C) 33
    (D) 82

Practice Test #2

30. A coin is tossed 5 times. The table shows the possible outcomes and the probability of each outcome.

Number of tails	Probability
0	$\frac{1}{8}$
1	$\frac{1}{8}$
2	$\frac{1}{4}$
3	$\frac{1}{4}$
4	$\frac{1}{8}$
5	$\frac{1}{8}$

What is the expected number of tails?

(A)   0

(B) $\frac{1}{8}$

(C) $\frac{1}{4}$

(D) $\frac{5}{2}$

31. The first five terms of an arithmetic sequence of numbers are shown.

$$7, 11, 15, 19, 23$$

Which expression represents the nth term of this sequence?

(A) $n + 7$
(B) $7n + 4$
(C) $10n - 3$
(D) $4n + 3$

32. Which expression is equivalent to the expression $\sqrt{144x^{16}}$?

(A) $12x^4$
(B) $12x^8$
(C) $72x^4$
(D) $72x^8$

33. The grid shows three vertices of a parallelogram.

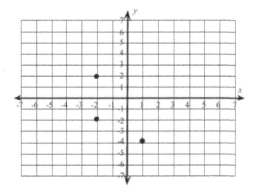

Which could be the fourth vertex of the parallelogram?

(A) $(0,1)$
(B) $(1,0)$
(C) $(1,1)$
(D) $(1,4)$

34. What is the solution set for $x^2 + 56 = 20$?

(A)   -6
(B) $6i$
(C) ± 6
(D) $\pm 6i$

35. The width of one side of a rectangle is 10 inches and the length of the diagonal of the rectangle is 26 inches, as shown.

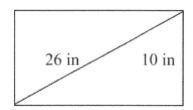

What is the perimeter of the rectangle?

(A)   34 inches
(B)   60 inches
(C)   64 inches
(D)   68 inches

36. What is the result of the expression

$$\begin{bmatrix} 9 & 9 \\ 9 & 9 \end{bmatrix} - \begin{bmatrix} 8 & 8 \\ 8 & 8 \end{bmatrix} ?$$

(A) $\begin{bmatrix} 17 & 17 \\ 17 & 17 \end{bmatrix}$

(B) $\begin{bmatrix} 98 & 98 \\ 98 & 98 \end{bmatrix}$

(C) $\begin{bmatrix} 0 & 0 \\ 0 & 0 \end{bmatrix}$

(D) $\begin{bmatrix} 1 & 1 \\ 1 & 1 \end{bmatrix}$

37. Deion tracked how many glasses of water he drank each day for one week. The results are shown below.

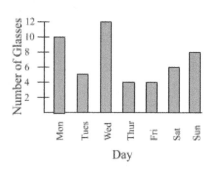

What was the mean number of glasses of water Deion drank each day?

(A)   4
(B)   5
(C)   6
(D)   7

38. Triangle LMN is shown. The length of $\overline{LM}$ is 5 units. The measure of angle MLN is 25°.

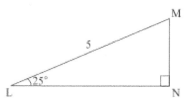

The value of which expression is equal to the length of side $\overline{MN}$?

(A)   5sin65°
(B)   5cos65°
(C) $\dfrac{\sin 25°}{5}$
(D) $\dfrac{\cos 25°}{5}$

Practice Test #2

39. The formula for the surface area of a right pyramid is $SA = \frac{1}{2}pl + B$, where p is the perimeter of the base of the pyramid, l represents the slant height of the sides of the pyramid, and B represents the area of the base of the pyramid. A right pyramid has a surface area of 85 cm², and the perimeter of its base is 20 centimeters. What is the slant height of the right pyramid?

    (A)   4.5 cm
    (B)   6.9 cm
    (C)   20.2 cm
    (D)   25.7 cm

40. The solution set of which inequality is shown on the number line below?

    (A) $|\, 2x - 6\, | < 2$
    (B) $|\, 2x - 6\, | > 2$
    (C) $|\, -2x - 6\, | < 2$
    (D) $|\, -2x - 6\, | > 2$

41. Which graph represents the solution set of the inequality $-4 \le -2x + 4 \le 10$?

    (A)

    (B)

    (C)

    (D)

42. The graph of a line is shown.

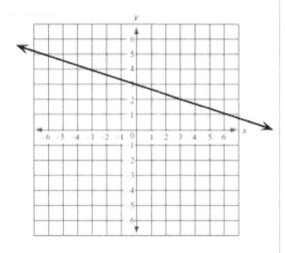

Which of the lines below is perpendicular to the line shown on the graph?

(A) $y = -\frac{1}{3}x + 4$

(B) $y = \frac{1}{3}x - 5$

(C) $y = -3x + 1$

(D) $y = 3x - 2$

Part VII
Answer Keys &
Interpreting Your Results

Chapter 9

Answer Keys

Quantitative Reasoning Answer Key - Upper Level (32 Items)
Practice Test #1

Item	Key	Your Answer	+ if correct	*Type		Item	Key	Your Answer	+ if correct	*Type
1	C			G		17	C			N
2	A			N		18	D			M
3	B			A		19	B			A
4	B			D		20	B			N
5	C			M		21	C			N
6	B			A		22	D			N
7	D			A		23	A			D
8	D			M		24	A			A
9	A			D		25	C			D
10	B			G		26	A			G
11	D			A		27	D			A
12	C			N		28	B			N
13	C			D		29	A			A
14	D			N		30	B			D
15	D			D		31	A			M
16	D			A		32	D			M
						Total Correct				

*Key to Type of Item

N = **N**umbers and Operations
A = **A**lgebraic Concepts
G = **G**eometry
M = **M**easurement
D = **D**ata Analysis and Probability

Quantitative Reasoning Answer Explanations - Upper Level (32 Items)
Practice Test #1

1. (C) Triangles ABE and ACD are similar. From $\overline{BE}$ and $\overline{CD}$, we know the ratio between the triangles is 1 : 2. If $\overline{AE} = 8$, then $\overline{AC}$ must be double that length.

2. (A) The second range contains 2 integers that the first range does not: 66 and 67. Therefore, the second range will be equal to the first range + 66 + 67.

3. (B) Isolate y by subtracting $4x$ from both sides of the equation and then dividing both sides of the equation by 2.

4. (B) Set up the formula for averages and solve. $\frac{240 + 90}{4} = x$. You can also think about this logically. Her average score on the first three tests is 80. If she scores a 90 on the fourth test, it's impossible that her average will go up to 100 or down to 79.25. Since she scored 80 more often than she scored 90, the total average will be closer to 80 than 90.

5. (C) Start with a triangle whose base and height are both equal to 10. The area is 50. If the base increases by 20% to 12 and the height decreases by 40% to 6, the area of this triangle is 36. You can use the percent change formula to find the total percent change: $\frac{14}{50} \times 100 = 28\%$.

6. (B) The temperature of a frozen pizza will be about 32°F, so you can eliminate (A). You can eliminate (C) and (D) because the temperature of the pizza will not continue to increase after it is taken out of the oven.

7. (D) Plug in 3 for # and solve. $6(3) - 4 = 14$.

8. (D) To maximize perimeter, the shape must be as flat as possible. If the area is 65, you can set the width to 1 and the length to 65. Then, add up the four sides.

9. (A) Think logically. There are more scenarios in which Weishun can score a point, therefore she has a higher probability of scoring a point.

10. (B) Try imagining this cube in your head. The two circles on the middle strip and the square on the right flap of (B) will fold to form the given cube.

11. (D) You can see on the graph that Joffrey stops moving between .75 hours and 1 hour. Draw a line directly to the left, and you'll see that it crosses 5 miles on the y axis.

Quantitative Reasoning Answer Explanations - Upper Level (32 Items)
Practice Test #1

12. (C) Rearrange so that all the bases are the same: $\dfrac{2^5(4^2+8^2)}{16(2^3+2^6)} = \dfrac{2^5(2^4+2^6)}{2^4(2^3+2^6)}$. Distribute the term

outside the parentheses: $\dfrac{2^9+2^{11}}{2^7+2^{10}}$. Pull out the greatest common factor on the top and bottom:

$\dfrac{2^7(2^2+2^4)}{2^7(1+2^3)}$. Cancel 2^7 and simplify the remaining parts of the expression.

13. (C) $\dfrac{8+4+1+x+3+6}{6} = 5$. Solving for x results in 8.

14. (D) g(-2) = -8, f(-2) = -4, f(-.5) = -1, and g(-.5) = -.125.

15. (D) The range will not change at all. The original range was $71 - 50 = 21$. The new range is
     $81 - 60 = 21$.

16. (D) FOIL $(x + 4)^2$ to get $x^2 + 8x + 16$. $8x$ corresponds to bx, so $b = 8$.

17. (C) Try plugging in the maximum and minimum possible values of x, as well as 0. Plugging in -3
     results in -9, 0 results in 0, and 1 results in 1.

18. (D) On these questions, if the objects begin in the same location but leave at different times
     headed in the same direction, you need the difference of their speeds.

19. (B) These expressions look the same at first glance, but distributing the 4 in the second
     expression results in $4x + 16$. Any number you plug in to these two equations (negative, positive,
     zero, fraction) will result in a larger value for Column B.

20. (B) The three consecutive odd integers are 3, 5, and 7. Column A = 3 and Column B = 5.

21. (C) $7 + 4 \times (2 + 6) = 7 + 4 \times 8 = 7 + 32 = 39$. The two columns are equal.

22. (D) If you plug in 0, the two columns are equal. If you plug in 1, Column A is greater.

23. (A) The probability of selecting two white shirts (with replacement) is $\frac{4}{6} \times \frac{4}{6} = \frac{4}{9}$. The
     probability of selecting a black shirt is $\frac{2}{6}$ or $\frac{1}{3}$.

Quantitative Reasoning Answer Explanations - Upper Level (32 Items)
Practice Test #1

24.   (A) The area of the shaded region is $f^2 - g^2$. Because you are finding area, you can assume all variables represent positive numbers. Therefore, $f^2 + fg - g^2$ must be greater than $f^2 - g^2$.

25.   (C) The probability of flipping a heads or tails is $\frac{1}{2}$ regardless of what you roll on the die.

26.   (A) Perpendicular slopes are negative reciprocals of one another. If the slope of b is perpendicular to 2, it must be $-\frac{1}{2}$.

27.   (D) It is impossible to determine the relationship between y and x.

28.   (B) The value of Amalia's portfolio rises to $1,200 in 2015 and then falls to $1,080 in 2016.

29.   (A) The piggy bank contains 25 nickels and 50 pennies ($1.25 + $.50 = $1.75). The value of the nickels is $1.25. Column A is greater.

30.   (B) The largest possible range is 10 (70 – 60). The smallest possible range is 6 (68 – 62). The mean must fall somewhere between 60 and 70. Even though you cannot determine the precise value of the range or the mean, because none of their possible values overlap, you can state with certainty that the mean will always be greater.

31.   (A) The perimeter of Rectangle A is $3x + 3x + x + x = 8x$. If $8x = 40$, then $x = 5$. The area of Rectangle B $= 3y^2 = 48$. $Y = 4$.

32.   (D) The perimeter of the rectangle could range from 146 (if the rectangle is 72×1) to 34 (if the rectangle is 9×8).

Quantitative Reasoning Answer Key - Upper Level (32 Items)
Practice Test #2

Item	Key	Your Answer	+ if correct	*Type		Item	Key	Your Answer	+ if correct	*Type
1	C			N		17	C			M
2	D			D		18	C			A
3	C			N		19	D			A
4	B			M		20	B			A
5	D			A		21	C			G
6	B			G		22	A			A
7	C			N		23	B			N
8	A			N		24	C			A
9	A			A		25	B			G
10	D			A		26	A			A
11	C			D		27	B			N
12	B			A		28	D			A
13	B			M		29	A			A
14	B			A		30	C			M
15	C			M		31	B			A
16	C			G		32	A			A
						Total Correct				

*Key to Type of Item

N = **N**umbers and Operations
A = **A**lgebraic Concepts
G = **G**eometry
M = **M**easurement
D = **D**ata Analysis and Probability

Quantitative Reasoning Answer Explanations - Upper Level (32 Items)
Practice Test #2

---

1. (C) Rearrange so that all the bases are the same: $\dfrac{5^3(5^2+5^3)}{25(15+10)} = \dfrac{5^3(5^2+5^3)}{5^2(5^2)}$. Distribute the term outside the parentheses: $\dfrac{5^5+5^6}{5^4}$. Pull out the greatest common factor on the top and bottom: $\dfrac{5^4(5^1+5^2)}{5^4}$. Cancel 5^4 and simplify the remaining parts of the expression.

2. (D) You can make up some scores to help yourself visualize this question. If the students originally scored 50, 70, and 80, and the teacher increased the highest score to 90, the range would increase from 30 to 40.

3. (C) $y = x - 10 - 12 + 32 + 34 = x + 44$. $y - x = (x + 44) - x = 44$.

4. (B) If the original radius = 10, then the area of the circle = 100π. Increasing the radius by 10% to 11 will result in a circle with an area of 121π. The area increased 21%.

5. (D) FOIL $(x + 11)(x - 11)$ to get $x^2 + 11x - 11x - 121$. Simplify to get $x^2 - 121$. $n = 121$.

6. (B) Imagine a circle that has 24 equally spaced radii extending from its center. A circle has 360°, so the measure of each angle is 15°. However, the answer is not 24. Consider that each radius is actually one half of a diameter. In order to draw this figure, you would only have had to draw 12 diameters through the center of the circle. Therefore, the answer is (B).

7. (C) Plug in the biggest and smallest possible values of x, as well as 0. In this case, you will plug in 0 and 3. Plugging in 3 results in 11.

8. (A) Try assigning values to each variable. One possible combination is $w = 4$, $x = 2$, $y = 3$, and $z = 6$. (A) is the only correct answer.

9. (A) Subtract 4 on both sides to get $\sqrt{2x + y} = 2$. Square each side to get $2x + y = 4$. Subtract $2x$ from both sides to get $y = 4 - 2x$.

10. (D) Assume each person took exactly 13 pictures. $273 \div 13 = 21$.

11. (C) Look for the portion of the graph that contains the steepest slope. From 3 - 4 hours, Vincent traveled 60 miles.

12. (B) When objects travel toward each other along the same path, you need the sum of their speeds.

Quantitative Reasoning Answer Explanations - Upper Level (32 Items)
Practice Test #2

___

13.   (B) The box on the bottom of this figure is very wide, so it would fill slowly at a constant rate. Once the water reaches the cylinder, it will abruptly start to rise very quickly at a constant rate.

14.   (B) This is a time consuming question; on the real test, you should circle this one and come back to it only if you have time. Otherwise, you should guess. If the volume of Pyramid A is 3 times the volume of Pyramid B, the numerator must be three times as large for Pyramid A as it is for Pyramid B. In answer (B), length is tripled while width and height are held equal. (B) is the correct answer.

15.   (C) The ratio of the big triangle to the small triangle is 2 : 1. If the length of the hypotenuse of the large triangle is $5x$, the hypotenuse of the small triangle must be $2.5x$.

16.   (C) Each side of the square pen is equal to 8 feet. $8 \times 4 = 32$.

17.   (C) FOIL $(2x + 2y)^2$ to get $4x^2 + 8xy + 4y^2$. Rearrange to get $4x^2 + 4y^2 + 8xy$ and then plug in the values of these expressions to get $52 + 48 = 100$.

18.   (C) Replace r with 2: $\dfrac{3(2)^2 - 5}{5} = \dfrac{12 - 5}{5} = \dfrac{7}{5}$.

19.   (D) Whenever you see exponents in the Quantitative Comparisons section, try plugging in positive numbers, negative numbers, zero, and fractions between 0 and 1. In this question, you'll see that the answer changes depending on what you plug in.

20.   (B) Each angle of an equilateral triangle measures 60°, while each angle of a square measures 90°.

21.   (C) 5% of 10 is .5, and 10% of 5 is also .5.

22.   (A) The four consecutive even integers are 2, 4, 6, and 8.

23.   (B) $4 + (2 \times 3)^2 - 10 = 4 + (6)^2 - 10 = 4 + 36 - 10 = 40 - 10 = 30$.

24.   (C) The length and width of the prism are equal to 5, because $2 \times 5 \times 5 = 50$. The product of the length and height, therefore, is equal to 10.

25.   (B) The probability of choosing a penny is $\dfrac{2}{20}$ or $\dfrac{1}{10}$. The probability of choosing a nickel, putting it back, and then choosing a quarter is $\dfrac{8}{20} \times \dfrac{10}{20} = \dfrac{2}{5} \times \dfrac{1}{2} = \dfrac{2}{10}$.

Quantitative Reasoning Answer Explanations - Upper Level (32 Items)
Practice Test #2

26. (A) This is a tricky question that you should make an educated guess on when you're taking the test. Because Column A will contain larger values than Column B, it's safe to guess A. To find the exact answer, you will need to use some pretty complicated formulas. For Column A, the average of the set is 150 and there are $\frac{200-100}{2} + 1 = 51$ total integers in the set. The sum is $(150)(51) = 7,650$. In Column B, the average is 50 and there are 101 total integers in the set. The sum is $(50)(101) = 5,050$.

27. (B) $\left(\frac{1}{4}\right)^2 = \frac{1}{16}$. $\left(\frac{1}{4}\right)^{-\frac{1}{2}} = 2$.

28. (D) x could be equal to -6 or 3, so the answer is (D).

29. (A) Maximize area by making the rectangle a square. The area is 64.

30. (C) In June, the price drops to $2.40. In July, the price rises to $2.64.

31. (B) Solve for x by multiplying each side of the equation by 7. $x = 27$.

32. (A) Change Column A to base 2 to compare: $16^3 = (2^4)^3 = 2^{12}$. Column A is greater.

Mathematics Achievement Answer Key - Upper Level (42 Items)
Practice Test #1

Item	Key	Your Answer	+ if correct	*Type		Item	Key	Your Answer	+ if correct	*Type
1	A			A		22	D			N
2	D			N		23	D			A
3	B			A		24	A			D
4	B			A		25	C			A
5	C			D		26	B			A
6	C			D		27	D			G
7	D			M		28	B			A
8	A			M		29	A			N
9	C			A		30	D			G
10	A			D		31	D			D
11	D			A		32	C			A
12	B			N		33	C			D
13	D			A		34	B			D
14	C			D		35	A			M
15	B			D		36	D			M
16	B			N		37	C			A
17	A			M		38	A			A
18	B			N		39	D			G
19	B			D		40	A			G
20	C			M		41	C			N
21	D			G		42	D			N
						Total Correct				

*Key to Type of Item

N = **N**umbers and Operations
A = **A**lgebraic Concepts
G = **G**eometry
M = **M**easurement
D = **D**ata Analysis and Probability

Mathematics Achievement Answer Explanations - Upper Level (42 Items)
Practice Test #1

---

1. (A) You can work backwards on this question. If $5x = x$, the only possible answer is 0.

2. (D) Start with the fractions. For (A), $\frac{1.5}{9} = \frac{1 \times 1.5}{6 \times 1.5}$. These fractions are equivalent. For (B),

    $\frac{.5}{3} = \frac{1 \times .5}{6 \times .5}$. These fractions are also equivalent. Now, you will have to divide the decimals by

    hand. $\frac{1}{6} = .166666666667$.

3. (B) You cannot have 0 in the denominator, so 6 and -10 won't work. This allows you to
    eliminate (C) and (D). Both 4 and -4 will result in 0 in the numerator, so (B) is correct.

4. (B) This is a combinations question. Set up your four slots: ____ × ____ × ____ × ____. There
    are 7 options that you can choose for the first slot, 6 for the second, and so on. This results in 840
    possible permutations. Now, you must account for repeated permutations (for example, lettuce,
    tomato, pickle, cheese is the same as cheese, pickle, tomato, lettuce). To do this, divide by $4 \times 3 \times 2 \times 1$, which results in 35.

5. (C) $\frac{16 + 18 + 12 + 12 + 24 + 20}{6} = 17$.

6. (C) This is a general survey about all of the students in a high school. It is not specifically about
    males, females, students in a certain class, athletes, etc. Therefore, the most reliable survey is a
    random sample of students in the entire school.

7. (D) The area of a square is 9 in^2. Carefully count the total number of squares. We recommend
    writing a number inside each square so that you don't lose count. There are 10 squares, so the
    area is 90.

8. (A) Set up your fractions using the given rates: $\frac{.305\ meters}{1\ foot} \times \frac{5,280\ feet}{1\ mile} \times \frac{1\ second}{13\ meters}$. Feet

    and meters cancel out, leaving you with seconds per mile. Notice that you have to flip the last
    fraction so that meters will cancel. Finally, convert from seconds to hours.

    $\frac{.305\ meters}{1\ foot} \times \frac{5,280\ feet}{1\ mile} \times \frac{1\ second}{13\ meters} \times \frac{1\ minute}{60\ seconds} \times \frac{1\ hour}{60\ minutes}$. When you cross cancel all

    your units, you end up with $\frac{.305 \times 5,280\ hours}{13 \times 60 \times 60\ miles}$. The question asks for miles per hour, so you must

    flip this fraction.

Mathematics Achievement Answer Explanations - Upper Level (42 Items)
Practice Test #1

9. (C) FOIL. $(x)(x) - (x)(5) + 4(x) - (4)(5) = x^2 - 5x + 4x - 20 = x^2 - x - 20$. You can plug in 1 for x if you don't feel comfortable with FOIL. $(1 + 4)(1 - 5) = -20$. Plugging in 1 for x in (C) also results in -20.

10. (A) Set up the equation for averages using the information you have: $\frac{94 + 94 + 94 + 94 + x}{5} = 80$. Solve for x to get 24. You can work backwards on this question if you don't feel comfortable finding averages.

11. (D) You can work backwards on this question. You need 0 in the numerator, but not in the denominator. Plugging in -8 results in 0 in both the numerator and denominator. Therefore, there are no values for x that will solve this equation.

12. (B) Rewrite $4.5 \times 10^3 + 3.2 \times 10^4$ in standard notation and then add: $4{,}500 + 32{,}000 = 36{,}500$. Only one of the answer choices starts with "365," so you don't need to convert back to scientific notation.

13. (D) You can work backwards on this question. Plugging in 9 for y in $yx + xy$ results in $9x + 9x$. This is equivalent to the given equation.

14. (C) The median is the easiest thing to find in a box-and-whisker plot: it's always the line in the middle of the box!

15. (B) There are 25 total data points in the sample. The median, therefore, is the 13th data point. Students with 1 absence account for data points 10-15, so the median is 1.

16. (B) You should know the definitions of these four terms. Complex and imaginary numbers both use i, and irrational numbers cannot be expressed as a simple fraction. A composite number is a positive integer that is the product of two smaller integers. Therefore, (B) is correct.

17. (A) Inches are units of length, so eliminate (B). Measuring a coffee cup in pounds is illogical, so eliminate (C). Milliliters measure volume, so eliminate (D).

18. (B) $\sqrt{36 + 64} = \sqrt{100} = 10$. Do not make the mistake of finding the square roots of 36 and 64 and then adding them together.

19. (B) Median means middle. Line up the values from smallest to largest and identify which number is in the middle. The values are 3, 6, 6, 12, and 15. The median is 6.

Mathematics Achievement Answer Explanations - Upper Level (42 Items)
Practice Test #1

---

20.   (C) If the diameter of the circle is 16, that means each side of the square is 16, and the area of the square is 256. You can eliminate (A) and (B). The radius of the circle is 8, so the area of the circle is $\pi r^2 = \pi(8)^2 = 64\pi$. Subtract 64π from 256 to find the area of the shaded region.

21.   (D) Quickly sketch this graph to help yourself visualize. The distance between (2, 9) and (-3, -3) forms the radius of the circle, and it also serves as the hypotenuse of a right triangle. Finding the two legs of the triangle will allow you to use the Pythagorean theorem to determine the length of the hypotenuse. One of the legs is 5 units tall, while the other leg is 12 units long. Therefore, $5^2 + 12^2 = c^2$. $169 = c^2$. $c = 13$.

22.   (D) The least common multiple of 4, 5, and 2 is 20. Only one answer choice contains 20, so you do not need to do any more work.

23.   (D) Rewrite the expression without parentheses. Make sure you distribute the negative sign. Then, carefully combine like terms. $5n^3m^6 - 7n^6m^3 - (3n^6m^3 - 4n^3m^6) =$ $5n^3m^6 - 7n^6m^3 - 3n^6m^3 + 4n^3m^6 = 9n^3m^6 - 10n^6m^3$.

24.   (A) In this question, you must consider the probability of Glen choosing a red jelly bean independently of Isaac choosing a blue jelly bean. If Isaac chooses a blue jelly bean, there are 24 jelly beans remaining: 7 red, 4 black, 5 yellow, and 8 blue. The probability of Glen choosing a red jelly bean is therefore $\frac{7}{24}$.

25.   (C) Rewrite as two separate inequalities:

$$2x + 4 \geq 10 \qquad\qquad\qquad\qquad 2x + 4 \leq -10$$
$$2x \geq 6 \qquad\qquad\qquad\qquad\qquad 2x \leq -14$$
$$x \geq 3 \qquad\qquad\qquad\qquad\qquad\quad x \leq -7$$

26.   (B) To solve algebraically, let x = the speed at which Kerry writes her essays, and let $2x$ = the speed at which Dan writes his essays. Therefore, $2x + x = 24$, and $x = 8$. You can also work backwards on this question. If Kerry wrote 8 pages, that means Dan wrote 16 pages. $8 + 16 = 24$, so you know this answer is correct.

27.   (D) This is a ratios question. Set up your ratio: $\frac{9}{3} = \frac{x}{2}$. Solve to find $x = 6$.

28.   (B) $\sqrt{36} = 6$, so you can eliminate (C) and (D). $\sqrt{x^{36}} = x^{18}$.

Mathematics Achievement Answer Explanations - Upper Level (42 Items)
Practice Test #1

29. (A) $\sqrt{16-9} = \sqrt{7} = 2.65$, which is not an integer.

30. (D) Triangle XYZ is isosceles, so the remaining two angles are congruent. Each angle is equal to 75°. Straight lines contain 180°, so the value of angle m is $180° - 75° = 105°$.

31. (D) The probability Andrea will choose a black shirt is $\frac{3}{16}$. When she puts that shirt in the hamper, there are 15 shirts left. The probability she will choose a green shirt from the remaining shirts is $\frac{4}{15}$. To get the probability of both events happening in succession, multiply them together.

32. (C) The line has points at (-6, 0) and (-5, 4). Slope $= \frac{rise}{run} = \frac{4}{1} = 4$.

33. (C) Expected values. Multiply across and then add the products:
$(0 \times \frac{27}{64}) + (1 \times \frac{1}{4}) + (2 \times \frac{1}{16}) + (3 \times \frac{1}{64}) = 0 + \frac{1}{4} + \frac{2}{16} + \frac{3}{64} = \frac{27}{64}$.

34. (B) Rewrite the general equation with the information you know: $42\pi = 2\pi r(4) + 2\pi r^2$. Simplify: $42\pi = 8\pi r + 2\pi r^2$. Factor out 2π: $42\pi = 2\pi(4r + r^2)$. Divide both sides by 2π to get $21 = 4r + r^2$. Plugging in 3 for r results in $4(3) + (3)^2 = 21$.

35. (A) The tallest student is 74 inches and the shortest student is 51 inches. $74 - 51 = 23$.

36. (D) If the height is 16, then the radius is 4. Plug these numbers into the equation: $V = \pi(4)^2 16$. Solving results in 256π.

37. (C)
$$-2 \leq 4x - 2 \leq 18$$
$$0 \leq 4x \leq 20$$
$$0 \leq x \leq 5$$

38. (A) Create two separate inequalities:

$\frac{x}{2} - 3 < 1$ $\frac{x}{2} - 3 > -1$
$\frac{x}{2} < 4$ $\frac{x}{2} > 2$
$x < 8$ $x > 4$

Mathematics Achievement Answer Explanations - Upper Level (42 Items)
Practice Test #1

39.   (D) For (A), there will be two points that are "up 3, over 4" with respect to point (1, 1). For (B), there will be two points that are "down 3, over 4" with respect to point (-3, -2). For (C), there will be two points are "down / up 3, over 4" with respect to point (1, 1). For (D), point (-3, -2) is "up 3, over 4" with respect to point (1, 1), and point (3, -2) is "up 3, over 2" with respect to point (1, 1). Therefore, placing a point at (3, -2) will *not* create an isosceles triangle.

40.   (A) Angle B is given, as is the side opposite angle B. You are asked to find the length of the adjacent side. The trig function that uses opposite and adjacent is *tangent* (TOA). $\tan 35° = \frac{10}{x}$.

Multiply both sides by x to get $x\tan 35° = 10$. Divide both sides by $\tan 35°$ to get $x = \frac{10}{\tan 35°}$.

41.   (C) Matrix addition. Add the integers in the corresponding locations of the two matrices.

42.   (D) x^2 is equal to -100, which eliminates the integers 10 and -10 as answer choices.

$$(10i)^2 = 100i^2 = 100(-1) = -100$$
$$(-10i)^2 = 100i^2 = 100(-1) = -100$$

Mathematics Achievement Answer Key - Upper Level (42 Items)
Practice Test #2

Item	Key	Your Answer	+ if correct	*Type		Item	Key	Your Answer	+ if correct	*Type
1	B			A		22	C			A
2	B			A		23	D			M
3	B			D		24	D			M
4	C			N		25	D			A
5	A			A		26	B			G
6	B			A		27	A			N
7	B			A		28	D			A
8	A			A		29	D			D
9	C			N		30	D			D
10	C			M		31	D			N
11	B			N		32	B			A
12	B			G		33	B			G
13	D			D		34	D			N
14	A			M		35	D			G
15	C			N		36	D			N
16	C			G		37	D			D
17	D			M		38	B			A
18	A			D		39	B			M
19	B			D		40	C			A
20	D			A		41	A			A
21	C			D		42	D			A
						Total Correct				

*Key to Type of Item

N = **N**umbers and Operations
A = **A**lgebraic Concepts
G = **G**eometry
M = **M**easurement
D = **D**ata Analysis and Probability

Mathematics Achievement Answer Explanations - Upper Level (42 Items)
Practice Test #2

---

1. (B) The formula for percent change is $\frac{change}{original} \times 100$. In this question, fill in $\frac{.50}{1.25} \times 100$ to get 40%.

2. (B) You cannot have 0 in the denominator of a fraction, so eliminate all answer choices that contain 4. Plugging -4 into the numerator results in 0.

3. (B) The mode is the number that shows up the most in a data set. If you were to rewrite the chart as a set of numbers, it would look like this: 0, 0, 0, 0, 0, 0, 1, 1, 1, 1, 1, 1, 1, 1, 2, 2, 2, 2, 2, 3, 3, 3, 4, 4. The number 1 shows up more often than any other number.

4. (C) Deal with the left and right parts of the equations separately. $\frac{6.0}{1.5} = 4$, so you can eliminate (B) and (D). $\frac{10^6}{10^2} = 10^4$.

5. (A) Rewrite the equation without parentheses, and make sure you remember to distribute the negative sign: $3a^7b^2 - 3b^4a^5 - 7a^7b^2 - 5b^4a^5$. Combine like terms.

6. (B) $60 \times .45 = 27$. You can also use logic if you don't feel comfortable working with decimals. Half of 60 is 30, and 45% is a bit less than half. 27 is the only answer that makes sense.

7. (B) This is a combinations question. First, find the number of permutations: $6 \times 5 \times 4 = 120$. Then, eliminate any repeats by dividing by $3 \times 2 \times 1$.

8. (A) You cannot have 0 in the denominator, so 8 and -4 will not work. You can eliminate everything except (A).

9. (C) Create a factor tree. The factors of 30 are 1, 2, 3, 5, 6, 10, 15, and 30. Of these integers, 2, 3, and 5 are prime.

10. (C) There are 32 sides to the figure and the total perimeter is 96, which means the length of each side of a square is 3. Therefore, the area of each square is 9. There are 19 squares, so the total area is $19 \times 9 = 171$.

11. (B) Simplify like terms. $\frac{5}{30} = \frac{1}{6}$. $\frac{x^4}{x^6} = x^{-2} = \frac{1}{x^2}$. $\frac{y^3}{y^2} = y$. $\frac{z^{10}}{z^4} = z^6$. Recombine everything to get $\frac{yz^6}{6x^2}$.

Mathematics Achievement Answer Explanations - Upper Level (42 Items)
Practice Test #2

---

12   (B) The triangles are similar. Side $\overline{BC}$ corresponds to side $\overline{YZ}$, and the relationship between the lengths of the sides is $\frac{7}{10.5}$. Set up a ratio to solve for $\overline{AB}$: $\frac{7}{10.5} = \frac{x}{6}$. $42 = 10.5x$, so $x = 4$.

13.   (D) Set up the equation for mean and input the information you know. Bessie took 6 tests. On one test, she scored a 37. We don't know exactly what she scored on the other 5 tests, but we know her average was an 82. $\frac{5x + 37}{6} = 82$. Solving for x gives you 91.

14.   (A) Set up your fractions using the given rates: $\frac{1\ foot}{.305\ meters} \times \frac{3{,}250\ meters}{1\ second}$. Meters cancel out, leaving you with feet per second. Now convert seconds to hours:

$\frac{1\ foot}{.305\ meters} \times \frac{3{,}250\ meters}{1\ second} \times \frac{60\ seconds}{1\ minute} \times \frac{60\ minutes}{1\ hour}$. When you cross cancel all your units, you end up with $\frac{3{,}250 \times 60 \times 60\ feet}{.305\ hours}$.

15.   (C) You'll need to use long division to solve this one. The result is $.\overline{111}$.

16.   (C) The equation for the volume of a rectangular prism is $l \times w \times h$, where l = length, w = width, and h = height. In a cube, these three measures are all equal to one another. If the cube's surface area is 96 in^2, then each face of the cube has an area of 16 in^2. Therefore, each edge of the cube has a length of 4 inches. $4 \times 4 \times 4 = 64$.

17.   (D) If the area of the square is 100, each side is equal to 10. Cut the square in half along its diagonal to create a 45-45-90 triangle. The relationship between the lengths of the sides is $x : x : x\sqrt{2}$, so the length of the diagonal is $10\sqrt{2}$. Therefore, the diameter of the circle is $10\sqrt{2}$, and the radius of the circle is $5\sqrt{2}$. The equation for the area of a circle is $A = \pi r^2$. In this circle, $A = \pi(5\sqrt{2})^2 = \pi(5^2)(\sqrt{2})^2 = \pi(25)(2) = 50\pi$.

18.   (A) $\frac{5}{40}$ or $\frac{1}{8}$ of the students like sandwiches. Set up your ratio: $\frac{1}{8} = \frac{x}{360}$. Cross multiply to get $360 = 8x$. $x = 45$.

19.   (B) Scores ranging from 50 to 75 account for the first two quartiles of the plot (the left whisker and the left box). Each quartile contains 25% of the data points. There are 40 total data points, so 20 scores fall within this part of the plot.

Mathematics Achievement Answer Explanations - Upper Level (42 Items)
Practice Test #2

20. (D) Add 3 to each part of the inequality to get $-3 \leq 3x \leq 9$. Divide each part by 3 to get $-1 \leq x \leq 3$.

21. (C) Non-replacement probability. There is a $\frac{2}{15}$ chance that Emil will pick a pair of red socks the first time. If he does this, there will then be 1 pair of red socks and 14 total pairs of socks remaining. In this situation, the odds he will pick red socks are $\frac{1}{14}$. The probability of picking red socks both times is $\frac{2}{15} \times \frac{1}{14}$.

22. (C) Simplify $(3.44 + 2.56) = 2x$ to $6 = 2x$. Divide by 2 on both sides. $3 = x$.

23. (D) The parallel lines x and y are cut by a transversal. Vertical angles are congruent, and consecutive angles add to 180°. Angle A is therefore congruent to the angle next to the 30° angle. That angle measures 150°. Twice that angle is equal to 300°.

24. (D) Kilograms are a measure of mass, not length, so you can eliminate (B). It is most logical to measure the length of a car in feet.

25. (D) There are $1 + 3 = 4$ total "pieces" in this ratio. $\frac{428}{4} = 107$. The multiplier is 107. To find the actual number of children at the event, multiply 107 by 3 to get 321.

26. (B) Set up a ratio: $\frac{4}{14} = \frac{x}{24.5}$. $(4)(24.5) = (14)(x)$. $x = 7$.

27. (A) $\sqrt{81 + 144} = \sqrt{225} = 15$. Do not make the mistake of finding the square roots of 81 and 144 and then adding them together.

28. (D) FOIL. $(2x)(x) + (2x)(-4) + 2(x) + (2)(-4) = 2x^2 - 8x + 2x - 8 = 2x^2 - 6x - 8$. You can plug in 1 for x if you don't feel comfortable with FOIL. $(2(1) + 2)(1 - 4) = -12$. Plugging in 1 for x in (D) also results in -12.

29. (D) There are 19 data points total, so the median is the 10th data point. In this plot, the 10th data point is 82.

30. (D) Expected values. Multiply across and then add the products:

$$(0 \times \tfrac{1}{8}) + (1 \times \tfrac{1}{8}) + (2 \times \tfrac{1}{4}) + (3 \times \tfrac{1}{4}) + (4 \times \tfrac{1}{8}) + (5 \times \tfrac{1}{8}) = 0 + \tfrac{1}{8} + \tfrac{2}{4} + \tfrac{3}{4} + \tfrac{4}{8} + \tfrac{5}{8} = \tfrac{5}{2}.$$

Mathematics Achievement Answer Explanations - Upper Level (42 Items)
Practice Test #2

31.   (D) When $n = 1$, the expression equals 7. When $n = 2$, the expression equals 11. When $n = 3$, the expression = 15. The only expression that matches these points is $4n + 3$.

32.   (B) $\sqrt{144} = 12$, so you can eliminate (C) and (D). $\sqrt{x^{16}} = x^8$.

33.   (B) (1, 4) would create a trapezoid, so eliminate (D). The bottom right point is "down 2, over 3" from the bottom left point. That means the missing point must be "down 2, over 3" from the top left point. Trace this out on the graph to get (1, 0).

34.   (D) x^2 is equal to -36, which eliminates the integers 6 and -6 as answer choices.
$$(6i)^2 = 36i^2 = 36(-1) = -36$$
$$(-6i)^2 = 36i^2 = 36(-1) = -36$$

35.   (D) If you've memorized your special side triangles, you may recognize that this is a 5-12-13 triangle in which the length of each side has been doubled. Therefore, the missing side is 24. $24 + 24 + 10 + 10 = 68$. You can also use the Pythagorean theorem to find the length of the missing side: $10^2 + x^2 = 26^2$. $100 + x^2 = 676$. $x^2 = 576$. $x = 24$.

36.   (D) Matrix subtraction. Subtract the integers in the corresponding locations of the two matrices.

37.   (D) Set up the equation for mean and solve: $\frac{10 + 5 + 12 + 4 + 4 + 6 + 8}{7} = 7$.

38.   (B) Angle L is given, as is the hypotenuse. You are asked to find the length of the opposite side. The trig function that uses opposite and hypotenuse is *sine* (SOH). $\sin 25° = \frac{x}{5}$. Multiply both sides by 5 to get $5\sin 25° = x$. This is not an answer choice! You haven't done anything wrong, it just means the test makers want you to use a different reference angle. Triangles have 180°, so Angle M equals 65°. Based on this angle, you are given hypotenuse and need to find adjacent, so you should use cosine (CAH). $\cos 65° = \frac{x}{5}$. Multiply both sides by 5 to get $5\cos 65° = x$.

39.   (B) Rewrite the general equation with the information you know. If the perimeter of the base is 20, then each side = 4, and the area of the base is 16. Therefore, $85 = \frac{1}{2}(20)l + 16$. Simplify: $85 = 10l + 16$. Subtract 16 from both sides to get $69 = 10l$. Divide by 10 on both sides to get $6.9 = l$.

Mathematics Achievement Answer Explanations - Upper Level (42 Items)
Practice Test #2

40. (C) Create two separate inequalities:

$-2x - 6 < 2$ $-2x - 6 > -2$
$\quad -2x < 8$ $\quad -2x > 4$
$\quad\quad x > -4$ $\quad\quad x < -2$

41. (A)

$$-4 \leq -2x + 4 \leq 10$$
$$-8 \leq -2x \leq 6$$
$$4 \geq x \geq -3.$$

42. (D) The line intersects (0, 3) and (3, 2). Slope $= \frac{rise}{run}$. The line rises -1 and runs 3, so its slope is $-\frac{1}{3}$. Perpendicular lines have opposite reciprocal slopes, so a line that is perpendicular to the given one must have a slope of 3.

Chapter 10

Interpreting Your Results

Interpreting Your Results

Once you've completed a practice test, check your answers using the answer key. Place a "+" next to each correct answer to determine your raw score (the total number of questions you answered correctly). Then, look at the Conversion Table to find your Reported Range. Using your Reported Range, look at the appropriate grade level on the Scaled Score Quartiles chart. Finally, use your quartile to determine your stanine.

Example: A student applying to 10th grade answers 27 questions correctly on the Quantitative Reasoning test. This gives the student a reported range of 898 to 928. A score of 900 puts a student applying to 10th grade in the 75th percentile of students taking the test. The lowest end of this student's range is just below the 75th percentile, while the highest end would put the student above the 75th percentile. A percentile rank of 75 would convert to a stanine of 6. Because this is the lowest range of the student's scores, he or she would receive a stanine score of approximately 6 to 8.

Quantitative Reasoning Conversion Table - Upper Level

2016 ISEE Practice Tests Scaled Score Ranges (Min. = 807 and Max. = 945)						
Raw Score	*Reported Range			Raw Score	*Reported Range	
32	915	945		16	861	891
31	912	942		15	858	888
30	908	938		14	854	884
29	905	935		13	851	881
28	901	931		12	847	877
27	898	928		11	844	874
26	894	924		10	840	870
25	891	921		9	837	867
24	888	918		8	833	863
23	884	914		7	830	860
22	881	911		6	827	857
21	878	908		5	823	853
20	874	904		4	820	850
19	871	901		3	817	847
18	868	898		2	814	844
17	864	894		1	810	840
				0	807	837

* Minimum reported range is 30 points wide

Comparative Data			
Scaled Score Quartiles			
Based on the 2015-2016 ISEE Norms			
Applicants to Grade	75th	50th	25th
9	895	880	867
10	900	883	871
11	901	888	872
12	903	888	875

Percentile Rank	Stanine
1-3	1
4-10	2
11-22	3
23-39	4
40-59	5
60-76	6
77-88	7
89-95	8
96-99	9

Mathematics Achievement Conversion Table - Upper Level

2016 ISEE Practice Tests Scaled Score Ranges (Min. = 807 and Max. = 950)						
Raw Score	*Reported Range			Raw Score	*Reported Range	
42	920	950		20	861	891
41	917	947		19	858	888
40	915	945		18	855	885
39	912	942		17	853	883
38	909	939		16	850	880
37	907	937		15	847	877
36	904	934		14	845	875
35	901	931		13	842	872
34	898	928		12	839	869
33	896	926		11	837	867
32	893	923		10	834	864
31	890	920		9	831	861
30	888	918		8	828	858
29	885	915		7	826	856
28	882	912		6	823	853
27	880	910		5	820	850
26	877	907		4	818	848
25	874	904		3	815	845
24	872	902		2	812	842
23	869	899		1	809	839
22	866	896		0	807	837
21	863	893				

* Minimum reported range is 30 points wide

Mathematics Achievement Conversion Table - Upper Level

Comparative Data			
Scaled Score Quartiles			
Based on the 2015-2016 ISEE Norms			
Applicants to Grade	75th	50th	25th
9	897	883	869
10	903	887	872
11	906	891	875
12	908	892	877

Percentile Rank	Stanine
1-3	1
4-10	2
11-22	3
23-39	4
40-59	5
60-76	6
77-88	7
89-95	8
96-99	9

Made in the USA
Coppell, TX
02 November 2021

65075399R00162